The Dialectical Meaning of Offshored Work

Studies in Critical Social Sciences Book Series

Haymarket Books is proud to be working with Brill Academic Publishers (www.brill.nl) to republish the *Studies in Critical Social Sciences* book series in paperback editions. This peer-reviewed book series offers insights into our current reality by exploring the content and consequences of power relationships under capitalism, and by considering the spaces of opposition and resistance to these changes that have been defining our new age. Our full catalog of *SCSS* volumes can be viewed at https://www.haymarketbooks.org/series_collections/4-studies-in-critical-social-sciences.

Series Editor
David Fasenfest (SOAS University of London)

Editorial Board
Eduardo Bonilla-Silva (Duke University)
Chris Chase-Dunn (University of California–Riverside)
William Carroll (University of Victoria)
Raewyn Connell (University of Sydney)
Kimberlé W. Crenshaw (University of California–LA and Columbia University)
Heidi Gottfried (Wayne State University)
Karin Gottschall (University of Bremen)
Alfredo Saad Filho (King's College London)
Chizuko Ueno (University of Tokyo)
Sylvia Walby (Lancaster University)
Raju Das (York University)

The Dialectical Meaning of Offshored Work

Neoliberal Desires and Labour Arbitrage in
Post-socialist Romania

Miłosz Miszczyński

Haymarket Books
Chicago, IL

First published in 2019 by Brill Academic Publishers, The Netherlands.
© 2019 Koninklijke Brill NV, Leiden, The Netherlands

Published in paperback in 2020 by
Haymarket Books
P.O. Box 180165
Chicago, IL 60618
773-583-7884
www.haymarketbooks.org

ISBN: 978-1-64259-197-2

Distributed to the trade in the US through Consortium Book Sales and Distribution (www.cbsd.com) and internationally through Ingram Publisher Services International (www.ingramcontent.com).

This book was published with the generous support of Lannan Foundation and Wallace Action Fund.

Special discounts are available for bulk purchases by organizations and institutions. Please call 773-583-7884 or email info@haymarketbooks.org for more information.

Cover design by Jamie Kerry and Ragina Johnson.

Printed in United States.

10 9 8 7 6 5 4 3 2 1

Library of Congress Cataloging-in-Publication Data is available.

Contents

Acknowledgement   VII

Introduction: The Post-socialist Workforce in the Global Offshoring Networks   1
1 The Post-socialist Workforce in Global Production   3
2 Offshoring Studies   7
3 Social Reproduction and Offshoring   9
4 Ethnography of Foreign Investment   11
5 The Investor and the Region   13
6 The Structure of this Book   15

1 Romania's Systemic Transformation: Chaos, Austerity and Imposed Neoliberal Reform   20
1 Ad-hoc Transition (1989–1996)   23
2 The Period of Market Orientation (1996–2004)   27
3 The Period of European Integration (2004–2009)   31
4 Global Economic Crisis and Neoliberal Rule (2009–2014)   35
5 Conclusions   39

2 The Arrival: Global Assemblage of Neoliberal Production   42
1 Nokia Village Plans   48
2 Factory Closure in Germany   53
3 The Opening   56

3 A Journey onto the Shop Floor: Cultural Specificity of the Offshored Plant and Workforce Adaptation   60
1 Joining a Capitalist Workplace   62
2 Cultural Specificity of the Workplace and Worker Socialisation   64
3 Workplace Adaptation   68
4 Cultural Specificity and the Offshored Workplace   79

4 Shop Floor Culture and Routine Production Process   82
1 Lubricating the Taylorist Workplace   84
2 Limiting Control and Political Intimacies at Work   87
3 Epistemic Holes, Humour and Storytelling   94
4 Conclusions   98

5 **Familial Involvement in Offshored Labour**   101
    1   Prior to Investment   103
    2   Mutual Dependencies   106
    3   Emancipatory Forces   109
    4   Intergenerational Exceptionalism   111
    5   Mutual Dependency in a Broader Context   115

6 **Employee Reactions to the Plant Closure**   120
    1   The Good Investor's Bad Decisions   123
    2   Social Mobilization   126
    3   What the Plant Changed   133

7 **Coping with Loss: Local Agency and Offshored Labour**   137
    1   The Secrecy of the Contract   141
    2   Smartphone Controversy   145
    3   Romania in the Global Economy   148
    4   The New Investor   153
    5   Discussion: National Reaction to the Issue of Relocation   156

Conclusions: Labour Arbitrage, Modernity and the Realities of Offshored Labour   159

Bibliography   167
Index   188

Acknowledgement

This book would not have been possible without kind support from my home institution, Kozminski University, Poland and the Ryoichi Sasakawa Young Leaders Fellowship (SYLFF) that I received while being a doctoral student at the Institute of Sociology, Jagiellonian Unviersity, Poland.

I am grateful for comments, ideas and feedback I received, especially my doctoral supervisor Jacek Nowak and committee members Andrzej Bukowski and Waldemar Kuligowski. I also thank all of the colleagues for the tremendous support received during my work and research at the University of Surrey, University of Oxford, Columbia University, NY and University of California, San Diego.

As this book is a final step in my completing my research of offshored work, I am grateful to everyone who supported my work, especially the following earlier publications: a book in Polish (*Etnografia Globalnego Kapitalizmu*), and articles in *Critical Sociology* ('Global Production in a Romanian Village: Middle-Income Economy, Industrial Dislocation and the Reserve Army of Labor') and in the *Journal of Organizational Ethnography* ('Labour Arbitrage: the Lifecycle of a Global Production Node').

My warmest thanks to my respondents, who tolerated my presence among them, answered my questions and posed new questions and leads.

Most importantly, I would like to thank my wife, Emma Greeson for the never-ending amount of love and support.

INTRODUCTION

The Post-socialist Workforce in the Global Offshoring Networks

In the last few decades, the mobility of production processes has intensified. The industrial workplace has evolved over time, but it has never been as mobile as it is today. The hypermobility of production has become one of the biggest challenges for the workforce, whose mobility is disproportionately more limited. Recent times have brought an increased number of industrial factory closures in industrialised economies. Detroit, the motor city, with its collapsed industry and immense scale of social problems, is the most dramatic example of these changes (LeDuff, 2013; Galster, 2012). A growing number of communities have witnessed factory closures. Continuing industrial restructuring changes cities and regions, including those traditionally regarded as industrial. In some places, production plants are turned into fashionable lofts, while in others rust and remain forgotten. Geographically dispersed industrial production is also intensifying. Even highly recognised manufacturers, often considered symbols of nations and their values, such as the British clothing producer Burberry, end up offshoring their production cycles (Blyton and Jenkins, 2013). Information technology, expansion of global value chains, decreasing trade barriers and economic integration have stimulated changes in the way organisations are governed and how work is organized.

The workforce in more advanced economies loses out to newly industrialised ones. Production is undergoing globalisation, and as a result, the workforce is highly dependent on the condition of international markets. Regardless of the sector, the competition on the global labour market evolves. Offshoring refers to the business activity of sourcing and coordinating tasks and business functions across national borders. The central mechanism of offshoring is labour arbitrage, which might be defined as a business strategy of fulfilling the same work processes by the workforce in one locale, which is paid less than the workforce in a different locale (Hollinshead et al., 2011). Based on reduced tariffs and the removal of barriers to capital flows, the increased mobility of goods and services has contributed to the emergence of the "new, imperialist stage of capitalist development" embedded in complex production networks (Smith, 2015). Labour arbitrage is applied in a variety of industries, from simple production activities to high-tech capital-intensive tasks and R&D activities (Levy, 2005; Getto and Amant, 2014). By bypassing intermediation, suppliers and channels, this strategy serves as a way of ensuring savings and broadening human resources and capital at a lower cost (Ghemawat, 2003). In the manufacturing sector, which has experienced tremendous growth in recent years, the process of labour arbitration has strongly relied on de-industrialisation of advanced economies and offshoring of production to less advanced ones. The competition also concerns destination locations, for instance newly industrialised economies win over the more advanced ones (Brecher, Costello and Smith, 2006). As a result, corporate profits and decision-making concentrated in wealthier economies of the global north, while the labour force of the manufacturing sector, chronically underpaid and facing insufficiencies, in the less advanced economies (Foster, McChesney and Jonna, 2011).

Offshoring leads to wealth creation for organisations but not necessarily for countries, regions, or, most importantly, employees (Levy, 2005). Nation states, progressively integrating economically and politically, struggle to control production processes. With offshoring, their sovereignty remains challenged in a vast number of spheres (Sassen, 1996; Krasner, 1999; Cohen, 2012). Diminishing amount of external control over the production processes leads to the intensive cost-competition race between hosting populations (Rudra, 2008; Brass, 2011). Advanced Western economies, with long industrial pasts, face factory closures (Rousseau, 2011; Mollona, 2009; Blyton and Jenkins, 2012), adapt to service work offshoring (Nadeem, 2009) and try to cope with industry re-structuring. The competition contenders, usually less powerful economies, actively expand their global engagements by offering incentives and lower costs of labour. Since this competition has no end, it is known as the "race to the bottom" in labour costs (Rudra, 2008; Collins and Mayer, 2010). The further down the costs go, the bigger the potential net profits. The decrease in costs is proportional to the decrease not only in salary levels and work conditions but also in the scope of labour movements and workers' rights (Clawson, 2003; Silver, 2003). Labour arbitrage effectively reduces the bargaining power of employees. Offshoring practices, the relocation of businesses from one place to another, transform not only organisations but also the way employees engage in work. In the new locations, the introduction of new regimes of production offers lower labour costs, new organisation of work and improved efficiency (Brass, 2011).

In this book I concentrate on the cultural meanings of offshored labour, giving voice to the affected community, and showing the changes in the region where the investment was located. In studying offshored labour, I am particularly interested in the relationship between the global political economy, offshoring and social reproduction. Throughout this book, I show that expanding studies of offshoring to the processes of social reproduction introduces an important perspective on the globalisation of production, allowing for enhanced interpretation of the local population's involvement with global production through familial and local solidarities. Studying these processes helps to understand how firms through offshoring generate relationships with local communities, labour markets, and national economies. This perspective relies on the examination of the local dynamics aimed towards the offshoring investment. It formulates an approach of studying offshoring "from below" to counterbalance the bottom-down mainstream interpretations of global production and to show how local communities participate in global production. I show local outcomes and ways of understanding of global production. My empirically informed analysis helps to describe how the creation of a production node might be understood and what social settings it generates. The perspective of this work is strongly inspired by the writings of critical management studies, which show a different side of the dominant discourse of business, development and neoliberalism.

In the following chapters I present different aspects of global engagement and offshored investment at various stages of their functioning. I take the reader through the process of localization and show the different stages of the industrial node's lifecycle: from the physical infrastructure, to the prestige of the location or the locally understood significance of industrial labour. I also describe local economic strategies and how the presence of the plant generated specific changes in the local dynamics. Throughout my study, I show the tensions that those processes caused, while stimulating further changes. Finally, I explain the effects of the node's relocation. Despite the fact that the plant disappeared from Romania, the experience of offshored investment influenced the self-perception of the community and enforced social ties. The investor's departure shows how accurate this process is for describing those dependencies. What was left in the village was a mobile phone factory waiting for someone to use it as well as a devoted labour force. However, there are other assets that were developed, including important infrastructure such as roads, street lighting, etc. that improved the lives of the people in the community and connected them to a broader economic system. Even without the foreign investment, the connection to a global market continues.

1   The Post-socialist Workforce in Global Production

By opening the national economic systems after 1989, formerly isolated socialist economies have been reconnected with the global economic system. One of the most important propellers of this change has been foreign investment. Since the structural transformation, the former Eastern bloc has become a major destination for industrial offshoring. Foreign investors participated in the privatisation of former state companies, merged with local firms, established joint ventures and subsidiaries, and developed green field investments (Weresa, 2004). Investors have been attracted by the low-cost of labour, the stability of the political situation, state-led initiatives supporting foreign investors, and geographic proximity to Western markets (Ellingstad, 1997; United Nations Conference on Trade and Development, 2012; Smith et al., 2008). The opening of previously isolated economies to foreign investors brought internal optimism and economic growth in the region as well as instantaneous restructuring of any former poorly functioning state enterprises (Bandelj, 2004; Clark and Soulsby, 2012; Fabry and Zeghni, 2006; Weresa, 2004). The effective actions of investors resulted in an uncritical view of offshoring from local populations and policy makers. Also known as "the obsession with foreign investors", this manifested in an indifference to the distinctions between investment types and their outcomes as well as the lack of consideration for their adverse effects (Pavlínek, 2004). The enthusiasm for investments also occurred among the workforce. Experiencing adverse effects of market reforms, low-skilled populations idealized investors, seeing them as saviours from the troubled, sometimes bankrupt, industrial entities. Throughout 25 years of change, the presence of international investors has completely re-structured the manufacturing sector in the region. Investors have become key players, not only leading economic growth, but also introducing new workplace practices and bringing international management trends, up-to-date technology, and industry standards (Uhlenbruck, 2004; Clark and Soulsby, 2012). In effect, the post-socialist manufacturing sector became an important element of the global offshoring system, dynamically growing in automotive, consumer electronics, and wood processing industries (Sturgeon et al., 2008; Bohle and Greskovits, 2006).

The offshored investments employed a large portion of an even greater population of workers laid off in the process of market transformation. Following the transition, masses of industrial workers faced lay-offs and experienced difficulties in re-entering the industrial workforce (Torres, 2011; Brainerd, 2000; Bohle and Greskovits, 2007). Prior to transition, former socialist enterprises were very significant employers. Most of them, when confronted with market reality, proved to be rather unsuccessful in adapting to the contemporary realities and failed, leaving large and unqualified populations unemployed (Crowley and Ost, 2001; Marin, 2006). Many of those laid off in both the industrial and agricultural sectors were forced to maintain their existence with state support or early retirement programmes. Following the initial shrinkage in manual jobs, a change was brought on by foreign investors, who initiated new production processes and hired a small number of workers desperate to continue employment. In seeking a low-waged workforce, this process first took place in urban centres, expanding to more peripheral areas. The ability to find these opportunities has become a *modus operandi* of international investors desiring competitive advantage in post-socialist Europe.

Low demand for industrial labour in states such as Romania therefore translated into the progressive degradation of employment practices, which, to some degree, was exploited by foreign investors (Woolfson, 2007). At the same time, local conditions were coupled with external trends, reflecting the progressing global degradation of industrial employment (Blyton and Jenkins, 2012; Cowie, 2010; Hochschild and Machung, 2012; Mollona, 2009). Since the 1970s, the geographical pursuit of lower production costs has intensified, causing a deepening power imbalance between local workforces and industrial producers (Silver, 2004). When after 1989 the economies of the Eastern bloc opened to outside investment, the cost-based race led investors to seek profits in these disadvantaged regions. Practices used by investors have often taken the form of "social dumping", causing the depreciation of wages, preventing upward mobility, increasing reliance on weakening state support and limiting opportunities for a long-term career path (Lillie, 2010; McGovern, 2007). Industrial manufacturing to a large degree contributed to the deregulation and decentralization of trade unions as well as a weakened representation of the working class (Lee and Trappmann, 2014; Varga, 2014). This has led to an expansion of the "working poor", an active labour population falling below the poverty line (Kopinak, 1996; Salzinger, 2003; Pun, 2005). The labour force in the global manufacturing sector has also been increasingly composed of the female workforce, often facing no work alternatives and migrating to industrial zones as a result (Cravey, 1998; Brooks, 2007; Mills, 1999; Ong, 1987; Ong, 1991). Change occurred also in the managerial techniques used in investments. Investors often relied on efficiency maximization techniques, effectively removing worker involvement and expanding control (Silver, 2004). This global trend has been significantly reflected in the position of the post-socialist workforce.

Adopting market freedom brings to question social stability, which was broadly addressed by Karl Polanyi in *The Great Transformation* (Polanyi, 1957). Polanyi shows through the history of capitalism how competitive advantage was becoming the primary logic governing social relations and how societies responded to it over time. Polanyi's insight was visionary as it helps to frame the issues emerging from the spreading and localizing of neoliberalism through economic globalization. Polanyi saw the transformation to market society through the process of "disembedding". Disembedding was the effect of the process of commodification, so putting elements of social life on the market. At the same time, society defended itself against this process, creating the "double-movement of history", which oscillated between moments when the market was disembedded from social norms and controls and a social countermovement, which re-embedded the free market in the society. In other words, the social status quo is either pushed towards free market development and short-term profit domination or social protection that is based on a responsive action to the domination of economic rationality. A regulating component in the double-movement lies in the hands of the nation-state, which works as a buffer by regulating the amount of freedom of the market. For a state, in order to be a part of the global market, it is necessary to enable the preliminary process of economic integration. As I demonstrate in Chapter 4 of this book, it is mainly up to the national legislative and state policy in the transforming economies such as Romania to do so.

The most important assumption is the inability of the market to provide any form of social and environmental protection. Polanyi's framework proves that throughout history the reactions to the market can be seen as "an essentially disconnected set of national movements, each with goals and strategies determined by the place of its own nation state within the larger global market" (Evans, 2008: 273–274). As the market cannot be properly protected and disciplined, people who are connected by it are left to fend for themselves and cannot be protected from the potential chaos of the unregulated circulation of capital. Moreover, today this process intensifies with globalization. My work is inspired by Polanyi in that it provides a perspective on the market participant, such as a worker who cannot defend his social well-being in the market context. It means that in a Polanyian perspective we can put into the matrix issues such as: health care, family leave, living wage campaigns, consumer boycotts, improved working conditions or wages. As Michael Burawoy noted, "Polanyian-type struggles invite alliances among communities facing commodification of social existence"(Burawoy, 2010: 182). It is unlike the issues concerning the unification of the class of exploited workers, like in the case of Marxism, which in terms of the industrial relations focuses mainly on exploitation in the workplace. Additionally, the Polanyian point of view, unlike Marx's perspective, also includes those who are not on the payroll but who are influenced by the capitalist activity, including people facing water-privatisation, degradation of the environment or effects of the economic activity. In practice, adapting the view suggested by Polanyi permits us to think in the categories of actors, rather than focus on the externally driven mechanisms of history or the economic system. We might even say that it is a more ethnographic point of view; the research tries to grasp the set of contextual conditions in order to see the interaction.

Eastern Europe provides a specific case of internationalization, introduction of the market economy and economic globalization. By all means, its systemic transformation was among the biggest neoliberal experiments that have ever happened. Many of its outcomes, reformed according to the plans made by economists, were very successful, including the implementation of a number of policies and reformation of collapsed economies permitted social change and advancing social conditions provided decency, even though for some it meant being thrown to the margin of society. Elizabeth Dunn wrote one of the best accounts of this process. Her excellent book *Privatizing Poland* describes a transitory environment of workplace connected to the implementation of the new managerial standards. Dunn writes that her research provides "the opportunity to rethink the consequences of these isolating and privatizing practices: the products people in market buy and the self-audits they perform, the kinds of moral balance sheets they construct and the relationships they invest time in" (Dunn, 2004: 173–174). Dunn's account explicitly shows the ways of coping and making meaning of the new, lived practices. The perspective that I present goes beyond the simple category of systemic transformation, even though it clearly has its elements. By describing the presence of the new investment, I posit the economic influence over the ongoing systemic transformation in Eastern Europe taking place for 25 years as well as the change connected to participation in the global economy.

2   Offshoring Studies

This book bridges theoretical arguments addressing the processes of degradation of employment in the manufacturing industry and studies of post-socialist industry transformation by depicting their intersection with familial organisation and the changing dynamics in the private lives of workers. Taking up the perspective of the workforce (Pun, 2005; Mills, 1999; Dunn, 2004) and considering working class families' livelihoods, I observe that offshoring in the former Eastern bloc largely relies on local resources, which are made available in the moment of taking up employment, and they function as enabling mechanisms for industrial activity. My approach assumes that local culture, faced with challenges connected to structural limitations caused by the investment and stemming from the transitional reality of post-socialist Europe, mobilizes its own resources to achieve economic progress. In this book I show how offshoring influences and affects organisational culture in the workplace, the organisation of a worker's family structure, and the influence of offshoring labour in the region on the situation of those not directly on the payroll, such as other household members.

In addressing offshore investments, mainstream literature has predominantly concentrated on the economic dimension of the process, giving attention to a number of employee and labour-related topics. Firstly, a core part of this research has focused on interdependencies and networks that embrace both the sending and host economies, such as global value chains, global production networks (Lakhani et al., 2013) or theories of multinational enterprise (Guillen and Garcia-Canal, 2009; Marginson et al., 2010). Studies have also concentrated on issues concerning sending and receiving economies, such as labour agency shifts (Rainnie et al., 2011; Riisgaard and Hammer, 2011); challenges to organised labour (Kshetri and Dholakia, 2009); casualisation of employment (Barrientos and Kritzinger, 2004); or implications of a firm upgrading for labour (Barrientos and Rossi, 2011; Knorringa and Pegler, 2006). Secondly, an important research focus has been placed on the offshoring workplace and issues connected to distinct national institutional contexts (Meyer et al., 2011; Figueiredo, 2011) and the intercultural aspects of offshoring projects (Nicholson and Sahay, 2001). This included studies of the governance process (Gooris and Peeters, 2014), organizational adaptation (Asmussen et al., 2016), and organizational change in both home and host firms, for instance occurring over time and differing in many cases from their initial objectives and expectations (Jensen, 2009, Lewin and Peeters, 2006). Thirdly, a key area of study has been on new workers in receiving economies (Woodart and Sherman, 2015) and issues that arise there, such as the employees' attitudes towards the offshoring of labour in hosting states (Linder, 2011; Sengupta and Gupta, 2012) or worker reactions to a high level of supervision and control (Budhwar et al., 2006). Most of the literature on offshoring has produced research that fosters a better understanding of the dynamics and relations within the offshoring network and almost exclusively focuses on interfirm and firm-employee relations. Very little has been done to address the familial implications of offshoring in the receiving populations, especially on the micro-level.

This work intends to supplement the research by providing an empirical and theoretical contribution. It addresses the processes of employment degradation in the manufacturing industry and global workforce transformation by depicting the intersection of these processes with familial organisation practices and the changing dynamics in the private lives of workers. The theoretical foundation of this book underscores that a thorough study of offshoring requires the researcher to not only examine the workplace, worker and employment relations, but also to focus on familial relations, which, as I demonstrate, add an important dimension to the analysis of global accumulation and offshoring. The main argument rests on the assertion that local populations in offshoring destination countries that are facing challenges connected to structural limitations that stem from both the investments' labour conditions, such as low-pay and precarious work conditions, and the reality of destination countries with social instability and economic turbulence, mobilises its own resources for the sake of socioeconomic progress of its members. In this book I show how these two types of limitations affect the organisation of a worker's family, leading to the creation of mutual dependencies between the offshoring firm and receiving workforce. My analysis articulates the mutual dependence of family and offshoring process, understood as a set of mutual relations that are based not only on financial gains and social protection from offshoring work, but also on the worker's reliance on familial support, which, for instance, allows young adults to pursue employment.

This book provides a new perspective on the global labour market participant: the worker who cannot defend their social well-being in the market context and who by participating in the labour market extensively involves, or heavily relies upon, his or her family. Familial involvement should be recognised as a significant part of global industrial production employment, as it is related to widely recognised issues such as health care, family leave, living wage campaigns, consumer boycotts, working conditions and wages. By including family in this analysis, this book demonstrates another type of a Polanyian struggle understood as a response to the commodification of social existence (Polanyi, 1944; Burawoy, 2010). Therefore, this analysis supplements critical literature concerning the global exploitation of the workforce (Seidman, 2007; Webster et al., 2011) and studies that have addressed offshoring's reliance on low-skilled employment, low wages and how this process translates into the progressive degradation of employment practices (Cowie, 2010; Hochschild and Machung, 2012; Woolfson, 2007). This literature notes that since the 1970s, the pursuit of lower production costs has intensified, causing a deepening power imbalance between the local workforces and industrial producers (Silver, 2004). It has been extensively demonstrated how the cost-based race led investors to seek profits in disadvantaged regions, what employment practices were used, and how they translated to the depreciation of wages, prevention of social mobility, increase of reliance on weakening state support, and the limitation of long-term career path opportunities (Lillie, 2010; McGovern, 2007). None of this literature has however explicitly identified the role of familial support in this process, and this book responds to that gap.

3   Social Reproduction and Offshoring

This book proposes a critical examination of offshoring by adapting a political economy framework and concentrating on the relationship between global offshoring production, offshoring labour, and the worker's position in a market society. Even though mainstream literature demonstrates offshoring's role in generating economic growth, restructuring local industries, or producing spillover effects (Fabry and Zeghni, 2006; Winkler, 2013; Pavlínek, 2004), it has been extensively shown how offshoring leads to the exploitation of the working class, motivated by lowering labour costs. Especially within the manufacturing sector, the majority of the labour force is composed of women, often facing zero work alternatives and migrating to industrial zones as a result which leads to exploitation (Cravey, 1998; Brooks, 2007). Power inequalities in this industry manifest not only in employment conditions but also in the managerial techniques used in the investments. Investors often deliberately deepen workers' commitments, for instance by expanding knowledge about the workers' family lives (Mills, 1999), extensive control over private and free time (Lee, 2007; Pun, 2005; Pun and Smith, 2007) or through loss of workers' control over work time and scope (Cravey, 1998; Fernández-Kelly, 1983; Salzinger, 2003).

The power imbalance between offshoring and labour has its roots in structural limitations that stem from both the investments' labour conditions, such as low-pay and precarious work conditions, and the reality of destination countries with social instability and economic turbulence. In Eastern Europe free market reforms provoked a radical decrease in the number of industrial jobs (United Nations Conference on Trade and Development, 2012), accompanied by broader social turbulence, such as crumbling state support and shrinking state welfare (Deacon, 1992; Haney, 2002). This has limited formerly extensive social services, such as medical and child-care or labour protection. In effect, the systemic shift has resulted in deepening social problems, strongly impacting disadvantaged populations of industrial and agricultural workers (Brainerd, 2000; Bohle and Greskovits, 2007; Funk and Mueller, 1993; Pascall and Kwak, 2005; Einhorn, 1993; Fortuny et al., 2003; Torres, 2011). In this book, I consider these realities by examining the familial adaptations to the conditions of offshoring labour.

Existing literature on structural problems in transforming economies has attempted to identify coping strategies, and a strong accent has been placed on the household. For instance, defunct state care was replaced by family support, including taking care of children and providing resources to those who faced layoffs in state-owned industries and playing a key role in organising livelihoods by reallocating at-home labour to household members (Rajkai, 2015; Pine, 2002). Unemployed family members pursued informal work at home (Rudd, 2006; Szalai, 2000; Bridger and Pine, 1998) and took care of children and the elderly (Haukanes and Pine, 2005; Szelewa and Polakowski, 2008) or participated in subsistence farming (Pine, 2002; Mathijs and Noev, 2004). This at-home organizational balance was based on bridging salaried labour of household members active in the labour market and the at-home duties of the others. Using an empirical example from this context, my work uniquely demonstrates the reliance of offshoring labour on these strategies activated by the transformational environment.

I propose to incorporate the dimension of family in order to expand the existing theories on the political economy of offshoring. This perspective attempts to produce a picture of offshoring organisation that goes beyond the workplace and offshoring networks, and it is crucial for studying receiving communities. My proposal is based on identifying the paradoxical relationship between the structure of market society and its incompatibility with social reproduction (Bezanson and Luxton, 2006; Peterson, 2005; Vosko, 2002). Drawing on feminist political economy (Meaghar and Nelson, 2004; Jefferson and King, 2001), which predominantly studies intra-familial dynamics within the capitalist system, this book theorises "mutual dependency" between offshoring labour and a worker family. On the one hand, this orientation permits observing how offshoring labour relies on at-home support, and on the other, allows for observing the effects of offshoring's production on local populations. Offshoring destination countries provide an important case study, where both global financialisation and progressing degradation of employment coincide with privatisation and commodification of formerly non-marketed spheres of social reproduction in transition countries. This approach shows how offshoring produces what Nancy Fraser has termed "the social-reproductive contradiction of financialised capitalism" (Fraser, 2017: 22). The findings of this book allow for further consideration of the ethics of offshoring, the future of receiving populations, and social reproduction of the global workforce.

4   Ethnography of Foreign Investment

The ethnographic data used in this book was collected from interviews with workers and their families. Despite the relative proximity to the city, the hosting community, as well as the communities that the majority of the workforce was recruited from, some features of a traditional rural village, in which there are still elements of *Gemeinschaft* solidarity networks, communal social relations and the residents are often connected through kinship and religion (Tönnies, 1934). Remotely located, with a history of collective socialist enterprises organizing local life, these rural populations maintained a traditional lifestyle, largely based on multi-generational households and reliance on semi-subsistence agriculture. Their region witnessed Romania's biggest foreign investment at the time, which provided over four thousand low-skilled positions for workers from the region. The investment was created in 2007 on the initiative of the investor and co-sponsored by the local government, which provided the land and developed the infrastructure.

Another topic that this work addresses is the issue of the global mobility of production nodes, as parts of global production systems. Despite the wealth of literature analysing the outcomes of labour arbitrage, there is still a gap in studying "on the ground" effects of the mobility of workplaces. My work seeks to explain how industrial relocations shape local communities. In this manuscript, I focus on the lived experience of labour arbitrage by showing the changing situation of workers during a manufacturing plant's location, presence and relocation.

Ethnographic studies of workplaces have proven to be a helpful tool in framing encounters with overseas organisational cultures. Anthropologists and sociologists have widely addressed how foreign investors have either transformed existing workplaces or created new ones, for instance by introducing new management systems, bringing in foreign management staff or increasing efficiency. This transformation is taking place on a global scale. Labour studies have commented on the problems of workers in a global context, for instance by referring to the industrial workplaces in Mexico (Fernández-Kelly, 1983; Salzinger, 2003), Thailand (Mills, 1999), or China (Lee, 2007; Pun, 2005). Understanding global phenomena is possible only through the experiences of the people who live it. Michael Burawoy argues that the ethnographer has privileged insight into the lived experience of globalization (Burawoy, 2000). For Burawoy, global ethnography signifies "releasing fieldwork from solitary confinement, from being bound to a single place and time" (Burawoy, 2000: 4). For Burawoy, global research requires that researchers pursue ethnographic work globally. Comparing this stand to classical ethnography, fieldwork still plays the leading role. However, the diversity of sources and the number of materials increases due to the complexity of global phenomena. Because of the very dynamic and changing character of global problems, a larger number of levels and changing perspectives might be required. Similarly, the nature of fieldwork evolves, pushing the researcher towards "multi-sited fieldwork" and requiring "multi-levelled single-site fieldwork", which can mean studying one phenomenon from the perspective of different social groups or studying one site at "several levels of abstraction from ongoing social process" (Eriksen, 2003).

My 16 months of research took place in 2011 and 2012. My goal was to learn how the global investment is understood locally and how the presence of the production plant generated change. Initially, my research plan included exploring the outcomes of the global node's presence. However, after about three months of my work in the field I was surprised by the investment's relocation. This required adaptation, and in effect, I re-designed my research in order to showcase the outcomes stemming not only from the investment's location but also from its departure. As a result, I built a comprehensive ethnographic study of the factory's influence. I studied the hosting community, the workforce, and the workers' families, and I complimented this data with content analysis of press publications that addressed the investment. In the next chapters, I provide limited information on the interviewees in order to protect their identity.

5 The Investor and the Region

Nokia was once a symbol of prestige and technology that was globally recognized for excellent quality and innovation. Since the early 1990s the company was growing, focusing on digital solutions in mobile communication and competing with its main rivals Motorola and Ericsson (Steinbock, 2005). The company came up with a unique design for its products, created new trends as well as generated technological standards that were cutting edge. At the same time, the usability of Nokia devices made them available for virtually everyone, not only business people (Lindholm et al., 2003). Year after year Nokia's product portfolio was growing and the brand became a symbol for popular mobile telecommunications (Steinbock, 2001; Häikiö, 2002). Even though Nokia had Finnish origins, its growth made the company truly multinational (Ornston, 2006; Lattanzi et al., 2006; Daveri and Silva, 2004). Its large network of suppliers obtained a truly global character that spread to all continents. In 2005, every third mobile phone used in the world was produced by Nokia. The corporation introduced phones with cameras, selling the highest number of camera lenses in the world, as well as popularized wireless protocols in mobile phones. The world fell in love with Nokia.

Nokia's investment took place in Transylvania, in proximity to one of the most important cities of Romania, Cluj-Napoca, with a population of about 400,000. The literature has extensively reflected on this region's multicultural past, consisting of large populations of Romanians and Hungarians as well as the existing historical tensions between them (Brubaker et al., 2006; Mitu, 2001; Verdery, 1983; Kovács Kiss, 2011). For the last eighty years, the population of Hungarians, representing the more privileged and educated urban class, has significantly dropped due to extensive migrations to Hungary. Cluj's important chapter under socialism included high industrialisation and development of production facilities as well as extensive involvement in manufacturing. This resulted in a growing working-class population, mostly consisting of rural immigrants of Romanian origins occupying low-skilled positions. Their large numbers created worker neighbourhoods, symbols of the city's new development and evolving public space (Lazar, 2003), with their inhabitants being significantly reliant on factory labour. At the same time, part of the socialist workforce remained in the countryside, commuting on a daily basis and fulfilling the function of peasant-worker, while also working in agriculture. The emergence of the working class was strongly linked to party planning and the process of rapid industrialisation. Outside of the city, the region has a strong agricultural past with a large number of collective farms and extensive involvement in the country's agriculture sector.

With the collapse of socialism, a wave of unemployment severely touched the region. Rising prices and high unemployment stemming from the collapse of state farming and industry caused a deep crisis of the working class (Neef and Stanulescu, 2002; Kideckel, 2008; Petrovici, 2012). The post-socialist crisis had profound consequences as the Romanian systemic transition, more explicitly addressed in Chapter 2 of this book, produced high levels of turbulence and social problems, especially affecting the most vulnerable populations in the region. Many in the workforce were pushed to re-migrate to rural areas and semi-subsistence agriculture in the countryside, and they faced the process of self-selection and destruction of existing trust networks (Petrovici, 2011, 2012). The transition for the region signified the sale of some of the former state-owned enterprises to investors and expansion to new activities by foreign investors. Due to the presence of leading universities and active academic life, in addition to the low-skilled workforce, the city's population is also composed of educated graduates and much of its labour market is in the service economy (Petrovici, 2013). The arrival of the multinational corporations, such as the Nokia Corporation, which was among the largest employers in the region reliant on low-skilled labour, opened new opportunities for this region, also playing a significant role in the shifts in the national economy.

The contribution of this book is threefold. Firstly, a lot of empirical work regarding the process of industrial relocation has been concentrated on Western urban centres and has analysed economies with an industrial past (Rousseau, 2011; Mollona, 2009; Blyton and Jenkins, 2012). This work refers to a case in Eastern Europe, a region which has not been previously studied in the context of industrial relocation and which can be considered a semi-periphery of European industrial production. Secondly, this case argues in support of the theoretical position of uneven geographical development, expanding it to the issues typical to the region, such as social reproduction. Once an industrial zone was built, it constituted "a space of global capitalism" and brought intensified neoliberal activity to the region (Harvey, 1990). The eventual relocation of the plant proves that the journey was part of the ongoing spatial restructuring of production. According to Harvey, this process of "accumulation by dispossession" propels the informalisation of labour and results in a global decline of workers' rights and entitlements such as wages, social benefits or job security (Harvey, 1990). As my case illustrates, the workers' lack of ability to achieve upward mobility pushed them to seek alternative sources of income during employment in the plant and to use the support of other household members. Industrial employment was thus closely tied to workers' private lives and at-home care and support. Thirdly, by referring to the consequences of the plant's closure, I show how the workforce and host community considered the industrial zone a "spatial fix" of the global capitalist production. By referring to the mechanisms of social support and solidarity following the relocation, the chapter demonstrates how different the reactions of the workforce in new geographies are compared to more advanced economies. Romanian workers' deep belief that the industrial production in the zone will promptly continue with another investor strongly reflects what Marx termed the expansion of the global reserve army of labour (Marx, 2001).

6   The Structure of this Book

I present how the local community participates in the investment and how they contribute their effort, commitment and resources. Central to this process are the ties between local workers, their families and global value chain, and even the global economy. My work shows how this connection is created and how it matures over time. I organize my findings in a chronological way in order to show how a global production node was understood and how its relationship with the receiving population changed over time. The major focus of my enquiry is to observe and present how locally generated dependencies emerge, how they persistently grow, and finally what happens with these resources once an investor leaves. The short period was enough to not only develop brand new infrastructure but also entirely change the scalar positionality of the region and the workforce. Specific desires, hopes, benefits as well as new cultural capital transformed not only the workforce but also the village and changed the understanding of foreign investments and globalization in Romania. I consider the short period of the lifecycle of a production node as a metaphor for changes that communities are bound to face in today's reality and an attempt to conceptualise the ways in which nodes of production penetrate societies.

Chapter 1 analyses Romania's integration into the global economy and sets up the background of the events described in the book. This chapter shows the process of systemic transformation of a post-socialist state. By giving attention to the economic opening of Romania, it chronologically focuses on the political events and the role of external organizations, such as the World Bank or IMF, and how they enforced Romania's global economic integration through loan mechanisms. This part also addresses the inflow of foreign direct investment, which reflects the investors' trust and Romania's political and economic adjustment to the global production market. The analysis is divided into four periods. Firstly, it starts with the initial period of transition and shows how Romania's post-communist ruling class failed to reform the state. Then, throughout the mid-1990s, it shows the country's struggles with the reforms, followed by waves of transitional fevers. Thirdly, since 2004, Romania's transition sped up because of the prospect of membership in the European Union. During this time, the economy grew, thanks in large part to the wave of foreign investments, including Nokia's. Fourthly, the global economic crisis and mounting debts of the state forced the government to introduce strong austerity measures. The difficulties included mass street protests and the attempt to impeach the President. This is when Nokia closed down the factory and moved production to China. The analysis of this chapter shows the socioeconomic dimension of the internationalisation of a state in transition, addressing shifts in labour law and orientations of political class, providing a historical context for the investment addressed in this book.

Chapter 2 opens the ethnography-based part of this work. It demonstrates how the local population reacts to the plans of the investment and the global production node. The analysis explains the establishment of the global assemblage (Ong and Collier, 2004) and addresses the process of scalar changes in two geographical contexts, where production formerly took place in Germany but closed to re-locate to Romania and the new location of the plant in Romania. This description starts from the moment when the decision to build a plant in Romania is announced and considers the initial plans of establishing a cluster – named by the investor the Nokia Village. Further analysis considers the negotiations process (the initiative came from the investor), reactions of the hosting community to the process of construction of the industrial zone and the plant, and commentary on how the German public took the news of the investment in Romania and perceived the Romanian side. The chapter is concluded by an extensive description of how some hosting community members participated in the opening of the plant by the investor.

Chapter 3 is a study of the workplace. It demonstrates the cultural specificity of work in the plant, and it addresses the adaptation efforts of the workforce. It considers the process of recruitment, describes hiring policy and salaries, as well as challenges connected to formalised application of work. Its main part analyses the process of worker socialization and adaptation to the highly regulated and formal environment of the plant. I show how important the cultural specificity of the plant was and how it contrasted with existing experiences of the workforce by using the metaphor of the "journey". I also describe the efforts connected to adjustment to new organizational culture and language, learning terminology related to production, acclimating to the work attire as well as invariable temperature and lack of windows. In this part I argue that despite the hardships, manual labour and the relatively low salary, the plant was perceived mainly in positive terms. The distinctiveness, almost exoticism, popped up in nearly all assessments of the workplace by the workers who highly valued the all-encompassing experience of a highly clean and modern environment and specific workplace rules and procedures.

Chapter 4 examines the context of the workplace by concentrating on shop floor culture and mechanisms of coping with routine production. As I show, a key part of the coping strategies to the realities of work was played by humour and storytelling. In my analysis, I relate to the existing literature on shop floor cultures (Korczynski, 2011; Collinson, 1988; Ackroyd and Thompson) and consider functions of humour in the workplace. The first fulfils the function of "lubricating the Taylorist workplace" (Korczynski, 2011), producing mechanisms of coping with boredom from repetitive tasks and the physical demands of the work. Using empirical data, I show how talking, laughing, and provoking funny situations was among the biggest attractions during the long working days. Secondly, I describe the role of shop floor culture in coping with the oppressiveness of control, which in the plant included a complex surveillance system, physical control of the workers' possessions and extensive monitoring of all worker activities through CCTV. A key strategy for coping with oppressive invigilation was storytelling. Using humour, for instance by discussing the alleged attempts of stealing memory cards by a hypothetical worker, provided a platform to develop personal autonomy from the oppressive supervision. I argue that this type of coping mechanism shows significant parallels to socialist joking (Lampland and Nadkarni, 2016), based on specific antagonism between the socialist everyman and the oppressive power structures of the state. Both similarly have humorously and critically described everyday hardships and realities, as well as openly criticised power structures and existing procedures. Thirdly, I describe workplace storytelling, which played a significant role in the plant, by providing descriptions of improbable and controversial facts or events related to plant's functioning. Even despite their anecdotal character, I argue that the function of this mechanism was to fill epistemic holes connected to the functioning of the global value chain, such as the lack of access to information regarding the key decisions made in the plant, the role of the plant in the global corporation, and the relationship of the investor with the Romanian state.

Chapter 5 problematizes worker family organization, which was influenced by the investment. This part concentrates on the mechanisms that emerged in response to the structural limitations existing in the region and the reaction to investors' activity. In this part I argue that offshoring production in the region created mutual dependencies along with existing models of family organisation. These dependencies triggered familial agency that enabled upward economic mobility and allowed for changes in lifestyle and purchasing power for its worker-members. I argue that offshoring labour was highly reliant on familial support, which played a key part in enabling offshoring work by providing social reproductive functions to the workers. Otherwise the employment in the plant would not have been possible because a single operator's salary was insufficient for life. At the same time, I describe how this relationship was interpreted on the family level. It played a crucial part in the fulfilment of aspirations connected to inter-generational economic mobility. By referring to these dynamics in this part I discuss evidence of how foreign investments rely on this type of local agency and familial involvement, and I problematize gender and age in the context of the region's rural traditions of bridging industrial work with semi-subsistence agriculture and desires of modernisation and urbanisation.

Chapter 6 concentrates on the events following the decision to re-locate the plant from Romania to Southern Asia. It examines the reactions of the workforce and the events following the announcement of the plant closure in 2012, including often-positive opinions, despite the termination of production, and, in fact, understanding the decision as rational and cost effective. But this section also shows the precarious situation that the closure of the plant left families in, including those who had taken up bank loans and those who had expected to reach retirement age while working in the plant. The traditional rural household provided shelter from the potentially disastrous effects of the investor's decision by incorporating family members into the subsistence production and at-home duties. This part also addresses low mobilization against the investor's decision and puts forth the argument that the high number of short-term contracts contributed to a lack of trust in worker unions and the expectation that the job will not be long-term or stable.

Chapter 7 expands the study by focusing on the national and regional reactions of authorities, commentators and politicians. This chapter shows how the investment became a national issue, quickly moving to the front-page headlines of national newspapers. The analysis of the discourse allows for understanding how important the investment was for national self-perception and the image of the successful systemic transition of Romania. The investor's disappearance generated high expectations of finding a new investor, and the discourse depicts how the investor has incorporated local workforce into a global "reserve army of labour" (Marx, 2001: 707) reliant on external capital to achieve an imaginary fantasy of capitalist modernisation and future. In the empirical part I show the key themes of the public debate, including poor protections in the contract between the authorities and Nokia, which probably did not specify the minimum stay period of the company and controversies related to the role of Romania in the global economy and its relationship to other geographies of production, as well as the range of speculations regarding the new investor.

These chapters are followed by a conclusion that summarizes the book's findings and considers the twofold role of the offshoring investments in middle-income economies. It argues that on the one hand they support the desire for modernisation and Western-style livelihoods, and on the other hand, they expose local populations to tensions caused by global labour arbitrage based on global cost-competition, cost-cutting race and progressing degradation of employment.

CHAPTER 1

Romania's Systemic Transformation: Chaos, Austerity and Imposed Neoliberal Reform

Romania, like other Eastern European countries, went through a process of systemic transformation. From 1990 onwards, former socialist economies have slowly reformed and opened themselves up to the world. The end of the socialist era introduced the formerly isolated markets to the international economy (Balcerowicz, 1995). The new situation, strongly inspired by international economic and political pressures, influenced the developing democratic ideas and market freedom (Grzymala-Busse and Luong, 2002). The pace of reforms varied in different states and depended on the availability of the internal agents of transformation (Fish, 1997) and the amount of external support (Kovács and Zentai, 2012). The fastest advancing economies, such as Poland and Hungary, reformed through shock therapy which involved trade liberalization, price stabilization and removing state subsidizing practices through privatisations and re-structuring (Gligorov, 1994). The slower ones, including Romania, delayed their reforms, and as a result, focused on coping with structural turbulence, lack of consistency in local-level governance and an instable economy (King and Sum, 2011; Noutcheva and Bechev, 2008).

Romania's systemic transition was different from the beginning. The country was one of the few socialist countries that ended communism with a revolution. Its major effect was the abolition of the communist system and the immediate execution of Romania's communist leader Nicolae Ceaușescu and his wife Elena. From the first moments of transition, the state struggled with political consistency, which was fed by populism. Up until the mid-1990s it was unclear whether Romania will stay under the influence of Western capitalist democracies or rather the Eastern, Russia-led world. Once the state leaned towards the West, mounting difficulties emerged. The activity of the institutions known as Bretton Woods loan-givers, i.e. the World Bank, the International Monetary Fund (IMF), as well as the European Commission, officially attempted to support the country's systemic adjustment to the Western world, bringing in anti-communist narratives and promising the right to property, freedom, and prosperity. At the same time these states supported the regulation of global capitalism by connecting less advanced economies to the advanced ones and reproducing uneven development (Smith, 1990). These institutions, through loans conditioned by steered reforms, stimulated the country's engagement in global capitalism and co-organized the advancements of the implementation of the market economy (Vincze, 2015).

According to the external perspective, the transition was based on the introduction of neoliberal policymaking and continuous progress in the privatisation of public assets, including state-owned enterprises, land, housing and natural resources. In response to the pressures coming from the loan-givers, the Romanian political class continuously played a "two-level game", trying to satisfy both external and internal constituencies (Linden, 2004). To the discontent of many Romanians, loans and arrangements with the West did not bring lasting stability and caused heavily paid social costs. Throughout the years, Romania was able to stay on the Western course and slowly follow the path taken by other reforming Eastern European states. This process put a heavy burden on society and the workforce.

Throughout the next chapters, I focus on a case study that concerns the relationship established between the local population of Romanian workers and a foreign investor. Foreign Direct Investment (FDI) is an investment made by a company from an investor country in a foreign host country with the goal of creating a long-term relationship with significant management influence and investor ownership of at least 10 per cent (Bandelj, 2009). FDI's presence in post-1989 Eastern Europe is strongly connected to trade liberalization, advocated by neoliberal macroeconomists and the European Union. In the region, the amount of FDI inflows has strongly differed, as local governments demonstrated different approaches to their presence and the process of transition. Quite often, especially in the context of privatisation, FDI became a politicized issue of selling the "family's crest" (Sinn and Weichenrieder, 1997). A common view on FDI during transformation was based on an assumption that it plays a key role in generating economic growth, leading to long-term positive effects, such as the survival of domestic companies, or providing new workplaces with green field investments. This view has strongly contributed to "Eastern Europe's obsession with foreign investors" and an uncritical view, largely ignoring the diversity of the FDIs and their adverse effects, such as those on the balance of payments and the loss of sovereignty (Pavlínek, 2004).

In the following sections of this chapter, I introduce the process of Romania's integration into the global economy in order to paint the political context of the investor's presence in the country. The four sections of this chapter contain an analysis depicting the progress of state reforms and political struggles related to it. I divide them into four different stages. From (1) the early transition and start of slow reform (1989–1996); (2) the period of externally enforced but necessary reforms followed by a transitional fever (1996–2004); (3) the moment of international political integration and economic boom connected to the aspirations of joining the European Union (2004–2009); to (4) the economic crisis and extensive implementation of neoliberal measures (2009–2014). In my analysis, I pay attention to the process of economic opening and shifting of internal dynamics and legislation. Each of these stages brought different elements to Romania's political and economic transformation. As depicted in Figure 1, these periods are also characterized by different levels of the foreign investors' interest. The inflow of FDI steadily grew till 2009. Then, facing the global economic crisis, the inflow of investments radically dropped. As the figure indicates, throughout the post-communist years Romania sustained a very low outflow of investments. Similarly, in this period the level of imported goods completely outnumbered the amount of exported goods (Romanian National Institute of Statistics, 2011).

The introduction that I provide in this part is organized chronologically. Step by step I show the emergence of a new systemic framework, based on the neoliberal idea of a market state and its role in Romania's opening. Besides chronology, there are several elements that organize this introduction. Firstly, through an outline of the historic changes in political and economic climate of the country, I show the internal context of Romania's pace of transformation and internationalization. By addressing the continuing political tensions, I show how the country was coping with the mounting social problems and how they have had an effect on the externally influenced attempts to progress with

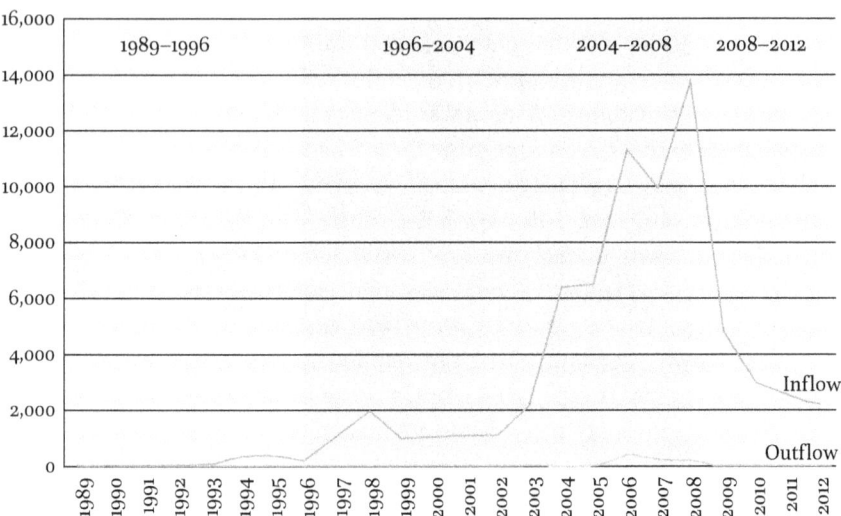

FIGURE 1   Inward and outward foreign direct investment stock in Romania, annual, 1989–2012
SOURCE: UNITED NATIONS CONFERENCE ON TRADE AND DEVELOPMENT (2012B).

systemic transition to the market economy. Secondly, I address the question of the role of external actors in this process. As I show, Romania's transition was largely stimulated by loan-givers and foreign advisory bodies, which under certain pressures imposed a certain progress in systemic changes. Thirdly, in addressing the internationalization process and describing the inflow of foreign investments, I shortly refer to the strategic investments that took place during this process and the dynamics surrounding those projects. Lastly, an essential part of the Romanian transition have been changes in local legislation, relevant to worker status and the role of their unions, as well as the elements of the strategy to attract foreign capital.

The time period of this investment in Romania, which is addressed in this book, was from 2007 to 2012. Nokia Corporation's assembly plant was among the biggest and the most spectacular FDIs in Romania. Its role in the hosting economy was enormous. The multinational was among Romania's largest exporters and its turnover equalled to roughly 1.5 per cent of Romania's GDP. Prior to describing the cultural dimension of this project in the further chapters, in this section I briefly address the investment only by reflecting on its significance for Romania's transformation.

1   Ad-hoc Transition (1989–1996)

The starting point of Romanian transformation was difficult, particularly when compared to the countries of Central and Eastern Europe. Although during Nicolae Ceaușescu's regime, notably in the 1970s, Romania became more integrated with Western Europe than the other ComEcon members, the last decade of the communist rule was disastrous both in social and economic terms. Before the 1980s, Romania's economic policy, especially in relation to other members of the Soviet Bloc, was a source of conflict and controversy with the Soviet Union. During the period of *détente*, Romania not only stayed connected to the West through economic agreements, especially through petrochemical exports and licenses for production technology, but also joined the International Monetary Fund (IMF) in 1972. In addition, its trade with other ComEcon countries was proportionally lower than of any other member state (Mureșan, 2008). In the 1980s, the Socialist Republic of Romania took an $11 billion loan from the World Bank and the IMF, which was entirely paid back over the decade. The $11 billion debt was equal to 20 to 30 per cent of annual gross domestic product (GDP). The repayment was based on cutting down imports and imposing the burden on the population by high taxation of consumption. Romania struggled. The 1980s were an era of political extremism and economic collapse. Economic growth was based on outdated industrial production in large factories for the domestic market. In the literature this stagnation of the 1980s is also called "immiserizing growth" (Daianu, 2004). It manifested in economic collapse, malfunctioning economic allocation and wrong choices in central planning, and this translated to the radical worsening of the living conditions of Romanian population.

The implications of this "immiserizing" growth for the upcoming period of transformation were twofold. On the one hand, the policy of radical reduction of debt resulted in a relatively privileged situation for economic transition. Romania began it with no foreign debt. On the other, the lack of technological progress, no former experience with market freedom, no presence of foreign investments, and complete social exhaustion hampered the growth and decision-making. Moreover, the contribution of the private sector to the economy was much lower in Romania than in the other states of Eastern Europe, especially in those with more liberal policies in their last years of communism. The collapse of the communist regime in Romania took place in December 1989. Just like in the other countries of Eastern Europe, it was followed by a steep economic decline. The disassembly of the Eastern bloc stopped trade agreements and disrupted already slow economic flows. It resulted in Romania's dropping GDP: -5.6, -12.9, -8.7 per cent at the end of each of the first three years of the 1990s. It was coupled with four-year long hyperinflation (International Monetary Fund, 2012). Attempts to regulate inflation and stabilize the economy took over a decade. The issues caused by these processes have largely undermined all opportunities for economic growth and hindered the usage of Romania's advantageous geopolitical location or its large supply of natural resources and agriculture.

The first government was established by the National Salvation Front (FSN – *Frontul Salvării Național*) led by post-communist Ion Iliescu, who was elected for president in 1990. The ruling party's implicit vision for stabilizing Romania's situation was to base it on a pro-Western political orientation and financial assistance from the outside. The IMF loan in 1991 did not prevent the inflation from rocketing, mostly due to the chaos in financial spending. The initial loss of stability was not counteracted by the ruling party, which was about to face the next elections. The promise of protection from the free market reality was necessary for the FSN in order to keep its electoral base. The electorate's fear of deteriorating social conditions was very strong. It was fed by the experience of a difficult decade of extreme economic mismanaging of the 1980s. The success of the 1992 elections did not cause a shift in the government's practice. Although the program of the Party of Social Democracy in Romania (PDSR – *Partidului Democratiei Sociale din Romania*), the successor of the FSN, was more economy-oriented, the new Prime Minister Nicolae Vacaroiu did not express any initiative in revising the actions of the government and the course of the events. Instead of reforms, consecutive negotiations with the IMF and the World Bank for years became the element of political reality in Romania.

Taking a gradualist approach to transformation resulted in a chaotic route. This path manifested in problems caused by state-owned firms, unreformed law, the enormous grey zone and declining GDP. Political projects, such as land restitution to peasants and the creation of micro-farms, mainly served populist goals and were oriented to cater to short-term goals. Subsidization of state enterprises reduced potential unemployment but did not contribute to the overall fitness of the state. The post-communist political elite faced several governance problems during the early years of transition. There was no control over the government actions, and political opposition only started to amalgamate. At the cost of populist moves, such as increasing wages or introducing a five-day workweek, no improvements were made in the ways in which the state functioned in the new reality. Keeping influence over the economy was justified in order to hold the social costs low.

The chaotic transitional environment created the perfect conditions for pathologies. The elite of *nomenklatura* capitalists, composed of former a*pparatchiks*, have played an important part in the changes occurring in the Romanian economy. Thanks to preferential credits and government favours, this group benefited from its connections, for instance by receiving loans from state-run banks, developing economic activities in the grey zone or remaining in the state structures as managers of state enterprises (Gabanyi, 2004; Gallagher, 1998; Grosescu, 2004; Stoica, 2004). This situation strongly differed from the Central and Eastern European path, where the elites immediately entered the private sector and predominantly used their social capital to establish the first enterprises. The effect of Romania's lack of clear economic regulations was an eruption of clientelism and corruption. Along with the low reserves of the Central Bank, the weakness of the Romanian currency and no legislation for foreign investments, this chaos contributed to the negative international perception of the Romanian economy. It was reflected in a very low inflow of foreign investments. In 1993 it equalled only $94 million, compared to Hungary's over $2.4 billion and Poland's $1.7 billion (United Nations Conference on Trade and Development, 2012b). The only initiative oriented to the outside was the free trade agreement with the Republic of Moldova from 1994.

In 1993, the Romanian government tried to improve its financial discipline, starting with the goal of creating a working exchange market. This action was accompanied by other attempts of taking economic measures: tightening subsidization, reducing money creation and lowering the interbank exchange rate

(Radulescu, 2003). Although the interest rate shock in 1993 was followed by a relapse into inflation with a record of 256 per cent in 1993 (International Monetary Fund, 2012), the general outcome translated into economic growth. In 1995 the GDP reached its peak growth of 7.1 per cent with a low 32 per cent inflation (International Monetary Fund, 2012). The government delayed the reforms until the end of its term. Its lack of consistency and a failure of the voucher-based 1995–1996 Mass Privatisation Program (PPM – *Programul de Privatizare în Masă*) did not commit to the advancement of the reforms (Earle and Telegdy, 1998; Negrescu, 1999). Instead of creating an independent and market-oriented private sector, a group of loss-making enterprises was still controlled and financed by the state (Bacon, 2004; Tache, 2008).

Around 1996 the transitional explosion of the investments was soaring in the other parts of Eastern Europe. In 1996, the total amount of FDI inflow in Romania equalled $263 million, while Poland and Hungary, the leaders of the region, achieved respectively $4.5 billion and $3.3 billion (United Nations Conference on Trade and Development, 2012b). Throughout the period of 1990–1996, the FDI inflow in Romania was mainly the result of microscopic privatisations. The factors that kept investors outside of Romania included the absence of systematic policy in attracting investors, an overpriced exchange-rate stimulating imports rather than exports and economic patriotism of that time that saw state-run enterprises as "family treasures not for trade" (Bandelj, 2004; Bandelj, 2003). At this stage, unlike other states in the region, the Romanian state remained passive in opening the country to foreign investors. It neither took any active action to combat the prejudice against privatizing state property, nor tried to improve the framework for the greenfield projects. One of its few initiatives was the opening of the Romanian Agency for Development (ARD – *Agenţia Română pentru Dezvoltare*). It was created to promote foreign investments but soon proved to be highly bureaucratic and, as the indicators show, very ineffective. Until 1996, its activities were limited to issuing brochures entitled "Doing business in Romania" and administering a database of potential business opportunities in Romania (Pîrvu et al., 2008).

On June 22, 1995, Romania officially began its application for membership to the European Union. In the initial period of Romania's transition, the government did not actively try to integrate Romania into the global system and also failed at establishing the internal functionality. Despite the insistence of loan-givers, the World Bank and the IMF, which were bound to regulate Romania's process, and the support of external experts and advisors, Romania failed to implement the track of reform. Until 1996, the ruling parties neither strictly implemented the instructions from the loan-givers, nor enforced their own vision of recovery. As a result of this ad-hoc policy, 1996 brought a major economic setback. The economy was declining again; the inflation rate tripled beyond the predicted number, two state-run banks became illiquid and the GDP growth started to slump again. The trade deficit deepened significantly (United Nations Conference on Trade and Development, 2012a). Political and economic conditions for external investments were far from appealing and the internal situation did not give any promises for the economy to recover quickly. The tensions with Western states deepened, and in 1996, two tranches of the IMF credit were frozen to officially sanction the lack of reform progress.

2   The Period of Market Orientation (1996–2004)

In the autumn of 1996, the Romanian Democratic Convention (CDR – *Convenţia Democrată Română*) won the elections and established a new government with the Social-Democratic Union (USD – *Uniunea Social-Democrată*) with Victor Ciorbea as the prime minister. His goal, expressed in the program entitled "Contract with Romania" (*"Contractul cu România"*), was to put the country on "the road to Europe" through the market reforms. At this point, one of the biggest strategic disadvantages of an unstable economy was losing the perspective of the NATO candidacy and being sidelined from integration with the West. All the subsequent political aims concentrated on reaching for this goal, seen as a step forward for future European Union membership. At this time, the population dreamed of consumption and economic advances, which were almost impossible facing the ongoing internal impasse (Roman, 2003). The ongoing outside migration intensified.

Ciorbea's attempt to fight the corruption, the most burning problem of Romanian economy, was made in 1997. The National Council of Action against Corruption and Organized Crime was established, supported by the newly elected president Emil Constantinescu. Its actions showed precedential determination of political class, mostly directed towards the establishment of a liberal state. The plan of normalization and improving macroeconomic stability began with increasing the foreign exchange reserve, a return to indirect policy tools and the liberalization of prices. The result of this last-minute shock therapy was a deeply experienced transitional fever, similar to the one that shook Central and Eastern Europe in the early 1990s. In 1997 and 1998, the economy shrunk by 4 and 6 per cent. The inflation increased to 151 per cent in 1997 (International Monetary Fund, 2012). The deficit of trade balance deepened (United Nations Conference on Trade and Development, 2012b). The eagerness for reforms of Ciorbea's government was visible and intentions for privatisation and restructuring were backed by actions. One of its key actions was pushing through the new banking law (58/1998), which permitted the sale of state-run banks and free-market competition in the financial sector.

Another paramount step in opening the Romanian economy under Ciorbea was the introduction of laws, which finally regulated the activity of foreign investors in Romania. Prior to this moment the investments were not regulated and almost non-present in the other form than micro-privatisations based on share purchases. The new law provided the possibility for tax allowances for prosperous investors and a general framework for their operations. The purchasing of industrial land by foreign firms and repatriation of profits was permitted (Hunya, 1998). With the Government Ordinance 92/1997 approved by the Law 241/1998, foreign direct investments were ultimately recognized as part of the Romania's economic landscape. Their presence was understood as an important way of balancing the economy and stimulating demand on the labour market. Ciorbea's cabinet openly stated its hopes to finance Romania's growth and combat the raging unemployment with the help of foreign investors.

In the same year, Ciorbea started the belated reconstruction of the national industry. Selling stocks and streamlining large loss-making companies, mainly in oil-refining, machinery and coal mining, significantly contributed to the budget and directly resulted in a rise of FDI inflows. Among the strategic bids were the icons of Romanian economy exhausted by the extreme inefficiency and mismanagement. For instance, in 1996 the Brasov tractor-maker factory Roman, one of the icons of industrial production of socialist Romania, got its power switched off for not paying the bills with over 20,000 workers on board. A wave of privatisations brought buy-outs by foreign investors and rescued very few workplaces, mostly in the production sector. Since 1997, the amount of FDI started growing. Romania became an attractive business destination in Europe due to relatively low wages, geographic proximity to the Western markets and availability of well-trained specialists. Incoming investments initially concentrated in the heavy industry. Around that period there was still no effective official body providing support for foreign investors in Romania. The newly created Romanian Foreign Trade Center (RFTC) was operational but its activities concentrated on supporting the Romanian companies in exports.

The government also made some early attempts to promote trade with Romania internationally. A very meaningful moment was Ciorbea's 1997 visit to Budapest with the goal of inviting Hungarian investors to Romania and tightening economic cooperation between the two states. The relations between Romania and Hungary up until today stay rather chilly because of a dispute over Transylvania. Ciorbea's encouragement, although read as controversial inside Romania, was a symbol of openness for economic cooperation, even despite the difficult past (Phinnemore, 2001). In 1997, Romania joined the Central European Free Trade Agreement (CEFTA) and signed additional trade agreements with Israel, and in 1998, with Turkey. All endeavours of Ciorbea's government committed to the significant rise of the inward FDI flows. In 1997 they equalled $1.2 billion, and over $2 billion in 1998, which demonstrated progress, but still left Romania far behind the other post-communist economies (United Nations Conference on Trade and Development, 2012b).

Since 1989, the socioeconomic conditions persistently worsened. As an effect of restructurisation and decreasing output between 1997 and 1999 unemployment grew. It reached its peak in 1999 when it escalated to 11.5 per cent of the labour force (International Monetary Fund, 2012). Romania's delayed shock therapy caused a transformational recession and crisis and committed to the complete loss of social trust in political institutions. Deregulation boosted consumer prices and domestic demand strongly decreased. Raging corruption was eroding morale, and it caused strong protest. Worsening living standards, especially bad living conditions, poor nutrition and stress caused an epidemic of tuberculosis (Stillo, 2012). In response to all those difficulties, migration to Western countries and Hungary grew even more (Sandu, 2005; Ianos et al., 2010). The tensions in the government and protests against sales of drowning state-owned enterprises led to Ciorbea's resignation.

Inheriting the same systemic problems that made Ciorbea leave, subsequent leaders faced the same difficulties. The following Prime Minister, Radu Vasile, stayed in office for 1.5 years. He promised to re-name the Victory Square in Bucharest in the name of the person who could cure Romania's finances (Economist, 1998). The plan of continuing privatisation and land reform was enforced by the IMF in the summer of 1997 under the threat of freezing the funding. The Romanian side responded with "institutional mimicking", a very inconsistent way of introducing reforms serving the goal of satisfying the loan-giver (Daianu, 2004). In 1998, the reform progress slowed down again. That same year the government missed target after target, and again in order to sanction the existing agreements, the IMF and the World Bank stopped payments. These payments resulted in another round of negotiations, ending with the signing of the two-part PSAL (Private Sector Adjustment Programme) documents, followed by a Memorandum describing national privatisation plans, including bank restructuring and reduction of public sector losses.

Vasile's government was able to continue the privatisation process initiated by Ciorbea. The biggest successes included privatisation of the state telephone monopoly RomTelecom, with 35% of shares sold to Greek telecom OTE; the electricity company Renel; and banks, including the Romanian Bank for Development (BRD) with 59.35% of stocks purchased by French Société Générale and BancPost with 35% of stake acquired by American GE Capital and 10% by Portuguese Bank for Investment. In addition, 51% of shares in Dacia, the Romanian carmaker, were sold to French Renault. The progress of selling state-owned enterprises was complex and it targeted investors outside of Romania. Quite often the buyers were speculators, failing to maintain production and leading to failure. The results, the sale of only about half of the planned companies, kept it far from earlier set goals. In 1999 the FDI inflows dropped again, mostly as a repercussion of the ruble crisis in Russia and stayed at the same level of around $1–$1.1 billion until 2002.

Under Vasile, "restructuring" took place, including closure of many mines, with severance benefits offered to workers equal to 12 times the monthly wage ultimately resulting in layoffs of 83,000 miners (Varga and Freyberg Inan, 2015). The restructuring caused waves of protests, including clashes with the miners' movement, machine-building workers and white-collar workers. The wave of privatisations caused resistance from the unions, including sectors, such as metal, transport, education and health care organizing national protests (Kideckel, 2001; Martin and Cristescu-Martin, 2000). The counteractions against protests included arrests of union leaders and police force usage as well as concessions to prevent miners from joining the protestors. After Vasile's resignation, the government was led by Mugur Isarescu. In effect, until the elections in 2000, political rotations caused a failure in the reforms, and over and over again stopped the payments from the World Bank and the IMF.

In December 2000, the Prime Minister Adrian *Năstase* was appointed by the newly elected post-communist president Ion Iliescu. *Năstase* was the head of the government between 2000 and 2004. Although the implementation of reforms was selective, limited and delayed, the four years under *Năstase* and Iliescu rule was a period of economic growth. The growth was mostly based on the microscopic boom and bust cycles. The government's actions focused on "triage interventions" in the system in order to stimulate very short growth cycles, which resulted in a very slow plodding towards the reforms (Sum and King, 2011). The growth was also stimulated by competitively priced exports. In October 2003, the IMF enthusiastically evaluated Romania's efforts in the economic sphere and observed "sound macro-economic policies and progress in structural reforms" (International Monetary Fund, 2003).

Despite complete inconsistency in internal policy, economic growth was enough to attract foreign investors. The moment of stabilization permitted more privatisations to take place. Petrom refinery was sold to Austrian OMV, which until today is the biggest privatisation in Romania's history. The loss-generating steel company Sidex in Galati was sold to Mittal Steel Company in 2001. Agricultural Bank was bought by Raiffeisen Bank. Turkish investments, especially in manufacturing and financial sector, grew significantly (Culpan and Akcaoglu, 2003). The biggest success of this period was a significant gain in inward FDI flows which in 2003 equalled $2.2 billion and almost tripled in 2004, reaching $6.4 billion (United Nations Conference on Trade and Development, 2012b). A fraction of those numbers came from the established greenfield investments, often financially supported by the government. Their presence was partially possible thanks to the legal framework for industrial parks, namely the Government Ordinance no. 65/2001 and the Law no. 490/2002. Initial support from PHARE funds and government money stimulated the creation of the first nine parks and one industrial zone (Popescu and Ungureanu, 2008). Further industrial zone projects provided business infrastructure for greenfield investments. Moreover, the Romanian Agency for Foreign Investments (ARIS – *Agenţia Română pentru Investiţii Străine*), which operated since 2002, showed initiative and provided technical guidelines for potential investors. It also familiarized Romanians with the advantages of FDIs. A few years after opening, the ARIS quickly became passive and bureaucratic. The critics point out that its activity concentrated on issuing certificates to investors aiming to obtain long-term residence permits in Romania (Pîrvu et al., 2008).

In 2003, a new Labour Code was introduced which continued a dialogue with the unions, supporting their role in governance of the economy. Along with new privatisation laws, these regulations specified a need for new owners of former state enterprises (incl. foreign investors) to establish a "social contract" with unions. The contract was highly criticized by free-market commentators, who pointed out that it problematizes the process of short-term employment and firing and creates vast obligations for employers (Varga and Freyberg-Inan, 2015: 687). At the same time, the privatisations proceeded, causing waves of layoffs, high worker dissatisfaction and open conflict with unions (Varga, 2014). While the law supported unions' activities, the privatisations eroded their role. The drop down of industrial labour force, shrinking inability of unions to prevent pay cuts, growing liberalization have all contributed to lowering unions' influence over Romania's economic governance. (Varga and Freyberg-Inan, 2015).

3   The Period of European Integration (2004–2009)

The stabilization of the economy brought Romania closer to European Union membership. Romania had submitted an official application for accession to the EU in 1995; due to the absence of decent improvements in internal dynamics, it failed to meet the political and socio-economic measures for the Eastern

European accession in 2004. The difficult goal was proving to Europe that Romania is capable of reforms, especially that there was very little internal evidence of determination so far. The year 2004 was crucial in this campaign as it was a meaningful moment for the Romanian transition. First of all, in 2004 the country reached the level of GDP from 1989. This moment was proclaimed a big success and a symbolic end of the transition (King and Sum, 2011). Secondly, thanks to the strict guidelines from the loan-givers and the efforts of the consecutive governments, in 2004 Romania was called a functioning market economy in the European Commission's report (European Comission, 2012). Thirdly, in 2004 Romania officially joined the NATO alliance, thus finally confirming its Western orientation. The early and well-presented preparations for the accession and prosperity of the economy conjoined with a rocketing increase in FDI (United Nations Conference on Trade and Development, 2012b; Stefan and Sorin, 2011). This was noticed by many of the foreign commentators, who started to see the bright future of Romania as the EU state, even under the condition of externally guiding it to the completion of state reforms (Quayle, 2005; Gross and Tismaneanu, 2005). Most of the pre-accession period between 2004 and 2007 was aimed at keeping up with the requirements of the European Commission.

One of the most celebrated moments of this period was the successful single tax reform introduced in 2005. The income tax of individuals and corporate tax was set at the level of 16%. It was simple, transparent and prudent (Stănescu and Nedelescu, 2008). This change, in addition to the low level of wages and excellent human capital base, finally made Romania an equal player in the competition for offshoring and outsourcing in Eastern Europe. Between 2004 and 2006, Romania's FDI flows equalled from 6.6% up to 8.9% of the GDP (Eurostat, 2010). Cautious economic policy of the pre-accession period contributed to economic growth. The budget deficit was kept at low -2.2% of the GDP in 2006 (Eurostat, 2010). The prospering economy let the government undertake some initiatives in improving infrastructure, especially the devastated road system lacking expressways and highways.

The reform projects, although ambitious and fostered by the European Commission, still produced insufficient results. In effect, Romania's EU accession was quite uncertain even at the beginning of 2006. Up until the last moment, the state was monitored and measured in order to assess its eligibility. Facing the fact that Romania already did not fulfil the criteria for 2004 accession, the European Commission allowed Romania and Bulgaria, both struggling to reform, to sign conditional safeguard clauses. The precedential Co-operation and Verification Mechanism (CVM) was established in 2006 to address specific benchmarks in judicial reforms and stimulate the fight against corruption. It gave the Commission an option to suspend some of the benefits of the future accession and condition them with the progress (Noutcheva and Bechev, 2008). In January 2007, Romania and Bulgaria joined the EU on conditions based on their efforts rather than results. To a high degree, Romania's success was a result of its good image generated by the ruling coalition rather than by the real progress. Alina Mungiu-Pippidi, an influential Romanian opinion maker, wrote that EU accession was no "end of history"; the state was not reformed and society was underpaid and exhausted (Mungiu-Pippidi, 2007).

To confirm Mungiu-Pippidi's assessment, just after joining the EU in 2007 a conflict started in the coalition ruling since 2004. The two sides were Calin Popescu-Tariceanu, the ruling Prime Minister from the National Liberal Party (PNL – *Partidul Național Liberal*), and president Traian Băsescu from the Democratic Liberal Party (PDL – *Partidul Democrat-Liberal*). The conflict exploded when both leaders publicly accused each other of involvement in obscure multi-million-dollar energy deals. The confrontation put off the EU-parliament elections. Instead, the government organized a referendum on the president's impeachment. After the voting, Băsescu remained in his position and PDL withdrew from the government. The result of this course of events was dismissal of reform-oriented ministers, including independent justice minister Monica Macovei. For foreign commentators she was a symbol of the reforming potential of Romania. Macovei was responsible for a fight with politics-related corruption and positively contributed to the reform of the judiciary (Mendelski, 2011a). Again, the reforms were put aside by the chaotic political moves. Outdated or untested laws and lack of judicial independence committed to uncured corruption. In July 2008, a report on high-level corruption by Willem dePauw shocked European political commentators. The report diagnosed that if the effort against corruption "keeps evaporating at the present pace, in an estimated six months' time Romania will be back where it was in 2003" (dePauw, 2008). Because of the catastrophic chaos, a threat of freezing structural funds was issued by the EU. To rescue the situation, the state again concentrated on institutional mimicking in order to show the commitment and to convince the EU counterparts that the intentions of advancing the transition are genuine and the CVM was worth the European Commission's effort (Andreev, 2009).

The ongoing prosperity cycle was independent from the chaos on the higher level. The trust of the European Commission and progress of the EU-imposed reforms was enough to prove Romania's place in Europe and build the trust of investors. The European Union membership was the best assurance of Romania's stability. In 2006, a record amount of $11.3 billion of inward FDI flows was registered; both 2007 and 2008 also brought high numbers, like $9.9 billion and $13.9 billion (United Nations Conference on Trade and Development, 2012b).

This confirmed Romania's big potential in the region. Foreign investments played a vital role both in the structure of employment and in the contribution to the GDP. Financial help to families of Romanian migrants working in Western Europe also supported the growth of the economy. Partially because of almost two decades of extensive migrations, unemployment of the labour force declined. From 1999 when it equalled 11.5 per cent of the labour force, it reached a record 5.8 per cent in 2008 (International Monetary Fund, 2012). Between 2006 and 2008, the economy grew by 7.8, 6.3 and 7.3 per cent per year. In this period, the deficit of the balance of trade was deepening, reaching a peak of -0.193 in 2008 (International Monetary Fund, 2012). Unfortunately, the economic boom and the EU accession had a bitter twist in Romania. The wages remained only a fraction of those in Western Europe and fell far behind those in Central and Eastern Europe. GDP per capita in Romania 2005 was only $4,572 or about 50 per cent of the Eastern European EU average and about 17 per cent of the EU-wide average (World Bank, 2012).

From the longer perspective, the period of 2004–2008 was a moment of stability for the business environment in Romania. Even with terrible road infrastructure and increasing wages, the investors frequently chose Romania. The pull factors included sufficient economic stability, the fluctuating exchange rate, an unsaturated labour market, industrious and low-cost workers, a high level of multilingualism and a newly created private business sector. The investors already present in Romania expanded their activity. For instance, in 2004 French Renault started to produce the low-end Dacia Logan model in a town next to Pitești. Due to its low price, the Logan became a hit not only in Romania, where it became nation's trademark vehicle, but also in European markets. It entered the competition with second-hand cars. In effect over 80,000 Logans were sold in Western Europe only in 2007 (Economist, 2008). The success has been remarkable also because of the labour conditions, fortified by the union in the plant (85% of workforce), resulting in high increases in wages, high job security, and resistance to agency work (Adăscăliței and Guga, 2015: 8–13). During this period, more privatisations took place. They included the Romanian Commercial Bank (BCR), bought by German Erste Bank in 2006. In 2008 the majority shares of the car production factory in Craiova were sold to Ford, giving the American company 72.4 per cent of the shares (Reuters, 2007). Only one year before, the government had bought 51 per cent of shares in the plant from Daewoo Motor to rescue the factory from the bankruptcy. Ford's plans included employment reaching up to 7000 employees.

Green field investments bloomed. The most spectacular investment included opening the assembly plant of the Nokia Corporation, addressed in this work. The plant re-located to Romania from Germany and the investor openly motivated it with a cost-cutting strategy. In the first year of functioning, the plant's turnover was comparable to 1,3 per cent of Romania's GDP. The multinational quickly became Romania's largest exporter, competing for this position with Dacia-Renault factory. The plant initially gave work to more than 1500 people, then reaching a peak of over 4000 employees. The other greenfield projects included Emerson's outsourcing centre in Cluj-Napoca; Procter and Gamble's factory in Urlați; and the logistic centre of the retail giant Kaufland in Ploiești. In 2008, the ARIS was renamed to the Romanian Agency for Investments (RAI) with the goal of encouraging foreign investors and promoting the state aid schemes.

4 Global Economic Crisis and Neoliberal Rule (2009–2014)

The moment of economic confidence started to end with the global economic crisis; the global credit crunch noticeably impacted Romania. This period has also been used as an opportunity to fortify neoliberalism in the political economy of Romania, treating all-encompassing adoption of the free-market policy as a remedy for all problems of the state (Vincze, 2015; Trif, 2016). The initial moment of crisis has been dramatic; it caused the economy to shrink by 7 per cent in 2009 (International Monetary Fund, 2012), and the FDI inflows dropped down. The government, led by the Prime Minister Emil Boc from the PDL with no success, tried to stimulate the economy by selling bonds. In 2009, faced with no other solutions, Romania took a joint $26.4 billion loan from an impressive group of institutions: the IMF, the EU, the World Bank, the European Bank for Reconstruction and Development (EBRD), the European Investment Bank (EIB), and the International Finance Corporation (World World Bank, 2009). The main objective of the loan was to keep the deficit as low as possible foremost as the counterbalance to the dropping capital inflows and in order to strengthen the financial sector. Throughout the next years, neoliberalisation were very strongly backed by president Traian Băsescu, who in his public speeches opposed the idea of the welfare state, arguing for the efficient, neoliberal state (Vincze, 2015: 131–134).

The recovery from the global downturn took the form of far-reaching austerity measures. The cuts included an attempt to downsize pensions by 15 per cent, which was declared "unconstitutional" by the Romanian Constitutional Court. Additionally, the sales tax was increased from 19 to 24 per cent. Moreover, all public sector employees, including teachers and doctors, had their salaries cut down by 25 per cent. Unions proved to be helpless in renegotiating these conditions. Prices rose, more state-owned companies were dismantled, public subsidies for medication were frozen, price of utilities rose. New plans of privatisation included an entire health system. These changes caused political tensions, including Boc's confidence vote, and an exchange of six ministers. This situation caused a wave of protests and outraged public opinion due to increasing the cost of living. More than 42 per cent of the population was spending over 40 per cent of their wages for housekeeping (Vincze, 2017: 46). Large-scale waves of protests repeated in the major cities. They were connected not only to the austerity measures, but also to the proposed neoliberal reforms, disapproval of president Băsescu – the main promoter of neoliberalism in Romania through public policies, and many other issues, jointly expressed by the unified protestors.

In 2011, the New Labour Code was introduced. In contrast to the 2003 regulation, it was undermining national-level unionising and self-organisation as well as fully supporting fixed-term employment. In practice it signified the lack of the possibility of signing a collective agreement applying to all the workforce in the country (Hayter et al., 2013), which was important in processes such as setting the minimum wage (Adăscăliței and Guga, 2015). Labour Code made it difficult for unions to organise, because of the expanded usage of temporary contracts (i.e. expanding maximum fixed-term employment term from 24 to 36 months), elimination of mandatory pay of union officials for time to work on unions and allowing for their removal after their mandate expires, if they are not needed in the workplace. The new code also made it possible to reduce work time or overtime, as well as extend the maximum length of the probation period from 30 to 90 days for workers and from 90 to 120 days for managers (Clauwaert and Schomann, 2013). The unions expressed resistance to the code, but the mobilization against it was limited, partially due to their weakening influence over state policy taking place since the 2000s when privatisations and other events influenced the strength of the union movement (Adăscăliței and Guga, 2015; Varga and Freyberg-Inan, 2015). The code also eliminated immunity given to union leaders as well as put them under pressure and investigation by government-based anti-corruption bodies. Along with the Labour Code, the Social Dialogue Act was introduced, which defined stricter criteria for obtaining representativeness, creating administrative barriers for registration of new trade unions and destroying professional trade unions. Its most important regulations included the removal of national cross-sectoral agreements, changes to the criterion of representativeness of unions on the company level from 33 to 51 per cent of unionized workers as well as enforced obligatory conciliation before strikes, which prohibited striking if collective agreement provisions are not implemented (Trif, 2016; Hayter et al., 2013). Even though the labour code was in line with the neoliberal reform supported by the

IMF, it was not an explicit requirement of loan-givers. The code was drafted by the Council of Foreign Investors and the American Chamber of Commerce in order to increase employers' competitiveness (Stoiciu, 2012; Trif, 2016). Prime Minister Emil Boc argued at that time that the new legislation aims to "create a competitive labour market in relation to what is happening in Europe and in the world" (Vincze, 2015: 135).

Temporary economic stabilization was reached after cutting expenses between 2009 and 2010. Inflation was kept at 6 per cent (International Monetary Fund, 2012). Since 2008, unemployment grew drastically (International Monetary Fund, 2012). In the aftermath of the economic slowdown around the world, the cuts that took place in Western economies also influenced foreign investments in Eastern Europe. After 2009, when FDI inflows in Romania equalled $4.8 billion, partially thanks to the pre-crisis contracts, the next two years brought inflows on a level slightly below $3 billion (UNCTADStat, 2012). To compare, Poland noted at this time a score of only $9.6 billion and Hungary only $2.3 billion (United Nations Conference on Trade and Development, 2012b). In 2011 Romanian GDP went up by 2 per cent, which was a relatively good result for the region (International Monetary Fund, 2012).

Even though at this time the economy was stable, internal conflicts again tore apart the ruling government. Bottom-up pressures and tensions with the president led to the resignation of Emil Boc. In 2012, due to Băsescu's unpopularity, a referendum was organized to impeach the president. Its initiator was Victor Ponta – the prime minister from the Social Democratic Party (PSD – *Partidul Social Democrat*). Due to low participation rates, the referendum failed. The impeachment procedure caused a lot of controversy both inside and outside of Romania. Ponta's government ignored the objections of the Romanian Constitutional Court regarding the impeachment procedure; the protesting Ombudsman was dismissed; and the official state monitor, where major legal acts are published, was blocked by the government. In reaction, the European Commission issued a statement where it warned that the current events appear to reduce the effective powers of independent institutions like the Constitutional Court and might undermine the progress reached over the five years, especially judicial reform and anti-corruption measures in the context of the Cooperation and Verification Mechanism (European Comission, 2012). Some less radical ministers resigned after the unsuccessful impeachment, and Ponta's efforts concentrated on changing the constitution.

Although the Romanian economy survived the internal crisis relatively well, with a growth prognosis for the economy in 2012, the system remained unreformed and alarmingly in need of change. The most crucial and unfinished components of transition remain the same and include corruption on all levels, conflict of interest in the management of public funds, and fiscal crime, especially money laundering (European Comission, 2011). The role of the European Union's institutions in launching the reforms and enforcing more commitment of domestic actors is indisputable, and includes the Convergence Program 2011–2014, which was understood as a continuation of efforts for growing competitiveness, financial sustainability, privatisation of industry, public health and other state-own enterprises. It also included other measures, such as increasing the retirement age or strengthening the conditions of early retirement or reduction of healthcare and public official spending. The European Union's control is vital at all of the stages: beginning from the initiative of reform, through implementation and benchmarking. Even though some new mechanisms are adopted, resistance from various interest groups prevents their complete implementation. For instance, an uncompleted law reform is still pending due to what Mendelski termed "internal state capture by clientelism", in which state officials, high-level judges and political elites are caught up (Mendelski, 2011b).

The year 2012 was an unfortunate one for Romania also because one of the major exporters, the Nokia Corporation, closed its assembly plant and laid off about four thousand employees. The closure of one of the most significant and prestigious investors caused a national debate about the role and reliability of foreign investments in Romania. The investor's decision made Romanians upset. It also caused irritation among the rulers. Just after the investors' plans were announced in September 2011, President Băsescu commented that the decision came as no surprise, but also admitted that Romania's "bureaucracy and lack of courage in taking on important decisions" might cause low interest from investors (Capital, 2011, December 14). Later, in December 2011, facing a wave of protests supporting the president's dismissal, Băsescu strongly condemned Nokia for not keeping the plans and promises made to Romanians. In the same speech he angrily attacked Ford's under-hiring practices ("producing trailers in Romania, not cars") and argued that the private sector should be blamed for the situation of Romania, not the state (Capital, 2011, September 29).

At the end of 2012 Romania's situation did not meet expectations. The EU membership and general course are secured. Although in the long run the Romanian economy seems stable, the political class remains in an impasse. Up until today Romania notes the lowest level of the absorption of EU funds among the new member states (Goschin et al., 2012; Constantin, 2012). Internally, the social situation is difficult, especially outside of the largest cities. Romania is in urgent need of structural funds, as in the most spheres of life the standards are extremely low. The difficult social situation is caused by a high number of factors: very low level of wages; corruption, and extremely poor condition of infrastructure. Systemic paradoxes are Romania's calling card. Backwardness coexists with progress. While having the second fastest internet in the world, the country still has areas with no electricity and running water. The average road infrastructure is extremely poor, over 300 kilometres of highways are part of a devastated and dangerous network of post-communist express roads (Pando, 2012; World Economic Forum, 2010; Economist, 2011). Having extremely well educated, multilingual university graduates, the country struggles with bribery and fraud in higher education. Unending healthcare reform leaves Romanians with poor hospitals and wages, but on the other hand, well-qualified medical personnel. One of the symptoms of low confidence among Romanian citizens is the very high-level of migration to the other parts of Europe (Bartram, 2013). The estimates of the total number of migrants vary, ranging from 3 to 4 million people abroad, but the trend is significant for the population of a 21 million country (International Organization for Migration, 2008; Office for Labour Force Migration, 2006).

One of the remaining challenges for Romania's internalization is entering the EU visa-free Schengen zone, which after stark warnings from the European Commission seems to be out of reach for the next 2–3 years. The Netherlands and Germany are the sceptical voices, expressing their "concern about violations of the letter and spirit of the EU values [that may undermine – MM] the last steps to Romania's full integration in the EU" (Frankfurter Algemeine Zeitung, 2012). Romanian high officials had been sure the country would join the Schengen zone sooner than later, and the disappointment about the Dutch veto was expressed in numerous ways. Considering the labour market and potential in offshoring, entering Schengen might cause a boom cycle. For many investors, the proximity to Western Europe and high quality of the labour market are excellent reasons to establish production in Romania. The only question is whether Romania can finally stabilize and to what degree it can use its FDI potential.

5   Conclusions

The trajectory of systemic transition of Romania encountered many difficulties. Despite mounting turbulences, the dominating vision for Romania turned towards a state based on a capitalist, market-oriented social order. Extensive involvement of external actors and institutions, such as Bretton Woods loan-givers and the European Commission, sanctioned Romania's reform and pushed it towards a neoliberal vision of state. Faced with loan freezes, the rulers were pushed to integrate the country with the global economy, even at the cost of the local populations, exposed to precariousness and degrading labour standards. The loans were a tool of control. Borrowing was equal to an agreement with the external vision of the Romanian state. The constant process of evaluating and auditing the economy, and threats of stopping the financial aid committed Romanian rulers to stay on track of this form of change. The financing forced Romania to try to keep up with other countries in the region. A crucial driver of change was the stimulus of joining international organizations, especially NATO and the EU. Through the structural funds and reforms, based on the guidelines and haggling with the European Commission, Romania was able to partially reform its political institutions and join the EU in 2007 (Spendzharova, 2003). It was a credit backed by promises, which were yet to unveil during the economic crisis that resulted in the complete adoption of a market-based order and regulations exposing Romania to greater precariousness and liberalization.

The analysis of Romania's post-socialist transformation provides a picture of a system that struggles with adaptation to the global market reality, experiencing deep harm while attempting to adapt the externally imposed reforms. From the very first moments of transition, Romanians faced very deep social costs of the transition. With few exceptions, Romanian decision makers tried to balance social stability with the reform progress. Failure to do so for years stopped the Romanian economy from booming and kept the wages low. Progress strongly impacted the citizens, affecting the most disadvantaged populations of workers and rural zones. Because of shrinking workplaces, population outside of large cities was faced with no choice but migration. After twenty years of corruption in the many spheres of social life, tensions and frustration were deeply felt. Especially in the last years, Romania paid a high price for its economic stability by putting the burden on the taxpayers. Adapted austerity measures had an enormous social cost, deeply penetrating society and the labour market.

From the neoliberal perspective, Eastern Europe remains an important place for production. Since Eastern Europe started to transform, it was seen as a potential location of business, because of its low cost of labour and land as well as state support for investors. The process of transition that took place in Romania was also based on deep integration with the international economy. The neoliberal program had a number of social consequences. Brutal privatisations got rid of loss-generating enterprises. Despite being unreformed, Romania provided a relatively competitive investment location. Foreign investors very slowly started to appear in Romania. Until then, the state stagnated. Since the investments started to flourish, the economy started to grow but with no clear effect on the disadvantaged groups. The accession to the European Union stimulated the economy, despite a dysfunctional systemic framework and ongoing conflicts of the ruling class. The global recession caused a significant economic drop.

After twenty-five years that followed the revolution, Romania has generated strong ties to the global economy and dependencies on global value chains. Green field operations became an important element of the second decade of Romania's transformation. Investments and the creation of industrial zones were strongly stimulated by the state privileges given to the investors. Competitiveness of the local labour market was strengthened by the decentralization of industrial relations (Glassner, 2013; Varga, 2013), similarly to the other states of Central and Eastern Europe. Very controversial legislation relevant to labour law in 2011 allowed for greater flexibility but also precariousness among the workforce, removing central worker unions and strongly expanding employer powers (Adăscăliței and Guga, 2015). The investments, such as the one described in the book, have been an important point of reference for Romanian politics, a symbol of success in neoliberal rule achieved at the price of the worker populations. In the further chapters of this book I address the cultural effects caused by one of these investments, describing its interpretation by local populations and workforce, addressing its internal dynamics and outlining the outcomes of its relocation.

CHAPTER 2

The Arrival: Global Assemblage of Neoliberal Production

> It was a turning point for [the village], a turning point that nobody could predict.
> Community member, 52 years old

> After hearing the news [about the factory], it all seemed like a joke. I am happy that they chose our location, but let's be honest, they could have chosen from many different ones. So in many ways the region won a lottery ticket.
> Local official

Global industrial production is one way the world has changed over the past decades. Increasingly, production is highly dispersed and each process involved, including product development, design, assembly, production, marketing, branding, and support, might take place in different geographical locations. This complicated process, based on coordinating labour across the world, is a conceptual challenge. Immanuel Wallerstein's world systems theory has long been the basis of our understanding of geographically dispersed production (Wallerstein, 1974). In examining wheat production and the merchant fleet in the 18th century, Hopkins and Wallerstein note that, "forces were organizing production over a growing proportion of the "world" delimited by the scope of their operations" (Wallerstein and Hopkins, 2000: 158). Their approach interpreted geographically dispersed production as "a network of labour and production processes whose end result is a finished commodity" (Wallerstein and Hopkins, 2000: 159). This theory was subsequently broadened in order to understand these networks more deeply. Gary Gereffi, a leading theorist of value chains, observes that "in today's global factory, the production of a single commodity often spans many countries, with each nation performing tasks in which it has a cost advantage" (Gereffi and Korzeniewicz, 1994: 1). Gereffi's framework lays out four key areas that shape commodity chains (input-output, geographic, governance, and institutional) but one has received the most attention, specifically governance. Commodity chains fulfil different value adding functions, extensively organized in modular fashion that has the elements of both producer- and buyer-driven chains (Sturgeon, 2002; Florida and Kenney,

2004). Increasingly, producers, especially those in the electronics sector, pursue contracted manufacturing with a highly competent supplier. Each of the production facilities in a value chain has its own nature and characteristics. Moreover, production is based on uneven circumstances and differing conditions, negotiated in the network and among the local socioeconomic order.

The theory of "global value chains" is an important theoretical contribution to understanding of the complex networks of industrial production (Gereffi et al., 2005). Based on a new typology of chain governance strategies, it contains five different modules of governance (market, modular, relational, captive and hierarchy). Each of them is considered in the context of three variables, which refer to the relationship between producer and consumer. These variables include transaction complexity, transaction codifiability, and capability of the supply base. This renews the discussion about power in global chains and the role of their particular elements. The global value chain framework enables better insight into those complicated relationships and allows us to see how the governance of networks changes (Mahutga, 2012). As the literature proves, global production is not only based on simple division of roles between centre and peripheries. As the example of South Asia demonstrates, a region manufacturing for producers from around the world not only offers price-competitive services. Quite often the final products are based on importing parts and components not only from East Asia, but also from other parts of the globe.

Numerous theorists concentrate on understanding how global value chains are organized and work. They share the assumption that "various types of international, inter-firm networks have become central features of a wide range of contemporary industries" (Sturgeon, 2008: 21). Besides governance, at the heart of the debates connected to global value chains lay the issues of power and institution. The former refers to the firm, i.e. where the power of lead firms and suppliers is located, including "competence" power based on industry-specific know-how (Palpacuer, 2000; Milberg and Winkler, 2013; Brochner and Haugen, 2004). The latter focuses on institutional aspects of global value chains, namely economic integration. A number of institutional initiatives, such as NAFTA, the European Union or Chinese membership in the World Trade Organization stimulated the expansion of value chains. Also supranational bodies, such as the World Bank or the IMF, stimulate and strongly opt for foreign direct investment in the emerging markets. Publications of these institutions address how global value chains are positioned against political institutions outside of the value chain (Farole and Winkler, 2014; Winkler, 2013; United Nations Conference on Trade and Development, 2013). At the same time, comparative studies examine how local institutions enable or constrain how the entire chain functions (Sturgeon, 2007; Schmitz, 2004).

The above-mentioned notions appear in analyses of the economic activities taking place in various place around the globe and they address the challenged state sovereignty and inability of the nation-state to control labour processes and the other elements of value chains (Sassen, 1996; Krasner, 1999; Cohen, 2012); the cost-competition race (Rudra, 2008; Brass, 2011); and the forced evolution of labour movements (Clawson, 2003; Silver, 2003). Below, I position my approach in the literature. To study the investor's global value chain, I use on-the-ground research and the anthropology of globalization approach in order to understand the position, labour, and experience of a local community that witnesses and participates in the lifecycle of a production node. The relationship between global production and regional and local development is an influential aspect of labour studies (Henderson et al., 2002; Yeung et al., 2006). Other analyses include the study of the relationships between different nodes in the chain, including the distribution of profits (Fold, 2002;) or standards of labour (Barrientos and Andrienetta, 2004; Staritz, 2011; Lloyd-Evans, 2008). Just as Timothy J. Sturgeon concludes, the research concerning value chains shares "a focus on the organizational and spatial structure and dynamics of industries, the strategies and behaviour of major firms and their suppliers, and the need to identify scalable conceptual tools that help researchers move easily from local to global levels of analysis" (Sturgeon, 2008: 22). My work takes on a bottom-up perspective, examining participation in off-shored production.

The investor's decision to locate production in a village in Transylvania was motivated by economic interest. The proximity to markets and relatively cheap cost of labour were among the key factors that encouraged the investment. As opening passages above exemplify, the local population understood the investor's arrival as good fortune. After the initial announcement of the decision, a wave of excitement took over the public. It took several months to start the actual process of building the industrial zone, but the pace of the work was unprecedented. When construction began, the local population experienced an enormous undertaking. It was very well timed, orchestrated, and efficient and it was carried out by a variety of contractors from all parts of Europe.

The investor connected the region to its model of production, creating a binding relationship between its own operations and the local labour market, the families of workers and the Romanian economy. The new socio-spatial involvement mediated by the production node reflects how the FDI creates new relationships between different levels of human activity. One key way to describe the established relationships on these levels is the notion of scales, developed by human geographers. Typically, scales indicate different dimensions reflecting socio-spatial processes (MacKinnon, 2011). For instance, some phenomena, such as the distribution of products, occur on the local, regional or national scales. Despite the fact that those three dimensions are the most often referred to, scale theorists argue that the scales are not a given (Brenner, 1998). Scales are interconnected, and thus, they cannot be ordered hierarchically. Referring to Henri Lefebvre, Neil Brenner argues that instead of a *matrioshka* doll metaphor, which orders the scales from the smallest to the broadest, we should consider the scales in terms of relations, which are often very complex and chaotic (Brenner, 2001; Herod, 2011). Brenner argues that the idea of scales helps to create a vision of mosaics and collages rather than levels of pyramids based on size, scale or distance. Multiple spatial units are established, differentiated, hierarchized when scaling is used and, under certain conditions, these units are also rejigged, reorganized and recalibrated in relation to one another (Brenner, 2001). Involvement in different scales is embedded in social dynamics and reworked through every day routines and practices.

The location of the investment in Romania might be understood as a transformation of scales, known as re-scaling. Re-scaling might occur during socio-political transformations (Swyngedouw, 2000). The new scalar order created by the investor emerged not solely because of the investor's initiative. Its precondition, called "scalar structuration" in the literature, was the emergence of the Romanian economy on the global market and its coordination with it, which was described in Chapter 2 of this work. The structuration occurred through systemic transformation, namely the creation of free market legislation, as well as the legal framework for activity of foreign investors (Jessop, 2000; MacLeod, 1999; Smith and Dennis, 1987). In other words, it was necessary for the Romanian state to open new channels that permitted contact with external processes that were thus far unavailable to the country (Sassen, 2007). Creating new scalar positionality gave investors access to the Romanian labour market and internal resources. There is consensus that scales intersect in local processes and that this creates specific configurations that occur locally, no matter how globalized and transnational their nature is. Saskia Sassen gives the example of a financial centre, which is a local entity but at the same time is a part of the global market thanks to the production of electronic devices, which cannot be organized on a hierarchical scale (Sassen, 2007). The multiplicity of sources of capital, actors, and regulations involved as well as the electronic process make it impossible to name (and distinguish) any scale, but rather ideal types of local and global scales. A similar situation emerges when considering the production facility in Romania. Even though it is locally grounded, it connects phenomena located at different scales, making it sometimes even impossible to understand for those who organize the process of the plant and its operation in the global value chain.

Important for the locally materialized scalar order is the notion of "scalar fixes". Henri Lefebvre elaborates on the relatively long-standing crystalized scalar configurations (Lefebvre, 1991). A fix embodies a configuration, which becomes formed, stabilized, falls apart and is constantly under dynamic negotiation. In other words, "the current round of globalization can be interpreted as a multidimensional process of re-scaling in which the scalar organization of both cities and states is being reterritorialized in the conflictual search for "glocal" scalar fixes (Brenner, 1998: 465)". In the current conditions of capitalism, economic actors, such as foreign investors, establish scalar fixes through the development of their value chains. The scalar perspective allows us to understand two dimensions of the production node's scalar fix. From the top-down perspective of the global value chain, the production node functions as the space of global production and employs local resources for the purpose of capital accumulation. Managers of these firms have the power to choose the mobile processes basing their decision on rational calculations. Specific geographies and local conditions promise different profit margins.

On the other hand, there is the bottom-up perspective with locally involved parties in the scalar fix created by the global investor. On the one side, there was this large manufacturer of mobile phones, with over twenty factories around the world, a few dozen of suppliers and numerous retailers selling its products. On the other, there are the Romanians. Romanian workers and their families, who are disappointed by the reality in Romania, tired of austerity measures, dreaming about better consumption possibilities and migrating to Western Europe. But there are also the Romanian authorities, who are attempting to stimulate economic growth and worry about high unemployment. When the investor, seeking a new location for its low-cost assembly plant, showed an interest in investing in Romania, it was natural that Romanian negotiators did their best to accommodate its needs, from seeking out a location to sponsoring the infrastructure and supporting the investor's plans.

In order to frame my argument using the bottom-up approach, I employ the concept of global assemblages put forward by Aihwa Ong and Stephen J. Collier, who define a mode of enquiry that remains close to practice and is used to address situations where global processes cause social reconstruction and new social, material and discursive relationships (Ong and Collier, 2004: 4). The global, in Ong and Collier's understanding, refers to phenomena that are potentially not delimited by social, cultural or economic boundaries, but rather carry qualities of a universal nature, which in turn may be applied to phenomena such as the biological context or planetary scale. Following this line of thinking, global assemblages allow us to understand the lived experiences of phenomena that have global qualities. In that sense, my approach concentrates on the study of a specific model of production, which was an inherent part of neoliberal transformation of Romania. This change emerges from a specific historical situation, and it is a product of modern Western civilization and its model of development, which contains universal significance and validity. It is also highly encouraged by external institutions, such as the European Union, the IMF and World Bank. The program of systemic transformation is based on assumptions strongly tied to market-based rationality. According to this approach, locating and receiving the investment stems from profit-seeking behaviour. Yet, its effects are a central part of the lived experience, and as I show in the next chapters, often contrary to the rational interest, yet supportive of the investment.

Ong and Collier argue that global assemblages are "domains in which the forms and values of individual and collective existence are problematized or at stake, in the sense that they are subject to technological, political and ethical reflection and intervention" (Ong and Collier, 2005: 4). This approach is far from creating an ideal "global form", which is freed from its context. Instead "the ensembles of heterogeneous elements", or assemblages, are understood as articulation of the "global". Collier and Ong claim that phenomena have a global quality, when they:

(1) "have a distinctive capacity for decontextualization and recontextualization, abstractability and movement, across diverse social and cultural situations and spheres of life";
(2) "are able to assimilate themselves to new environments, to code heterogeneous contexts and objects in terms that are amenable to control and valuation";
(3) "are limited by the complex conditions of possibility of this movement";
(4) "are limited and delimited by specific technical infrastructures, or value regimes, not by the vagaries of a social or cultural field". (my selection; Ong and Collier, 2005: 11)

The value of this approach is that it concentrates on specific "on-the-ground cases", unlike grand narratives. Even though the observation that the global interacts with the local culture is not new, the idea of the global in the space of assemblage and describing the "contingent, uneasy, unstable interrelationships" is a way of bridging anthropology, ethnography, and sociology with large theorizations. Global assemblage provides a useful notion showing a product of multiple processes of temporary character, composed from a mixture of contexts and elements. Global assemblages permit for theorizing the cases of "global intervention" so specific and situated non-reducible effects resulting from multiple determinations of emergent nature. The approach of this stand is in staying close to the practices, which allows us to gain analytical and critical vision of the described forms by examining how actors reflect upon them or call them into question. I follow this approach in the next chapters of this book.

1 Nokia Village Plans

A woman in her mid-twenties who observed the process of construction of the investment and later joined the plant's shop floor gives the following account below. The quote indicates a rapid transformation of space and new life in the village.

> Nobody knew anything. All of the sudden there is information that [the investor] will come to the village. That company, wow! Most people did not have computers, did not have internet but a huge company, which makes advanced [equipment], will be in the village! It was like a dream. What could they possibly do here? I knew it will change things. I was jobless at that time. I am not from [here]. People were speaking about [the investor]. how [the company] will come; how it will give jobs. Some said it will be jobs for engineers. (...)
>
> And then the construction [of the plant] began. I am not from [here] originally. I thought it's a really quiet place. Since I came here, I saw absolutely no movement similar to what happened when they dug the hole for the [factory] building. Truck after truck would go from the back of the village and bring soil to the site. They had to put extra layers of soil, because it was damp there. Go there [behind a row of houses]. There is a small lake that they dug while doing it. People living in the house [located] near to where they were taking the soil got angry, because those trucks made their walls crumble. They worked twelve hours a day!
>
> Then [the construction] started. Delivery after delivery. They were bringing the components [for the factory]. All at a very fast pace. They were working to finish it. Once they started to deliver everything to where the plant was supposed to be, the trucks made sort of a dirt road by going through the field. It was dusty like hell, and they could not go fast on this road. Some would almost stop. There were holes like that [shows how wide]. Once it started raining, it all turned to mud, so they put gravel there. This is the road that leads to the plant from the roundabout, which was also made by them but later. So putting up the plant...that went fast. They put it up in less than a year. People did not know what was happening. I was starved for work too. I had shitty jobs before and even considering traveling to Cluj was a pain. My husband makes good money so there was no big hurry.
>
> But people wanted to know what is happening and when they will start to hire. For me it did not matter at all in which area, just to do something.

> Everybody felt warmly about the investor. Step by step people saw how the plant grew. People were getting curious, and they are always hungry for jobs, or maybe just crazy. All of the sudden you could see [the village] on the television, featuring interviews with people you see in the village shop. Journalists came to the village and started taking pictures and interviewing people. (...) Even our government officials would come here for a few hours to talk about the plans. (...)
>
> Once they settled, it was a gigantic operation. They moved employees from everywhere in the world. There was a Chinese woman in HR, the biggest boss was American. (...) They hired Romanians for assembly, but also for office jobs. The parts were coming on trucks, everybody worked on putting them together. (...) Then they sent it further, to Germany, Austria, France, Turkey, even to Africa.
>
> Female worker

The passage above depicts the investment as a stimulus that reshaped the local order. Physically, the industrial zone influenced local space from the moment that the new infrastructure was built. But it also generated a new narrative: a complex industrial construction, foreign and new workers, unique approaches to industrial production for the region. The production node connected local actors to a formerly unknown sphere of global production. From the construction workers to the company's staff, international managers, journalists, politicians, the village witnessed the presence of new actors. The local community experiences an entirely different organizational culture and a new pace of life. From the first moments, the scale and dynamics of the investment were impenetrable for local observers. All those changes immediately generated new ideas connected to the village's future, bringing forth a wave of excitement.

When the investor decided to negotiate a new plant location in Romania, it already had a very precise plan connected to its presence in the country. "The Nokia Village" was a complex plan based on a vision of creating an important European production centre. This plan included strategy drafts, architectural and zone development plans. At its heart, the Nokia Village had an assembly plant, also the first phase of the project. This plant's main purpose was processing the supplied components into a product ready to arrive to the shelves of the retail stores in the destination markets. Components arrived from contractors and included telephone parts such as screens, keyboards, motherboards and covers, as well as other elements of a consumer-end mobile phone set, including chargers, headphones, country-profiled manuals and boxing. After establishing the assembly plant, the investor plans included building facilities for component producers and, as a result, the creation of an industrial cluster specialising in consumer electronics. The last stages of the development plan included an apartment building for employees and a conference centre for incoming visitors. In the long-term vision, the Nokia Village had a designated direct road to the airport located about fifteen kilometres from the industrial zone.

The project proposed turning over 154 hectares of the former grounds of the state farmland into the industrial zone. The additional production facilities of the investor's suppliers were included in the initial plans of construction and used in the negotiation process with local authorities. The investor's plans were accepted with enthusiasm by the local authorities. The initial local costs were high. The local county sponsored the infrastructure of the zone in an effort to make it suitable for the Nokia Village. The authorities spent over $16 mln in order to build and equip the area, turning a former field into an industrial zone. Its road infrastructure included over 15 kilometres of asphalt lanes, a roundabout and two exits from the express road. All roads were equipped with streetlights. Large road signs marked the zone. The plan included establishing a train station in the Nokia Village as part of Nokia's labour force transportation system. Even though the investor was potentially eligible for state funding in the form of tax holidays, it did not use subsidies for its production activity.

One of the informants who participated in the negotiation processes remarked on the initial stages of negotiation:

> When [the investor] contacted us, it was clear that it will be a great and influential partner. The project was immense and impressive. We knew that it is either us or anyone else, so we really focused on getting them to choose Cluj. They were hard negotiators, but we did extremely well. A couple of times the negotiations almost stopped because they did not trust us. [The investor] had lawyers from Cluj who helped them and then lawyers from Bucharest who controlled those from Cluj. Literally every penny mattered, also when it came to crazy things that are not up to us, such as the price of electricity. They did not want to agree on the electricity price, but it was not up to us, obviously!
> Public Official

As I was informed by other officials, during the last stage of talks regarding the location, the investor considered a number of places offered by the local authorities. The final location was chosen because of its proximity to Cluj and to the airport. The investor evaluated the flatness of the terrain, railroad connection, proximity to the airport and access to the workforce. According to the

THE ARRIVAL: GLOBAL ASSEMBLAGE OF NEOLIBERAL PRODUCTION   51

agreement, the industrial zone was owned by the local county and leased to the investor. Quickly after the described negotiations process was complete, visualisations and detailed plans were presented to the media. Once the decision was made public, the bulldozers and heavy equipment arrived to the zone.

The construction site was organized as two separate projects. Firstly, there was the infrastructural development. The works included building basic amenities for the industrial zone, such as connecting the former field to power, gas, and running water, equipping it with a water purification station as well as creating lanes of asphalt. The infrastructural works were entirely financed and executed by local authorities and Cluj County. The zone was the third industrial park in the region. Officially, it was under the administration of the publically owned industrial park agency "Tetarom". The park obtained a code name "Tetarom III", which also appeared on road signs. The other part of the construction, building and equipping the assembly plant and its closest surroundings, was financed and realized by the investor.

When the construction started in 2008, a high density of traffic and uninterrupted construction work strongly contrasted with the quiet life of the village. Movement in the village, teams of workers and heavy equipment brought not only new hopes and dreams but inconvenience and tons of dust and noise. Tens of dump trucks transported soil used for foundation works. Prefabricated components were constantly arriving on trucks. As a young female inhabitant of the village recalls: "Any time their trucks would come by my house, I could hear my glass shaking in the kitchen. Talk to them [pointing], their house literally started to crumble from this heavy machinery" (female community member). One of the interviewees, who worked on the construction site as a security guard, recalled the army of workers and multitude of nationalities on the construction site in the village:

> At first a company from Bucharest hired me. There was two of us and we got the night shift [...]. That land was damp so they were putting up a lot of ballasts, truck after truck. Later the security company changed, and there were six of us for each shift because the material and construction firms were coming all the time. There were a lot of people, and [the contractors] were afraid of stealing. They brought concrete columns from Hungary by train, unloaded them right here, and Hungarians did that whole structure with cement. But there were also Czechs, Slovaks, and Poles working there. Poles did the roof. Everybody worked a lot. At the last stage, there were 25 companies and 550 people, and I was at the gate. I would ID them all to make sure they were supposed to be there. A lot of Germans, or maybe the Finnish, were finishing all that. The village has

never seen clamour like that. There was so much dust from all this that it looked like smoke.

Construction worker

The passage expresses the complexity of the investment. The man is amazed how many people worked on the site and how many nationalities were represented. To all those in the village, construction was realized very quickly, and continued on weekends. The large scale of the investment and the number of workers involved was unprecedented. But also, to the puzzlement of the observers, the highly regulated procedures and safety measures were enforced according to the international standards. The teams of construction workers, architects and supervisors cooperated. As one of the observers noted, construction was going on all the time: "They had artificial light and once one group finished, more would come". The effort and coordination were seen as a sign of the investor's determination and professionalism.

An empty field was slowly becoming an industrial plant of global quality. The observers have noted the occurring change. The earlier quoted security guard recalled:

There was no electricity there when I started. It was a completely empty field. I had rubber boots and sometimes the water will be up to here [points to his knee]. I would walk there, biking was impossible. Look, later they connected the electricity, like after a month. I was there when they [started the construction], until they finished everything. I was there the whole time as a security guard. When they planned to open, the zone was still under construction, but the inside of the plant was ready for the production to start. It took about half a year to get everything ready. It is a modern plant of the best quality.

Construction worker

As a result of the construction, a large up-to-date production facility of more than 375,000 sq. feet was built. The silver building was equipped with three gates, two for trucks and one for the employees. Outside the factory there was a private water reservoir, water purification station, football field and tennis court visible from the outside. Two parking facilities, one for personal cars and the other for white busses bringing the employees, provided the necessary transportation infrastructure. The close proximity of railroad tracks allowed for plans to include a covered train platform to transport workers from farther destinations. Elements of such magnitude and quality, visible from far away, have never existed in the village. When I visited the zone in early 2010, a man in his fifties told me when speaking by the industrial zone: "look at it, who would not want to work there?"

Once the industrial zone was built, it was visible from some gardens of the hosting community. Part of the village is on the hill and the zone was located in the valley. Steel-coloured, it stood alone in the valley surrounded by acres of empty space connected by asphalt lanes in the middle of what, in the socialist times, used to be the state farm's corn field. The newness of the zone contrasted with the forgotten surroundings. The newly laid black asphalt, a roundabout, glowing street lights, sidewalks, safety barriers and its own sewage system looked crisp even four years after the opening. At the time of the research in the village, there was no sewage system or pavements, and, with small exceptions, the village did not have streetlights. Some of the main village roads were covered with asphalt only in 2012. The community members living in the houses closest to the zone can see it from their windows. One of them, a retired woman, really did not like the lights installed in the industrial zone: "At night it is bright like during the day. I had to change the room in which I sleep. At night nothing goes on there. Do they have to keep those lights on?" The plant quickly became the subject of discussion and controversy.

The newly built industrial zone and its contrast to the surroundings was highly-noticeable. Every car using the express road going through the village passes by the zone. A passer-by observing local space in the village might see a reflection of systemic transformations that occurred during Romania's history. A shiny, steel-coloured modern industrial zone strongly contrasted with the rusty and collapsed buildings of the former state farm. Quite often farm animals rest inside the garages or buildings that used to be an important element of the village's life under communism. The collapsed buildings, uncultivated fields, and the village were covered in dust. Inside the plant, hundreds of workers assembled millions of mobile phones, which were picked up by foreign trucks and delivered internationally.

2   Factory Closure in Germany

The decision to locate Nokia's assembly plant in post-communist Romania, which was struggling at that time with economic reforms and awaiting membership in the European Union, was enthusiastically received by Romanian public opinion. When Romanian news programmes discussed the arrival of the prestigious investor, about a thousand miles away in Germany, the decision caused an eruption of protests and disapproval. In 2007, the investor decided to close its assembly plant in Western Germany. The reason officially provided by the investor was that the costs of labour in Germany increased too much. In Romania, the investor opened a similar big-scale assembly centre serving the European market. When the investor finally left Bochum in 2008, it caused a series of protests that were widely covered by German media. Compared to the plant that was about to be built in Romania, it was smaller in size, but its function in the producer's value chain was similar. The investor experienced a very strong reaction from both the community of workers and German authorities. The same process that brought enthusiasm and hopes of economic growth in Romania created social problems and budgetary issues in Germany. Roughly 2,300 direct employees and about 1,000 temporary workers were directly affected by the plant's closure.

Social mobilization against the relocation took numerous organized forms and embraced most of the factory's labour force. Worker unions organized meetings, local and national politicians issued strong statements condemning such practices, and German Chancellor Angela Merkel urged for boycotting the company. The rage was fuelled by the fact that in Germany the investor has previously received numerous funds from local and central government, and the decision to back off from this contract was considered shocking and unfair. Hundreds of workers marched on the streets in order to protest against the investor's decision and show disapproval of losing a plant that for more than a decade was part of the local life. German parliament debated on the actions of foreign investors. Strong action against the relocation was backed by workers' unions. IG-Metal, one of Germany's strongest unions, experienced inaction against the layoffs from the factories and opted for further negotiations. In the factory in Germany, union members were broadly represented and sat on the supervisory board of the investor's German branch. After tense negotiations, the redundancy payments amounted to a total of €200 million ($270 mln), with individual payment limited to €220,000 million ($300,000 mln). Moreover, a special placement organization was established for 12 months to assist redundant workers in their search for alternative jobs and training. The plant in Germany was ultimately closed at the end of 2007.

The storm in Germany caused anger and a sense of helplessness. Part of the attention of the local public was on Romania – the successor. The relocation of production to Romania garnered the interest of the Germans, who were strongly convinced that the decision to close the Bochum plant was unfair. In the Romanian hosting village, the community members remember German journalists arriving one after the other to collect material about the village.

Some of them emphasized that it was absurd to see elegant reporters filming in the mud of a quiet village and interviewing senior family members. Usually armed with a cameraman and a translator, Germans filmed the village and its everyday life and interviewed random villagers.

Some of the material took a more tabloid tone, using negative stereotypes of Romania and stigmatizing rural zones. Footage reliant on this narrative was polemic against the investor's decision and antagonistic to the Eastern European country that "stole" the plant from the Germans. In one of the satirical videos produced in the intermediary period, a German journalist arrives to the village in order to "find a job in the plant that was taken from Germany". The journalist, dressed in a neon-orange puffy jacket, walks around the village, shows off the autumn ponds full of chickens and mud, visits a disadvantaged Roma living in a nearby city, and goes to the plant's construction site asking the security guards in German if he could work there. The material created for the German television reflects the disappointment and frustration felt as a result of the closed plant. The video shows hopelessness and anger. As there were no instruments left to influence the investor's decision, the only action remaining was media violence: bitter reliance on stereotypes and emphasis on the much lower wages of Romanian workers. Some of the German media were less extreme. The common narratives were in solidarity with the underpaid workforce. The low wages, accounting for about 15 per cent of the wage of a German worker, the manual nature of work, and long work hours were the elements that German journalists discussed in their work. But at the same time, they pointed out the hardships of local life including the lack of heating in the local school, dirt roads, and the stagnation of the community, which had to rescue itself with subsistence agriculture, or use horse wagons, an alternative to motorized transportation.

Even though the production was relocated from Germany and the investor offered significantly lower remuneration for work, the idea of factory in Cluj was exciting for the receiving population. Romanians depicted the protests of the Germans against the relocation as unreasonable. The sense of insusceptibility prevailed. At the core of the Romanian understanding of the situation in Germany, there was one argument. Germans have a welfare state, better state support and job possibilities. I witnessed bar debates among Romanians about what happened in Bochum. Some people viewed the reaction in the German city, going to the streets and demanding compensations, as exaggerated. "They just want more money, so they made a big scene. But they can afford everything. They got millions of euros. If they don't like it in Germany [laughing], I can replace them there too" (male worker, 40). Romanians were convincing me that the situation of Germans was just better than theirs. Germans were at least living in an extremely wealthy state. "They can find work for euros, end of topic" (male worker, 45).

As mentioned above, in Romania the level of plant wages was significantly lower than in Germany, amounting to about 15 per cent of the German wage. As I show in the next chapters, the possibility of regular income and work for a prestigious investor was extremely attractive for the Romanian workforce. The common belief among the workforce was that because of the low price of labour, the investor would stay in Romania as long as the cost of production and labour remain low. One of the workers argued that in the long-term perspective reaching a higher standard of living would make it easier for people to live, even without the big investor. The shop floor workers got the salary of about 500 to 600lei (about $170–190). This usually served as an additional household income, which was often backed by other sources of the family income, such as traditional agriculture or pensions of the elderly. Under these conditions, the workers' agency was low and restricted by the production node's mobility, which created dependency. The investor's advantage in the village was partially tied to the economic immobility of the workforce who long-awaited the end of local stagnation. A common view held by many Romanians was that thanks to the investment Romanians were given a chance to work in Romania, instead of being forced to migrate and work in the low-skilled sector, often undocumented. However, as I saw in the village, migration was unpopular among the villagers because of the amount of financial resources, necessary skills, and cultural capital that it requires (for instance: Vlase, 2012).

3   The Opening

The construction of the plant finished in the winter of 2008. Around the time of the final works, announcements on television and radio introduced the investor and informed the public about upcoming hiring possibilities, starting from the spring. All of a sudden, the village appeared on television screens and in the newspapers. The media celebrated the success and described in detail the benefits of the investor's presence. The political class attributed the investor's presence to their merits and stressed that the newly established production node marks a new époque in Romania's history. The plant functioned as the symbolic end of the problematic transition to free market. The key moment in this process was the plant's official opening. For the local population it was the first time to engage with the investor. Prior to it, the village observed the construction of the factory and awaited new hiring possibilities. From the construction's start, there existed the expectation that the plant would be a key element of the local economy. One of my interviewees, who later worked in the plant, told me that he hoped to get a job in the plant, but it was a long waiting period, and in the meantime, he worked in a number of temporary jobs. "Everybody thought that there is a chance to apply, but it took a while to build the plant, like almost a year. You get less excited if you wait for so long. But I was busy with other tasks; I did not have any options anyway!" The local population remembers the construction period and circulating gossip about the plant's supposed opening. "Almost every couple of weeks somebody would say that in 3 months they are hiring (…) It was just gossip, completely not true" (female worker).

The final moment came in the late spring, when the work on the assembly plant was completed. Even though the surrounding zone was still under construction, the investor broadly publicized the official opening. Not only did the factory gain mass media publicity, but also, the information about the ceremony appeared on posters put up in the stores and on fences, which is a typical way of spreading the information in local villages. As my interviewee recalled, the message was short but concise: the local population was informed about the opening, the date, place and time were given. The opening ceremony is remembered very well because many of the local inhabitants were eager to respond to the advertised invitation and participate in the ceremony.

My interviewees, a group of retired women, gave me a detailed description of those events. Hearing the official invitation to the opening, they hesitated about going. However, the publicity gave birth to speculations that Nokia's mobile phones could be given away as presents for the attendees. Even though the news was not officially confirmed, their neighbours decided to attend, so the women made a plan to go to the event together. They needed to walk there, which from their houses took about 75 minutes. They recalled that when they were leaving, there were small groups heading there. Walking through the village, leaving it, entering the new road, not asphalted yet, they saw people concentrating in the zone. After a while, they entered the industrial zone. As one of them remembered: "It was all gated, and we were put in a large parking lot behind the fence. (…) Behind the fence there were journalists and a small scene. It took a while once the ceremony started. (…) There was a speech and some music". Unfortunately, to the crowd's disappointment, the investor did not give away phones. Only a few of them were handed to the local authorities. Once the ceremony was over, the villagers, including my interviewees slowly started to return. Another woman remembered: "There was not much disappointment, but they could have done something nicer for us. At least we had a nice walk".

The visual symbol of the investor's presence in Romania became a highly reprinted picture published in national and international newspapers. The frame contains three older village women walking with a large Nokia sign in the background. The picture was taken while they were walking back from the opening ceremony. It happened without their knowledge or authorization. It appeared in the press the day after the ceremony but also under many other occasions, often on the cover pages. As one of them remembers: "my daughter came from Cluj with a newspaper asking me how it happened. I was surprised, I saw cameramen then but why would they film us? Then it kept coming back again and again". The women agree that they don't like the picture and wish that it was not published. This very first encounter with the investor demonstrated ambiguity and distance from potential future relationships. The community expected immediate benefits. The idea of receiving freebies, gifts and profits continued throughout Nokia's presence.

Following the plant's opening, international media started to refer to the village as "the Nokia Village" and Romanian press referred to the industrial zone as "Jucu". The national narrative used the industrial zone as a symbol of change. To many Romanians their state stayed off-track the reforms for too long, remaining behind the other transiting states of the region. The plant's location followed Romania's European Union accession and was another step in building national optimism. The investor's arrival was interpreted as a symbol of the shift towards normality. Despite the negative campaign following the closure in Germany, the investor was perceived in solely positive terms in Romania. The investment appeared to be strategic to the country's growth. The statistics confirmed: Nokia's activity was one of the biggest investments in terms of the number of employees and the scale of exports. Undoubtedly, it was also the most prestigious investment. The global investor was very well received, reflecting the ambitions and dreams of Romanians. The brand image of Nokia contained the highly desired features: modernity, creativity, intelligence and dynamism. Since the plant started to operate, it was used by the political class as an example of Romania's good governance. The factory started to appear in political speeches, promotional materials and the national news. Political and media discourse depicted the investment as the national success. The opinion makers argued that "the factory is Romania's future"; "it will use Romania's human potential"; "it will bring at least fifteen thousand jobs"; and "that it will help to make Romania the seventh power of Europe" (Realitatea.net, 2011). The plant gave hope for future changes, a domino effect of positive consequences.

In the next chapters, I dissect global assemblages in order to study the local experience of the production node and how reorganization of local dynamics was soaked in the cultural meaning. The scalar fix created by the assembly plant functioned as a vehicle of change representing entirely new scales and connections. With the physical change that was taking place, along with the construction of the industrial zone, the village was connected to the global production system. Even though the industrial zone remained a separate entity that offered very limited access to the local actors, the investor's activity proved to be enough to involve the community in the new scales. Global industrial production inside the factory was locally experienced and lived by the community. The plant's presence and activity influenced new scalar positioning. Its effects, which I address in this work, produced new expectations and experiences, including transaction-specific assets that proved to be the cost of local involvement in the global production node.

CHAPTER 3

A Journey onto the Shop Floor: Cultural Specificity of the Offshored Plant and Workforce Adaptation

> The work [refers to employment in the plant] has resulted in an odd situation. For a while, I struggled with jobs. I felt cramped here with them [refers to parents and extended family living in the same house]. We had all we needed but no more than that. Living in a village has its downsides. Like, everybody knows you. Everybody talks about you if you want to make any change. It is also much harder to do things. For most of my life, I did what was expected of me; I helped my family in the field and with anything else that they undertook. I made sure that they were fine. (…) [With time] I was fed up with it. It is weird to think that you have an entire life in front of you but to feel that it all might be just the same. (…) When the factory was set up it not only changed my fortune by allowing me to work. It really brought about an entirely new life for me. It might sound really stupid, but it felt like I was a different person.
>
> What do you mean when you say that you felt like a different person?
>
> I know, but I'm not sure how to describe it to you. [sighs] It was just a job, but it had much more to offer than most jobs that I had. And I don't mean money. Maybe it was only my case, but I saw that I can live a life that was about more than being stuck in the village. The salary was actually not important to me at that point. I cared more about going there; (…) I never missed any of my jobs, but I remember that one time I caught a bad cold and stayed at home for a while. And I was really fed up with staying at home, but it was also connected to the fact that I missed my job! (…). I felt different there, needed, smarter, more needed than in any other job. Maybe it was not about the actual work but the people from my shift? (…) It was only a few kilometres from the house, and yet that made such a big difference. And I liked this difference. I enjoyed it, and I think to most people this was what ultimately mattered in this job.
>
> Factory worker

The industrial zone created thousands of jobs that were filled by locally recruited workers. Most positions offered in the plant were low-skilled jobs that were managed using efficiency-based techniques. Typical of the consumer electronics production process (Cowie, 2001; Danford, 1998; Kenney et al., 1998), the organization of production was very strictly supervised and regulated. Even though the shop floor produced mobile phones that were equipped with the most up-to-date technology, the nature of the work was relatively simple and based on Taylorist principles adapted to the assembly process, using efficiency-based techniques and reliant on Japanese management philosophy and methodology (Delbridge, 1998). Workers were provided with detailed instructions on highly-repetitive and manual tasks. In the opening passage, a shop floor operator describes how the investment provided an attractive work alternative, especially when compared to the stagnated local job market. This interviewee states that the opportunity to work for the investment influenced his sense of belonging and higher self-valuation. Other workers with whom I have spoken to reported similar effects, which were highly desired and appreciated by them. Work in the plant was perceived as an escape from the challenging situation, embedded in post-socialist stagnation and rural livelihoods. In this chapter, I consider the process of adaptation in the workplace, outlining the key steps of the workforce undertook to adapt and the factors that attracted employees to the job.

In this chapter I explore the relationship between the workforce recruited to the shop floor and the cultural specificity of the workplace. Focusing on the shop floor dynamics in the plant, I describe the significance that the factory jobs had locally. I analyse the actions performed in the workplace, and I describe how intense and complex the process of learning the organization of the shop floor was for local workers. Very few had previous experience in an industrial plant such as this one. Those who were previously employed in the manufacturing sector, either in Socialist enterprises or small-sized factories, described the strong contrast, including in the areas of safety, workplace procedures and organizational culture. From the first day the investment required workers to adapt to new tasks and procedures, such as security and safety regulations, and to understand the complex and highly regulated system of managing labour and production. The employer's expectations also included adjusting to the organizational culture and language, learning terminology related to production, and acclimating to the work attire. This was made difficult by the unexpected and newly experienced conditions, including the specific work clothes and diet, invariable temperature within the plant throughout the year or lack of windows. These conditions required adaptation. In this chapter I study the cultural specificity that was at the foundation of the workplace experience and the ways in which employees adapted to its distinctiveness. I depict a variety of factors that influenced the overall assessment of the workplace. This is followed by the next chapter, which addresses the issues and controversies of the workplace and the jokes and storytelling that were told to deal with them. Both are interpretations of the workplace and intend to demonstrate how the local community has taken to the offshoring work.

1   Joining a Capitalist Workplace

As soon as the construction of the plant was near completion, a few weeks before the official opening, the investor's plans and hiring possibilities were advertised. From posters on the old wooden fences around the villages neighbouring the industrial zone and advertisement posters in the towns, to long prime-time commercials on national television and announcements in local, regional and national newspapers. The TV commercials portrayed the plant and the investor enthusiastically. The media promoted the information that the plant is soon to become the largest employer in the region, and it showed the industrial zone and the newly developed offices, while providing instructions on how to apply. The widespread media attention exemplified how important this news is for the region. The investor offered low-skilled workers attractive employment prospects. One of the local inhabitants recalled: "People expected [the job offer's details] ever since they started building [the industrial zone]. Of course, people wanted to know as soon as possible. I saw [the advertisement] on TV, but I learned the most from people talking about it. From neighbours, church-goers, customers in the shop. You know how you just hear things around here" (community member). The job announcement by the investor was clear, and it left no doubts. Shop floor workers were needed in the factory and prior experience was not necessary.

The recruitment process was the first clue that this plant was different from other locally operating firms. Procedural and formal, it involved external agencies, standardized forms, and specific qualification criteria. In order to apply for a job, the candidates needed to submit an application form to the work agency in a neighbouring city. When asked, the hired workers usually recalled the job application process as stressful and requiring effort. For instance: "They wanted a CV and all I could write about is secondary school and that I was a [job position name] for 6 years" (worker). This quote shows the challenge some faced to detail their merits and experience. Older workers especially felt discomfort with the requirement, as they did not consider their work history to be impressive. Quite often, as in the situation of the worker quoted above, one's own qualifications and education were seen as inappropriate and almost embarrassing. Recruitment posed an intimidating barrier that required overcoming hesitation and timidity. The only group that did not experience deep concerns with the process were the youngest candidates with no prior experience. One of the first hires in the plant, who at that time was 20, told me that he had no problem applying as he had a computer and had already prepared his CV for a class at school. He later helped his mother to apply, and also typed and printed other people's applications. For him, as he has put it, there were no risks involved: "I just tried. I had no other plans, and I did not really have many other things to do [refers to having no work at the time of the application]".

After sending the documents, workers usually needed to wait for a subsequent recruitment stage. Those who were rejected did not receive any information from the work agency, and this initially caused some confusion, frustration and was sometimes considered impolite. One of the community members stated that "at least they could do something to tell people no, instead of making them wait for nothing" when recalling her son's application. People who were selected were invited to the city to take additional tests. "Testing was stressful, but it was clear what they were looking for and what they want from people" (worker). Information about what to expect on the tests and how to do well on them circulated throughout the village. Workers generally claimed that the tests were easy, and their main purpose was to check the ability to recognize colours, think logically, count, perform manual tasks, and prove one's resistance to stress. As one of them said to me: "They did not know me, so they had to make sure I am not crazy or that I can read". The tests were straight-forward and included a basic mathematical test, a series of puzzles and a short interview. Even though they were regarded as easy, some community members admitted to having failed them, especially the mathematical part. For most of those hired, it took about two weeks to receive notification and those who received a job offer were invited to an induction day. The plant was hiring on a regular basis and all recruitment was done in collaboration with work agencies.

Shop floor workers, called "line operators" according to the terminology used by the employer, were offered two types of full-time employment. The first type of contract was based on direct employment. This contract was the most lucrative and stable with a salary ranging between 600 and 800 lei ($200–$250). Employees were offered open-ended contracts, guaranteeing social security protection enforced by Romanian employment law. About 25 per cent of the shop floor workforce, as well as shop floor managers, administrative staff and higher managers were direct employees of the investor. Workers found it puzzling and ambiguous because there was no clear criteria on how to be moved to the direct hire. "You would never know why they decided to offer an open-ended contract to somebody. I got it after 13 months of work, and I am still unsure why they chose me. I always did my best, so this might be why" (worker). As this passage exemplifies, for most employees it was rather a matter of luck than skils or determination. I estimate that about 1500 employees with open-ended contract were employed at a time, of which about a thousand were shop floor workers.

The majority of line operators signed temporary contracts. Global offshoring largely relies on the intermediation of temporary work agencies, which support staffing and recruitment and play an important role in limiting the employers' responsibility towards employees, which often contributes to the degradation of the workplace experience (Kalleberg, 2012; Kinnie et al., 2008; Fudge and Strauss, 2013). The involvement of temporary work agencies is a type of buffer, often eliminating state-enforced social benefits, such as eligibility for sick leave or unemployment benefits as well as eliminating necessary compensation in the case of layoffs or closures. These agencies played a key role in the recruitment of the offshored workforce, testing as well as providing them with basic information about the workplace.

In the investment, flexible employment was based on the intermediation of Romanian subsidiaries of global work agencies who administered worker contracts. Typically, the contract was renewed every one to three months and officially depended on production needs, continuous employment was not guaranteed, but often continued for months. In many cases workers had their contracts extended, sometimes even for an unexpectedly long period of time. Uncertainty was the biggest problem for those on the shop floor. As one of the workers remarked: "I was never sure if in a month I would be unemployed. This was unfair. I won't even mention that no bank would give me a loan with a temporary contract". Some workers also pointed out that often the contract would not be extended, because of low staffing needs, while, at the same time, new workers would be hired. The sense of injustice was amplified by the lower salary. The salary of the group hired by the proxies was about 120–160 lei ($35–$50) lower than that of the direct employees. Their contracts also did not guarantee statutory benefits, such as maternity leave or redundancy payment. In the peak of production there could be up to 3500 temporary employees. In practice, both groups shared exactly the same responsibilities and duties. The only actual difference on the shop floor was the work agency's name on the identification tag. Additionally, the entire workforce received food vouchers. They were equal to 200–250 lei ($60–$70) and could be used in the local stores as well as in the supermarkets throughout the city.

2   Cultural Specificity of the Workplace and Worker Socialisation

The transition to the new workplace circumstances was a complex experience. Organisation scholars use the notion of organizational socialization to describe the process through which individuals obtain the knowledge, skills, attitudes, and learn behaviour required to adapt to a role in the workplace (Kramer, 2010: 17). In this process the workers shared the belief that this adaptation was driven by their interest and curiosity in the plant. As one of them summarised:

> I decided to choose [the investment], because I had a feeling that it could give something more [than other jobs]. I am sure that having it in my CV will be much better than [name of another workplace]. Everybody knew about [the investment]. That's already a good sign!
> Worker

For many workers the investment represented a unique, global workplace, different from most others that they have worked in before. An unfamiliar work environment, health and safety regulations, a large group of co-workers, unknown machinery and the high pace of work were only some of the factors that contributed to socialization-related anxiety. The first memories of the new workplace that were brought up by workers were related to the on-boarding procedures. In similar industrial workplaces, introductory activities are organised by the employer and their purpose was to familiarise workers with the work process and support coping with these new work experiences (Katz, 1978: 38). As the passage below describes, the presentations were very detailed and unentertaining:

> After we got our tests and signed the job contract, school started for us. They were crazy about all those details. They would tell us really basic stuff, but really basic. So basic! (...) Like how to use tools, where the exits are and what can happen if we do things the wrong way (...). I would not be surprised if [during the training] they would have reminded us to flush after taking a dump. Or wash hands with soap and use a hand dryer.
> Worker

For newcomers the level of detail often seemed unnecessary, even ridiculous. After signing the contract, every employee of the plant went through the above described basic induction process. It included health and safety instructions, outlined the production process and described the plant's rules. The same worker continues, arguing that perhaps the procedure comes from another cultural context: "This is because they are foreign procedures. Maybe in Germany you would get a fine from the officials for not communicating it. But it did not really matter; everybody just shut up and listened". Another worker also emphasised that the level of detail involved was meant to establish legal protection for the investor: "In case of an accident, Nokia could claim that the worker was not following the procedures". Although they were perceived as unnecessary, the safety procedures and materials were all considered a crucial element of the workplace. Employees understood that the training was part of the employer's duty.

After the formal induction, shop floor workers went through additional training, which took place inside the plant. Workers were shown how the phones are assembled. Each of the individual phone parts had a name that workers were required to learn. Typically, the operator's daily task was to assemble a phone. First, they would connect a motherboard with a screen, then add a keyboard, put the front and the back cover on as well as a battery, load software through the computer and put the completed phone into a box, which included a battery charger, the warranty card and a manual. The strategic elements, such as screens or motherboards, were marked with a barcode, which was scanned during the assembly process. Operators worked in groups of three to eight people. One of the workers describes the work setting: "I stood by the table, which was actually something between a computer desk and a complicated workbench with a lot of frames (…) next to me were other people on the line". In the production process, each of line operators was assigned tasks in the assembly process. The assembly program was set by an "order" (*comandă*), which defined how many phones ought to be assembled per unit of time. With time, the workers acquired the ability to pace their work and meet the employer's standards. One of the workers recalls: "It was sometimes hard to keep up; but I started to do it without thinking. We would even get some time to rest". A group of lines was supervised by a "line manager", who was also responsible for keeping up with commands. Each line manager was supervised by a "key manager", who oversaw up to a dozen lines. The parts used in the phones were delivered to a line by a "handler", who brought them from a warehouse, called by the workers "the supermarket".

One of the workers comments on the first impressions of the workplace and production process:

> I realize how surprising it was to me just to see that the building is not that flat and not as big on the inside as from the outside. The idea [of taking up the operator's position] was to work in a field in which I had no experience in. As a matter of fact, I did not know anything about it at all. I obviously was aware of the context, mobile phones, electronic parts. It was all crazy with the little screws. I did not know why, but I thought that I won't ever manage it. When I saw all the buttons, so many little parts, computers, and codes, I asked myself what am I going to do here? Those will all get lost. I won't manage. But listen, I learned all that gradually.

> I learned slowly, all that. And after a while, when new workers came, we saw how miserable they were. I think that I was even worse when I started. They were so amazed. They looked and did not know where to put their hands, what to do. But the thing is that they were not lazy at all. They simply did not know anything.
>
> Worker

This passage was shared by a woman in her late twenties who got hired at the plant after coming back from abroad, where she worked in the agricultural sector. As with this worker, very few employees had prior work experience in the manufacturing sector and their reflections on the learning process are similar to that above. Even though the formal training was tiresome and boring, the majority of new employees appreciated the care and professionalism of the trainers. It was something unique, as most local employers did not express such great care and attention to details to the initial stages of work. On-boarding efforts provided by the investor to facilitate the first days at work were called by the workers as "foreign" and "strange". One of them remarked that "[on-boarding] was really detailed, and the trainers would sometimes treat us a bit like children. Maybe you have to explain everything to a German twice, but I think everybody knew what a cloakroom was used for". Germany, the initial location of the plant, but also Finland or more broadly Europe, was referred to in such responses in order to rationalize the distinct character of the organizational culture inside the plant. The explanations provided to workers seemed rather simplistic to them, and the attitude of the trainers was perceived as overly cautious.

At the same time workers remarked that initially the investor could not do much to teach the actual job, as, in fact, only shop floor practice could allow new employees to gain the necessary skills on the shop floor. Below, one of the workers describes her experience:

> I don't know what to tell you about starting to work there [in the plant]. In a way it was hard at first. The training period was short. Maybe a couple of days of theory and practice. But it took me a while to get used to it. Maybe it was not a matter of learning the activity on the [assembly] line. It was more like getting used to the whole thing that came with it. Some people could not handle it. Too many cameras, too much hard work, too many norms. For me the first two months were the hardest. After that I was basically working without thinking. But before, oh boy! Look, it was painful, and sometimes I even cried at home after my shift.
>
> Female worker

As the passage shows, adaptation was a long and emotionally engaging experience. The worker, a mom of two, stresses that adapting to the workplace was exhausting for her. She points out that despite the relatively short period of induction and training, the biggest challenge was posed by adaptation to the demands of the workplace, including maintaining efficiency (volume) and quality of work. The experience of all new hires was similar and very distinct from what they previously experienced in the other jobs. Not only was this labour intensive but it was also paced by the phone assembly plans, highly supervised, and requiring long hours and shifts. These conditions were difficult to bear for some.

3 Workplace Adaptation

The initial experience of the workplace was challenging, but at the same time it proved to be attractive and provoked distinct emotions, usually positive. At first, many of the workers found the factory environment, co-workers, and daily work to be curious and interesting. One of them remarked: "It might sound weird but before [working in the investment], I never really felt like going to work, because it was usually the same boring bullshit. But when I got this job, it was all a new reality. I actually started to be curious, wanting something from life". This interviewee compares work in the investment to other experiences, describing how it sparked curiosity. He even mentions how the investment motivated him to take more interest in other activities.

Other workers described their first experiences related to their role clarification and the process of learning the organizational culture. As one remarked: "it was impressive from the first step. If you go [to the plant], inside there is an entirely new world". The first experiences with the plant were closely tied to the specific expectations of the offshoring workplace. Many workers perceived an extraordinary manifestation of Western modernity, in contrast to the local and post-communist everyday reality. What distinguished the plant was the highly formalised procedures, the interior space and its characteristics, and the work setting. As one of the workers recalls:

> When I entered the plant for training, I came in the morning. (...) They would not just let you in; there was a security officer and a lot of gates. They wrote down my details and gave me a temporary ID. (...) Not only was it something different but also you would immediately realize that they are doing something more than just dumb work. (...) They had secrets and parts they wanted to protect, innovations and products that

nobody but us [refers to the workforce] could see and take out. (...) They would also be obviously worried about people stealing or doing something unsafe. (...) It was an entirely new place with completely different dynamics.
Worker

The passage above further describes the uniqueness of the plant. Not only was it different from other available manufacturing jobs, which the interviewee calls "dumb", but the need for tighter security, which even involved metal detectors and strict security procedures also differentiated it from the rest. Even though the workers did not like it, some of them provided arguments supporting the existence of the security measures, such as the temptation to steal which was mentioned above or general safety. One of the workers remarked: "Upon entering, there were gates like in the metro, letting one person in at a time. (...) Then, when leaving, it was crazy strict. On the way out it was like at an airport. You have to put all of your stuff on a table: mobile phone, keys, or watch. (...) And if something beeps, they will search you, unfortunately". This interviewee uses the metaphor of metro entrance gates, while some other workers also used the airport comparison.

3.1   *Language*

The opening quote of this chapter reflects the hope for a change in life, and this is also a recurring theme in the responses of other workers in the plant. The narrative that develops among the workers indicates not only tangible difference, such as the workspace and infrastructure, but also the language used in the work environment. Language is among the most important elements of organizational communication in the management of offshoring projects (Clyne, 1994, Taylor and Bain, 2008; Kojima and Kojima, 2007). The corporate language used in the plant required the workers to adapt. The investor's policy was a universal top-down approach to shop floor language. Similarly to other offshoring shop floors, the specific terminology used was based on a production-specific variation of global English. Unlike the vernacular of professional groups (Philbin, 1996), which is produced and reinforced in a more democratic way, shop floor language at the plant was non-negotiable from the first day of training.

Global production had its influence on the way that the shop floor procedures were named and organized. They were all universal for all of the facilities owned by the investor internationally. The basics of the terminology to be used on the shop floor were transmitted during the on-boarding process, and workers would usually adapt to the vernacular enforced by the trainers. Once the specifics were communicated, the workers developed their own variations and phrases comprised of a mixture of English and Romanian phrases. Nouns referring to the specific phone parts and technical verbs were assigned English phrases, specific to the equipment and context of production. Similar issues were previously addressed in the literature, mostly in the context of transnational higher-level workers rather than the industrial labour force (Snell-Hornby, 1999).

An example of the shop floor vernacular is described below.

> The *object list* or *comandă* was a schedule of what to do, which models to do. *Enginul* was a telephone without anything else, just the motherboard. *Keymat* was a keyboard. *Display document* was an instruction manual ... Free time, *leisure*, and a person who would bring the parts [to the shop floor] was a *handler*.
> Male worker

In this factory, a job on the shop floor did not require knowledge of any foreign language. The workforce did not face serious problems learning new phrases. The workers reported that it was rather funny and strange at first. Communication among operators took place in Romanian on a daily basis. However, the working language of the organization was English, and it was the language of higher managers as well as the offices. Shift and line managers were required to communicate in English and Romanian. Administrative staff was comprised of transnational workers, including Romanian workers with high fluency in English. One of the prerequisites of becoming a key- or shift-manager was basic knowledge of English. A worker who started as an operator and became a shift manager within three years told me how English was a procedural language. "If somebody wanted to make a complaint or change the line, a protocol was needed. It would always be in English. It was a multinational corporation, so any member of the staff, also from abroad, had to have access to information about what was happening". The man told me that without knowledge of English, his promotion would have been impossible and his good language skills definitely helped him to advance so far.

There existed the general understanding that international managers working in the offices were recruited mostly from outside of Romania, and they implemented modern global management practices. For that reason, it was not only impossible to translate it to Romanian but also highly unnecessary. In the passage below, one of the female operators shares her impressions of using production-specific discourse.

> Everything on the computers was in English! The moment that somebody had something to do with the office, and there would be even one

foreign person dealing with the case, then they would always talk in English. The whole world there had to understand! And it's natural, no? It is an international company. There is no playing with words; they need to know what happens. Look, the engine [the telephone's motherboard] ... if we translate it to Romanian, what it would be? Motor? Which engine does it have? Where? People would get lost trying to understand that. [The managers] spoke English with each other. So there were [workers] who knew English. There would always be somebody around. Those who had the ability. Those who knew it from the internet. They were teaching us a bit. And I did learn a lot. And you needed to speak some, because at first [the managers] would come to the line and explain. So we watched. "If you don't understand English, I will show you how to do it". And they showed it, then left, and we continued working. In the worst-case scenario, you don't get any of it. That did happen to some people. But this was not a big problem, because then another person from your line who understood it would help you.
Female worker

Above one of the operators emphasizes that the establishment of informal networks helped in dealing with the language difficulties. In her view, adaptation to the vernacular of the organization was crucial and necessary, as the transnational management could not speak or learn the Romanian language. The other workers pointed at the fact that some managers started to learn Romanian greetings and basic phrases in time.

Different abstract names referred to the timing and organization of production. Each command, an order to assemble a number of specific phone models, was fulfilled under a nickname. Instead of using the trade names of the phone models, which in the particular production process were represented by numbers, such as the 6600 or the 3210, the workers used nicknames that were applied in the corporation's plants all around the world. The model nicknames were the names of world cities or Latin nouns – such as "Jakarta", "Delhi" or "Piccolo". All forty-two phone models produced in the plant had their nicknames. Dealing with linguistic adaptation was a crucial element of socialization. "They made sense. They were easy to remember, and maybe the numbers are different in various languages, but those terms [are easy to learn] for anybody from anywhere" (shop floor manager). Those who successfully completed the training did not have problems learning new words, even though, as they admit, at first it was confusing. Working with the interviewees, we built a dictionary of global words and phrases of the plant. We identified about 140 phrases that referred to names of telephone parts, factory rooms, work activities and the schedule, plus nicknames for the phone models. Despite the fact that most workers do not admit that it was a challenge to adapt linguistically, the process played a role in the entire work experience in the plant. Language contributed to the initial stress and anxiety of newcomers.

3.2   Work Attire

> When my sister saw a picture taken in the plant, she joked that we look like Smurfs [laughing] (...) We were all dressed in those blue and white aprons, and we looked a bit silly and innocent. (...) I think that it was a crucial part. It made us all a bit closer. I had no problem wearing it. I think everybody understood that it is just a part of that game.
> Female worker

The passage above addresses the work attire and considers it playfully. The Smurfs metaphor helped to integrate the workforce (while facilitating the production process). Work attire is an important element of any workplace and part of workforce identity and integration. The literature has extensively shown how attire substantially impacts how one operates within a role defined by work (Peluchette and Karl, 2007). Wearing appropriate clothing improves perceptions of work quality and performance (Solomon and Schopler, 1982), enhances self-perception of one's occupational attributes (Kwon, 1994a) and allows one to temporarily shed non-organizational roles (Rafaeli et al., 1997). Work attire might change self-perception to the degree that employees believe that they look significantly more responsible, knowledgeable, professional and hard-working (Kwon, 1994b). Workplace uniforms also contributed to the experience of cultural specificity of the workplace, which is exemplified in the passage above.

As shown below, the standardised uniforms on the shop floor helped to boost worker confidence making each worker in the workplace more anonymous and stimulated internal networking and team building. The specific environment of the plant, designed to protect the product, required keeping the body strictly away from production.

> We had to be really careful, because there was a cult of cleanliness. Everything had to stay shiny and fresh, because pollen was the worst enemy. If you got it on the screen, the phone would have to be put together again. People don't want to buy a phone with pollen on a display! This is why everything we wore had to be clean and dust-free. You would get a smock and shoes on your first day. Also, keys to your personal locker and an identity card to enter the factory, with a picture and your name. So

that they would know who you are through the cameras. After all, the workers all looked the same.
>   Male worker

As the passage above illustrates, the careful production process was enforced among the workforce. The workers considered the attire to be highly professional, safe for the equipment, protective or just comfortable. "It was all like in a laboratory. We all had white gowns and were dressed in a similar way". The gowns were designed in corporate colours. The white gown had blue elements on the elbow pads, four pockets, a collar as well as the investor's logo.

Leaving fingerprints, dust or any other traces on the equipment signified an error because the produced equipment would not pass quality tests. The two passages below illustrate those concerns:

> The new phones were supposed to look like they were made in a plant and not by a person. In order to prevent marking the pristine new models, the function of the work attire was to prevent direct contact. Touching any part could magnetize [the equipment] and break it, or it could become dirty even with clean hands.
>   Female worker

> You would get anti-static gloves made from fabric. Each worker was obligated to use them to protect the product. At first, I found it hard to use it; it's easier to drop things and you have a different touch.
>   Male worker

Separation of the body from the work set the tone for the workers' attitude to the product. This body-related alienation was learned through training. As part of organizational socialization, workers often repeated the following argument: "if you buy a phone, you want it to be perfect". From the toes to shoulders, the way workers dressed was regulated and imposed. The plant work required changing shoes upon entering. The workers used rubber thimbles so that they would not leave their fingerprints on the product when not using gloves. Workers were provided with cork sandals. The shoes were considered comfortable, sometimes even called slippers, and of good quality. The standardized shoes were worn with socks and all workers were required to wear long pants.

Clothing equalised and anonymized individual workers, who while entering the plant started to look alike. This proved to be very important to some of the workers. For instance, one worker commented that, "once I put on my work uniform, I felt like a part of that big family. (...) And when working with strangers, nobody would care who I am, as long as I kept things up. I seriously liked that". The workforce often emphasized that the uniformity of the clothing made every operator feel equal. The badge was the only distinguishing feature as those hired through the work agencies had different inscriptions on the badge, but this didn't make much of a difference. A female worker said that, "nobody would care about your contract and look at your badge. You just had to work well". The shared feeling of a common mission, despite different backgrounds and places of origin, was highly valued and considered a very positive component of the work in the plant. "Everybody, from the cleaning person to the manager, looked very professional! As one of the interviewees summarised in reference to workplace attire and the shop floor: "They made real Europe with all that". The reference to Europe, outlines the workers' perception of the workplace, signifying the high quality of the space and equipment as well as the strong contrast to local labour conditions. This reference also suggests that the time in the plant was perceived as unique; it was a distinct place, with special properties and qualities.

3.3 *Temperature and Light*

Air properties constituted another important element of the shop floor experience. A younger worker shared with me that he really enjoyed the temperature consistency in the plant.

> No matter what time of the year, it was always a really comfortable temperature inside the plant. T-shirt temperature. Because the computers could not overheat, they would keep the temperature stable. It was really pleasant, same temperature every day. No difference if it was winter or summer! Never too warm, never too cold! [laughing] (...) I actually had two pairs of pants and t-shirts, and I wore it all the time to work. In a way it was my uniform under the uniform. I just knew that this is the best set-up.
> Younger worker

Stable temperatures inside were independent of the conditions outside. Cold Transylvanian winters and hot summers during work were not felt inside the plant. Additionally, dust filters and air conditioning regulated the climate and humidity. For another worker, the stability of temperature seemed like a luxury. In her words: "you struggle to keep warm at home, and [the investor] had no choice. Obviously, it was not for us [the workers] but for the machines [production equipment]". Filtered and pollution-free air was among the benefits that

A JOURNEY ONTO THE SHOP FLOOR 75

were valued especially by workers who had experience in the manufacturing sector. A 34-year-old worker told me about how he had worked in a furniture company located nearby and compared it to the conditions of the plant.

> [In the other plant] saw dust was everywhere, in my hair, nose and ears. I was used to it, but still, a normal person would prefer to not to be breathing in dirt. It was harder anyway. Wood is heavy. It was really tough [...] And when I came to work here it was so clean. Do you know the smell when you get a new home appliance and open the box? Like plastic, or just like a new thing? This is the smell of the parts that we would put together. It's not bad! [smiling]
> Male worker

For this interviewee, with experience in the manufacturing sector, the plant provided safer, more comfortable conditions. When referring to the general order and cleanliness of the space, he mentions good quality of the work environment, even describing the smell and elaborating on its unique characteristics.

Another worker points out how radically different it would be to enter the plant: "The bus would always be really hot. So once you entered the plant and change, you would feel relief!" The same worker that told me about the work environment asked me if I have seen *Star Trek*. "It was like a starship. Do you think you would find dust in their rocket? I think that it would be impossible, and it was just as clean at Nokia". For all workers the ritual of starting a shift included changing clothes and entering a completely different environment. The shop floor with its own physical characteristics provided an alternative dimension to embodied experience. This feeling was also boosted by very few windows in the facility.

> There was no view of the outside from the shop floor, so I would lose track of what time of day it is. Listen, I would look at my watch and think, is it twelve – midnight or midday? This would happen especially when I got busy and tired.
> Male worker

For the employees, the only way of knowing if it's light outside was to look through the windows in the offices overlooking the shop floor, but these were visible from many spots in the plant. This lack of natural light was part of the work. Perception of time was distorted. One of the most important theorisations on time in offshoring work was Shezad Nadeem's study of an off-shored call centre in India. Nadeem uses this example to reflect on the workers' time perception, those who work between foreign time zones, experience long hours, an intense work pace, and temporal displacement. As Nadeem shows, working night shifts result in many of them facing health and safety problems and social alienation (Nadeem, 2009: 20). Similarly, the workers in the Romanian investment have faced challenges connected to time perception and the way in which the shop floor was organised. Lack of daily light, long working hours and the work pace caused a different perception of time inside the plant, contributing to the experience of cultural specificity.

3.4 *Diet and Well-being*

Factory canteens are a meaningful place for the workers and an important spatial and cultural component of the industrial experience (Marshall, 2005; Wallendorf and Arnould, 1991). In the studied facility, taste also fulfilled an important role in the workers' perception of the workplace. All shop floor staff, no matter what their function, received complimentary meals. The meals were served in the canteen, and depending on the shift, they were either a lunch or a dinner. The canteen was on the second floor of the plant. In short, the canteen was an open buffet and the workers lined up with trays for every meal and had a choice of a main course and a side salad. The canteen had windows to the outside, a red floor and rows of white tables, each with eight chairs. The majority of workers considered the food to be decent. For instance, one of the workers remarked:

> There [in the plant] the food was by all means good. I am sure, absolutely sure, that nobody would bring anything from home. Why would they? It was good and free! And other companies make you pay for that!
> Worker

The workers enjoyed the food as part of the work arrangement and considered the meals an additional bonus. Some of the interviewees gave me extensive lists of foods available in the canteen and the majority of them agreed that the food was monotonous and that it had the taste of industrial cooking. The poor effort undertaken to change the menu or make it more diverse was the object of jokes:

> When there was a Mexican Day, they gave us the same meals but everything had beans or corn in it. [laughing] All the same but more beans! Who ate the Mexican food? [laughing] Nobody! But Mexicans, they must use a lot of corn! Nokia did more of these international days. They were funny, because there was almost no difference!
> Worker

Another worker told me that the food was always warm and fresh but the only problem that would arise was that the canteen would be out of what you wanted.

The workers agreed that the foods offered were an attraction and that they provided something different to what most workers ate at home. Even though the food was not of superior quality, its distinctness, as well as the fact that it was free, provided an enjoyable distraction from daily activities. Eating at work was part of the workplace culture and was connected to the daily routines. It was an important ritual for the workers. "You would work from one break to another. Once I had a big meal and got my belly warm, the work was going much faster, because it would be the second half of the day" (worker). Similarly to other workplaces, workers combated boredom by counting hours to the upcoming coffee or food breaks (Grubb, 1975; Kass et al., 2001). Each workday consisted of two shorter breaks plus a lunch break. During one of the shorter breaks, usually referred to as coffee breaks, a sandwich was served. Workers also had the possibility of getting a coffee by putting an electronic key in a coffee machine. One person could take up to 33 coffees per month.

> Those breaks were short, but I enjoyed them. For shorter breaks, we had a little break room. There was a nice aquarium there and really comfortable deck chairs. Everybody would always stretch and talk there. I was running for a cigarette and a coffee. They had cappuccinos, lattes, even hot chocolates. It was good, but ten minutes was too short.
> Female worker

Even though the workers could only relax for ten minutes, the possibility of lying down and drinking a coffee created an atmosphere of closeness and togetherness.

The smoking lounge was located in a separate space. It was another important place for integration. As one of the workers commented, "I smoke, but I was aware that they won't let us smoke too much. It was not that bad, but sometimes I would [get worked up] from the urge to smoke" (male worker). Smoking is very popular in Romania, still cultivated despite the public smoke ban and other countermeasures introduced by the state (Ger et al., 1993; Trofor, A. et al., 2009). The desire to smoke was an element of the shop floor culture. Another young man told me that he would start thinking about going for a cigarette about an hour before the break. "There [in the smoking lounge] was always cigarettes and coffee in front of me; and a lot of laughter! It gave me a nice kick for the next couple of hours!" Smoking was fun and smokers kept together. The smoking lounge, with its atmosphere, created friendships and relationships. Smoking also became the theme of organizational myths and legends: a fictional hero would always try to hide the smoke but would get caught because of cameras and smoke detectors. One girl mentioned to me that some people, especially those who wanted to quit, used e-cigarettes, which is an alternative to smoking. "[The management] was restrictive [about the smoking ban], but some people would take an e-cigarette and smoke it in the toilet. It supposedly did not set off the smoke detectors". Some workers stressed that working helped them to control their smoking and thus either allowed them to be healthier or "made cigarettes taste better", because of the long breaks between a smoke.

The conversations around food and well-being of the workers also referenced the possibility of using the sports facilities. The plant had a football field and a basketball court, visible from the main entrance gate. Access was available to every employee. The sport facilities were equipped with lamps, new sports equipment, and were constantly maintained. For the workers this possibility of exercise was exciting. "New workers always stared at those [facilities], because you can see them from the outside. This cage of a football field and lights" (male worker). Indeed, many workers, when asked to describe the plant, would mention the field with the artificial lightning. Inside the plant there was also a fitness studio and a gym. "It looked really professional, like a real fitness centre in a luxury hotel, fully equipped" (female worker). Even though the equipment was excellent, very few workers actually used it. One of the reasons was the physical exhaustion from work:

> You could get a full body treatment there! But the thing is that you would be insane to stay after work to exercise. Not after the whole day! Or go there during a free day? Even more senseless! That's why those things were mostly used by the managers; nobody looked at their hands!
> Female worker

Because of the long workday and physically intense labour, the workers were too tired to do sports before or after work. Those who did not have a long way, such as the workers from the local area, were very disappointed because access turned out to be limited. A well-built young worker from a neighbouring village told me that his visits had to be scheduled in advance: "[the usage of] the football field was possible when two teams were registered and created. But it's hard to get ten people together and get everybody to come!". A young female worker told me that, "they were cheating, Whenever I said I want to go there, they said a different day or date is possible. It made me angry". Lack of access to the resources made workers think that those amenities are only available to everyone symbolically, but actually only management uses it.

4 Cultural Specificity and the Offshored Workplace

The daily experience of work in the factory provided a distinct cultural experience, which reflected a Taylorist organisation of the shop floor. Despite the hardships of daily work and the relatively low salary, the plant was perceived positively. This distinctiveness, almost exoticism, popped up in nearly all assessments and descriptions of the workplace. Unlike other available jobs in the manufacturing sector, the investment generated a strong and all-encompassing experience, which was tied to ideas of modernity, Western-style consumption and capitalism. The investor's practices imposed on the workforce, even the strangest, were treated as part of this experience and either accepted in their totality or rejected.

Entering any new workplace requires commitment and determination. Workers recruited for the job, especially those coming from rural areas and small towns, had a very intense experience. The initial stages, such as the job application, recruitment process and tests, were challenging. Filling out the standardised forms generated mixed feelings including doubts about the worker's potential and suitability for the capitalist production. Outlining one's own qualifications, work experience and main traits in a CV was uncomfortable for many workers, because it was considered private. At the same time, putting one's name out on the market was empowering and understood as the first step in the process. Those who did it and got the job felt appreciated, and their self-worth was boosted. They were initially committed to the investor. Going through the tests, even though they were simple, and succeeding supported the belief that even a person who does not have much experience and education could be a part of an exciting and impressive initiative that serves the international market.

Adaptation to the workplace was even a stronger experience. Workers invested a lot of effort to become part of the organization. Each of the workers underwent organizational socialization and learned how to overcome the initial stress and anxiety. The work separated the product from the human producing it, by requiring cleanliness and a machine-alike appeal of the product. Safety procedures, shop floor language and the formalisation of all dimensions of labour contributed to the general feeling of a foreign and distinct work culture experience. In response to the organisational requirements and dynamics, the workforce had coping mechanisms, including group support, a shared feeling of workforce equality and solidarity as well as the belief that persistence and determination can help to overcome issues with adaptation.

Shop floor work proved to be valuable on different levels. To many workers, the unique experiences rationalised the proportion of work to the wage. Another interviewee summarised this by stating:

> To be honest, it was not hard work. It was boring work. But it was not hard. It was just boring, but it was okay. The conditions that [the management] provided were good; they did treat us in the European way (…). It was so much better and different from what you would see in Romanian firms. I actually enjoyed it. This work was reasonable.
> Worker

Opinions similar to the one above showed that the plant was a type of refuge from daily life and obligation. Almost all workers considered the plant, work attire, and workplace organization as reasonable. It would not be rare to hear opinions that it was a comfortable job, with its temperature or canteen food.

The different environment, isolation from the outside world and repetitive tasks all influenced the workforce and amplified the contrast between the inside and outside world. As one of the interviewees explained, "shifting from my daily life to factory work helped me get focused, think over some matters and ignore my grey reality". Isolation from reality in the pristine conditions of the factory provided a unique experience. The monotony of the daily work helped the workers to reflect on their lives. For instance, a worker and part-time student mentioned: "I got the chance to think literally about anything. I started with some games, like adding up or multiplying [numbers,] but ended up just thinking about my future and about life in general [laughs hard]. The labour process was demanding and physically tiring but the overall assembly setting and labour conditions were considered positive. Workers considered the conditions to be exceptional, emphasising the different experience that the factory provided. Even though certain things, such as the monotony of food offered in the canteen or continuous standing throughout the day, were tiring, the plant offered an environment that contrasted with most workplaces that involved low-skilled labour. Its interior was well maintained and pristine, unlike the environment surrounding the plant. There was a cafeteria with an open buffet, serving slightly distinct foods from the ones served at home. The light and temperature were different; so was the coffee from the vending machine when compared to the coffee available at home. The composition of the workforce was diverse, and people of different ages came from all over the region.

Different aspects of the journey metaphor emerged from my interviewees' statements. Similar to the way journeys work for travellers, the workplace was a cathartic experience for the workers, who were provided with interesting challenges and for whom it brought balance to their daily lives. For many, work in the plant played an emancipatory role. This form of empowerment emancipated some from a stagnated village, their extended family, household duties or even everyday reality. Being needed in the plant, meeting new peers, gaining new experiences, reconsidering one's own role and perceiving oneself as contributing to global production all helped the process. In Chapter 5, I show how this empowerment worked in the familial context and address the relationship between family life and offshored labour.

CHAPTER 4

Shop Floor Culture and Routine Production Process

> You should meet [name of worker]. He was unbelievable. If he was born in America, he would be an actor. I met him in my second month and got put into the line with him, and there were a few people from [the city nearby]. At first, we worked very hard, it might have been the moment when I worked the hardest at this job. But once we knew each other well enough, like maybe after eight shifts, we started to fool around, or [name of the worker] started fooling around. He knew we were good, so he would make voices or pretend he is an (…) officer, asking to move faster (…). Believe me, I am not sure what was up with him, but his energy never fizzled. I remember a line manager, a really good guy, would be angry at us for giggling all the time – he worried that his boss would kill him, so we tried to keep it out of sight. (…) [The work] was killing my back and my legs, I would really struggle, but yet [in this period] I would be coming back home and feeling my muscles from laughing.
>
> Male worker

The quote above exemplifies the challenges of daily work in the plant. The interviewee describes humour in the context of the difficult and challenging production process, monotonous physically due to the repetitiveness of the task and precision of labour. The worker describes how his long working hours and the high amount of supervision were wearing down and impacting his well-being. In the same passage, he also reflects on two significant aspects of the work: the importance of humour on the shop floor and the role of social cohesion on his line. The interviewee shortly describes how friendly the atmosphere on his assembly line was and outlines how continuous conversations and fun played an important role in his positive assessment of the work. In this chapter I analyse the work culture in the investment by considering how social activities, mostly taking place during work shifts, influenced the understanding and interpretation of the workplace as well as facilitated daily labour.

Work life, humour and storytelling are important aspects of organizational culture. Studying them has a long tradition in the study of organisations. Beginning, with industrial plants, scholars have noted that "banana time" not only humanizes work and prevents workers from going "nuts", but also serves as a ground for oppositional acts among workforce (Roy, 1959). Especially in Taylorist plants, requiring repetitive movement and physical labour, laughing or manifesting non-conformity permits empowerment and allows "the illusion from an otherwise alienating situation" (Collinson, 1988: 185), working in a similar way to school environment when laughing is a tool of overcoming strict discipline. In "Manufacturing Consent" Michael Burawoy also addresses laughter, reflecting on his research in a Chicago plant and pointing out how humour works as a binding mechanism for worker community which manages to achieve work-related tasks, despite the outside divisions, such as racial prejudice (Burawoy, 1979). In similar tone, most early theorisations of humorous activities and shop floor labour in industrial plants conclude that humour provides an important counterbalance to mechanical, repetitive tasks and an important way to tackle boredom, which could be otherwise difficult to bear (Borman, 1988).

Marek Korczyński (2011) theorizes how workplace humour plays a key role in "lubricating" the routinized workplace, playing a twofold role: allowing an expression of a sense of resistance while simultaneously helping workers to cope with daily routines and repetitive tasks. Korczynski's perspective bridges two scholarly traditions which produce both arguments demonstrating how laughter has traditionally been used as a tool of resistance, for instance allowing for the critique of managerial decisions, opposing power structures (Ackroyd and Thompson, 1999; Bolton, 2004; Taylor and Bain, 2003) as well as showing how managers might use humour for motivation, acting as a stimulant for productivity boost uplifting the workforce (Avolio, Howell, and Sosik, 1999; Lytte, 2007). Studies of humour in the workplace identify a number of its psychological consequences, such as viewing one's self as more manageable, thus allowing better feeling of self-control at work and contributing to anxiety reduction. Humour simulates positive mood elevation and brings complex consequences to both thinking and behaviour (Isen et al., 1987; Lang et al., 2010). It improves morale, stimulates group-making and cohesiveness as well as facilitates adaptation to organizational culture (Gruner, 1997; Holmes and Marra, 2002).

While humour might bring a number of benefits to organizations, traditional literature concentrating on management of industrial workplace had considered it to be harmful to the discipline, and a source of potential conflict [refs!]. Contemporary studies have also identified a number of risks of humour in the workplace, such as offending co-workers (Quinn, 2000), increasing potential group exclusion for those who do not share sense of humour (Terrion and Ashforth, 2002) or eroding supervisor's authority and leadership potential (Forester, 2004; Holmes, 2000). In distinguishing the functions of those humour-related processes it is helpful to refer to Ackroyd and Thompson's (1999, p. 111) division, which outlines three types of humour employed in contemporary workplace. Jokes might act as (1) a satire, being aimed at control and reflecting tensions within hierarchical structures; (2) a way of teasing among peers, integrating the workforce but also exposing it to domination from employees holding similar positions in organisations; (3) take form of clowning, usually involving one person doing something extraordinary, for instance fooling around for a laugh. Even though Ackroyd and Thompson's typology identifies central types of workplace humour, its application might vary, for instance proving limited validity in the conditions of contemporary shop floor of the studied investment.

Industrial cultures undergo deep changes and contemporary workforce differs from those studied in the mid- and late-1990s. With the progressing disappearance of old Western working class, the shop floor in offshored investments in middle-income economies tends to be more democratic, more sensitive of diversity and interpersonally aware due to tight control and enforcement of workplace rules. Offensive behaviours, such as vulgar joking or humorous (but oppressive) bullying are less tolerated, thus making jokes such as vulgar and offensive banter in a lorry factory, described in a classical text by Collinson (1988), unacceptable and strictly reinforced by the management. The set of rules established by the investor in the studied investment strongly influenced the workplace. For instance, implementation of equality and diversity policy, strict rules of interpersonal conduct at work, and open prohibition of vulgar language have created boundaries protecting workers from upset and annoyance coming from the peers. The zero-tolerance approach for bullying and vulgarity were often highly appreciated by the workforce (and contrasted with local practices in the manufacturing sector in Romania). This made the workplace more inclusive, but also excluded direct teasing or banter. As a result of these regulations, workplace humour took a particular shape, not aimed at co-workers but rather to the process or joker himself. Later, I describe the role of humour and reflect on its role in production as well as its relationship to the history of the region and traditions of socialist political humour.

1   Lubricating the Taylorist Workplace

As the opening passage has shown, humour played an important role in coping with production-related activities and challenges. Repetitive tasks and work in production lines was tiresome for the workers. Most of my interviewees have experienced the shop floor in a similar way, pointing to the boredom or physical demands experienced. For instance, a female worker said: "You would spend the whole day there. Sometimes I worked and did a lot, then I looked at the clock and not even five minutes went by!" Phone assembly required attention and manual precision but also speed. Workers on the assembly lines coped with the completion of tasks listed as requirements on the "object-list". It was a source of tension: "there was always some stress because you never knew if you will complete [the object list]" (female worker). The high pace of assembly required concentration, precision as well as resistance to pressure. Even though workers did their best, sometimes they were not able to complete the object list. Despite the fact that the failure to complete was not directly sanctioned, it caused a feeling of disappointment and was understood as a potential factor that influenced the decision to renew a contract.

Making friends at work and establishing ties and relationships was a crucial part in adapting to the pace of assembly. "I liked going there. It was hard work, but it paid off and we had an amazing team. We still call each other" (male worker). To many workers coming to work was a tiring necessity, and boring and repetitive tasks of phone assembly were difficult to enjoy. Even though some workers argued that they are lighter than physical work in agriculture or construction, most of them stressed the fact that they are challenging, for instance because of the long hours of standing in one place. Lack of variation, constant concentration and general boredom were exhausting. However, as some workers argued, for the majority of the workforce, the daily work on the shop floor work was connected to pleasure of enjoying the company of other people. To workers it was an opportunity for establishing new friendships and broadening social circles. The recruitment strategy brought workers from different parts of the region into the plant. For instance, one of the workers remarks about his work mates: "we worked with two guys from [name of the town]. We had laughs all the time or would talk about the weekend all the time. We were not slow in doing so! (...) We were a good bunch, seriously, those were some good times". Similar reflections were shared by the majority of interviewees and many of them put an emphasis on social interaction and appreciated the possibility to meet people from other places. New friendships were among the most highly valued elements of the labour in the plant.

Organization of the shop floor work relied on teamwork and communication. The workers who worked together usually knew each other very well, spending long hours together and often chatting during work. Mechanical tasks that they performed made long chats easy and most workers discussed matters unrelated to production. Talking, laughing, and provoking funny situations, was among the biggest attractions of the long working days.

> I was working with a friend that I know from school and two other boys from [another village]. We had a lot of fun, especially on the night shifts

> where big bosses were in bed sleeping and nobody was in the office upstairs. One of the things that we often did was using rubber finger gloves and an air compressor to pump balloons. We called them condoms [laughing]. We would pump them and laugh, or make tits with them, you know. But really quickly: so that nobody can see [showing].
>
> Young male worker

Above, a twenty-year-old student, who worked in the factory for 5 months on an agency contract, told me about his line's entertainment methods. He told me that the job was boring for him, but he got used to it quickly. In his words: "my muscles knew what to do and my brain was sleeping at work". He stressed that he had no career plans in the plant but earned extra money over the summer break. He also argued that if he had worse company, he would not continue working in the plant for longer than three months. "The only moment to wake up was when we would joke or gossip. Or if a girl would come by!" He livens up every time he mentions a story about joking in the plant. He seems to miss the joyful atmosphere. Despite the fact that he stopped working in the plant almost two years ago, he still keeps in touch with his work buddies.

Another worker, a thirty-seven-year-old mom, shares the previously mentioned worker's point of view. "You work like a robot, don't even have to think. If you stand with somebody for ten hours a day, even in a factory, you know everything about the person, more than your wife or best friend". Below she speaks about the waves of laughter that were often erupting during night shifts:

> Because we had to rush [refers to high pace of work] for most of the time I could not really look around. But sometimes, being tired, there would be a peak [refers to an eruption of humour]. (...) Sometimes somebody would just start laughing and could not stop. And people would pick it and even the key manager would laugh just out of the blue or because of some stupid thing!
>
> Female worker, 37

Remarking on those situations, the interviewee also joyfully giggles. Her comments about the supervisor joining in the laughter exemplifies a similar dynamic to other Taylorised workplaces, where humour often includes supervisors and plays an important role in humanizing labour (e.g. Korczynski, 2011).

Another woman shares her favourite memory from the shop floor below. It was when the management put funny music on.

> We are working and usually there would be a radio on. Once somebody put *Manele* on. It was so much fun. They put it on, and everybody started

dancing and laughing. At the line we started dancing like real *Manelişti* with an instrument, still doing our job. But there was laughter all over the plant. Some guy danced electro while working! They switched it off quickly. I don't know who put it on and why! It was the funniest moment, we laughed about it several months later!
>
> Young female worker

"*Manele*" is a type of popular folk music in Romania. Highly criticized for its simplicity, misogyny and popular character, Manele is especially enjoyed in rural areas and among the urban working class, although the music was boycotted by the national media and only available through unofficial channels, like the internet. Manele is broadly known and embedded in the Romanian consciousness. As the quote above describes, hearing Manele in a tightly controlled and regulated plant loosened the atmosphere and engaged the workers on the shop floor, including managers, in laughter. The humorous bit was based on the fact that music did not suit to the strictness of the plant, as this music would rather be expected to be played late into the night of a wedding reception. Workers responded to the situation treating it as a joke and fully allowing themselves to enjoy the moment.

The examples above represent the most often remembered jokes, usually connected to the labour process. They typically were told on the assembly lines, providing a very short moment of. Humour provided relief from daily, monotonous activities connected to work routines. In response to the strict rules of production, the shop floor developed a culture of clowning and parody, which was not aimed at other workers but relied on making a fool of oneself. This was the important form of organizational culture lubricating the daily life and monotony of production. Clowning was a tool for integration, permitting the expansion of highly valued social networks. Most of the workers pointed to a particular person who used to be an entertainer and a social star on their shifts. This dynamic has greatly influenced the perception of the daily assembly.

2 Limiting Control and Political Intimacies at Work

> – A man that I knew was going to a pick up a coffee from the machine. He had his pen drive [refers to the personal electronic key used for vending machines], and he put it in the machine. But he was talking to someone and forgot to take the pen drive with him, leaving it by mistake in the machine. It took only twenty minutes for them to give it back to him. Security had cameras everywhere and as everybody had their badges visible, they could see his name [on the recording] and so on and then bring it to him.

– How do you know it was security?
– I don't know that for sure, but I know they were observing every move. So once there was a pen drive without an owner it took them thirty seconds to identify that person. It was just the matter of zooming into the picture and seeing his personal number. Then, they knew where he worked so after just a few minutes they were able to deliver it to him. (older male cleaning staff member)

Above, a worker repeats a version of a widely circulated story, which outlines the responsiveness and abilities of the security system. Even though this story is not a joke per se, it contains a dose of humour, and it was delivered in a jovial tone by the interviewee. Another aspect of shop floor culture was extensive interest of the workforce in the supervision and control practices. This interest translated into an entire body of myths, jokes and stories that were shared with humour and in confidentiality. The security system in the plant, as described in the previous chapter, was used to prevent stealing as well as a control mechanism of the workforce. In parallel to preventing theft, security also observed the workplace for any illegal or unsafe acts, such as smoking or not following health and safety rules. Stories, such as the one above, have been a part of the extensive descriptions of the security system that circulated in the plant. Typically, they included stories about incredible properties and fast reactions to the invigilation system.

Omnipresent cameras, physical control at the factory's entry gates, and careful and tight supervision of managers all caused workers to develop humorous stories describing either the outcomes of this control or elaborating on their mechanisms. Because security was among the biggest discomforts for the workers, permanent invigilation was often remarked upon. These stories extensively described how one of the workers attempted to steal and failed by being caught. Below a set of variations of the same story, detailing how one of the workers unsuccessfully tried to steal electronic parts.

An operator I knew wanted to steal memory cards.
1. At home he made a hole in his sandals between the rubber sole and cork. Then he put them inside, wrapped in foil. He failed because it set off the metal detectors at the gates. He got caught! (older male worker)
2. He put them in foil and put them to his mouth, but then at the gates the security officer asked him something and he wanted to reply but was so nervous that he choked. He got caught! (young male worker)
3. [about a female operator] She attached them to a hair band and put them in her hair. But once she could not pass metal detector, she started scratching and it fell out. She got caught! (older male worker)

An operator I knew wanted to steal [phone] batteries.

1. He wrapped the batteries and put them in a coffee cup. Coffee was inside it so nobody could see. The plan was good: the batteries in the coffee would be put on the table with other metal items, such as keys or belts. But he was so nervous that he spilled the coffee and got caught! (older male worker)

2. He hid them in a cigarette pack by cutting cigarettes so that you could open a pack and see a filter. He put the batteries at the bottom of the pack. During security check he put them on a table with other metal items, such as keys or belts. Cigarette packages would make the metal detector ring because they had the silver foil. But the security guard was nice and picked up the cigarettes in order to pass the items to him. He noticed right away that the pack was too heavy, and he got caught! (younger female worker)

In all of these stories, stealing always ended badly for the unfortunate and slightly stupid "operator that I knew". He tried to outsmart the oppressive system of control, break the law, and gain something valuable every time. The examples of jokes above demonstrate creative ideas of how to steal in the plant, and they all always end with an unfortunate conclusion. All workers agree that stealing in the plant was near impossible, very risky and could not bring that much profit (if not organized on a large scale). The market value of mobile phone batteries or memory cards was relatively low, but they were the best objects of potential theft, because of their portability, universality and relative ease in selling further.

Several factors related to organizational culture seem to explain the popularity of the myth of a criminal hero in the plant. Similar to the clowning around depicted in the first section, these stories provide a good laugh at work and their usage enabled a temporary distraction from the total control and supervision of the investor. Moreover, the humorous stories provide a platform for gaining personal autonomy from the oppressive supervision and plant culture. To many workers these fantasies of stealing provided a relief, even though they had absolutely no intention of doing the same thing. Instead, to majority of these workers the described attempts were an attractive means of building imaginary resistance – even though the investor has physically oppressed them by supervision, the fantasy of breaking these rules and penetrating the system through the cracks of a disrupted system seemed to be an attractive fantasy. Sharing those stories was also done in humorous conspiracy and treated like a fun moment of plotting against the oppressor.

This form of joking connects to the post-socialist history of Central and Eastern Europe. In a recent article, Martha Lampland and Maya Nadkarni analyse the convention of Socialist joking by studying how its slow disappearance might produce insights into how post-socialist politics and societies have transformed since the end of communism. Under Socialism, joking played an important role, fulfilling resistive functions and allowing for social integration. In the literature addressing their role, Socialist jokes have typically been understood as "a populist response to authoritarian repression: an act of everyday subversion" (Lampland and Nadkarni, 2016: 451). Their tradition is embedded in long local history of resistance to foreign rule, occupation and political authority in the region. The specific convention of Socialist jokes emerged as a form of opposition in the post-war period. It was usually based on a specific style of storytelling with a humorous and unexpected ending, usually containing a reference to a situation of the everyman living under Socialism. One of the very accurate examples of socialist joking that Lampland and Nadkarni give illustratively depicts the power dynamics of the convention:

> In joke after joke, the Socialist everyman was pitted against the powerful and incompetent party operative, whose unearned privileges made the vaulted claims of the party ring hollow. The simple formula well known from folklore – a clever servant or peasant outwitting the lord of the manor – was easily appropriated and elaborated upon by evoking the empty slogans and wooden jargon of the Communist Party.
> LAMPLAND and NADKARNI, 2016: 452.

Usually dark in their form, Socialist jokes use precise descriptions of Socialist realities, exposing the absurdities of the system, lack of equality between part members and the rest of society, poverty or specific coping mechanisms employed by society dealing with great lack and shortages. During the most repressive phases of Socialism in Central and Eastern Europe, storytellers might have faced repercussions from authorities for laughing at prominent figures such as Soviet leaders or local party officials, and they may have even faced imprisonment.

Socialist jokes have reflected a specific class conflict, which emerged in response to oppressive power structures. Socialist jokes have relied on a class antagonism, based on an exploitation of workers by the party and the state in clear and unequivocal terms (Burawoy and Lukács, 1992). In their analysis of the disappearance of Socialist jokes after transition, Lampland and Nadkarni argue that with the collapse of communism groups became sorted and the simple division "us" versus "the party", which lied at the basis of internal class conflict usually used in these jokes, lost its validity. Based on their research they argue that instead of joking about the ruling party and everyday disappointment, in post-Socialist reality the interviewees tended to blame themselves for being naïve and believing in the political promises of q variety of political actors and groups. One of the conclusions of this study is that democratization and systemic changes have allowed for a greater transparency of interests and actions as well as the dispersion of humour to camps representing specific political ideologies.

The material collected here on joking shows that there is a striking resemblance between the humour used in the plant and the convention of Socialist joking, both being reliant on the same binary model of "us" versus "them". Both the form and contents of the jokes bare a deep resemblance to the Socialist joke described in the literature. Here is another anecdote about the omnipresent invigilation system in the plant shared with me by a male member of shop floor:

> A guy told another guy confidentially that he had a beer for the bus in the cloakroom. It was during the cigarette break. After finishing the shift he changed and once he put his coat on, he noticed that the beer was gone. They would have microphones and listen all the time!
> Young male worker

This passage exemplifies the tension between worker and invigilation. Similarly, to the state police, plant security might (or might not) be observing every move or act of subversion. The workforce circulated the idea of a panopticon: everything done in the plant was observed by security who watched through the cameras in the plant. Even though, due to the high amount of staff and resources, such a close monitoring would be impossible, many of the workers felt oppressed and nervous about this system. The unpleasant condition of invigilation caused self-consciousness and discomfort, translating into extensive joking about security. As the camera lenses were observing the shop floor, corridors and other places in the plant, and the workers could not do much about it, the strategy of coping with this discomfort was laughing about it. Similar narratives used suspense to narrate the all-encompassing invigilation and the suspiciousness of security officers.

The interviewed workers repeatedly reported a high number of cameras and security guards watching the shop floor. These started from rough estimates, such as "about fifty [workers] at a time working in the factory", but also included humorous interpretations, such as:
– There is way too many security cameras so everything that happens here must be monitored from the outside. Security has connected the cameras to cheap places, and just like there are doctors practicing medicine in India

[refers to offshoring of medical services], the Finns pay people in India to watch us [laughing]
- You are joking right? I don't know if you are... [pulling my leg]
- [interrupted] Of course, I am serious, but I don't know any facts, that's the thing. I know zero people working in security. Nobody knows them really. Where did they bring them from? We don't know how they catch people, but I have told you there were weeks where there would be a police car every day at the factory.
- Why a police car? To take away thieves?
- Yes, to take away those idiots who shoved memory cards into their mouths [laughing]. (...) Did you know that police would just come into the factory? I had a friend who saw that they would always get a meal or sandwich from the canteen. They had an easy life with the factory, so many closed cases, and you know how smart our police is. This was great life for them [shows how a policeman shoves food into mouth]. (...) I did not really know what was true and what was not but in most cases there was some truth to those stories. (older male worker)

This example, with the interviewee being unsure what part is an exaggerated story and what actually relies on truth, well depicts the components involving the joking culture in the plant. Workers were unsure of the mechanisms, but they helped them to familiarize the unknown and establish some shared definitions, which, despite of being fictional, provided a shared vision that was useful and defined significant elements of reality.

The tension between the workforce and work organisation was also visible in the descriptions of the shift system. Work at night was considered lighter because workers felt that the control is lower, as the offices, overlooking the shop floor, were at that time closed. Even though the lights in the offices, visible from the shop floor through the glass walls, were dimmed, sporadically somebody from the office would stay longer. As the atmosphere was lighter at nights, workers would tell "scary" stories about invigilation, which in a way was also a disciplining tool. For instance: "on the night shifts it was looser because the bosses were not there. So some people would say that the director had a view from the factory at home! (...)" (young female worker). Not only were workers aware of the fact that there was omnipresent supervision, but some would also sometimes repeat that international managers are so hard-working that they would stay up late and watch the factory remotely. The workers agreed that the transnational office team was very career-driven and sometimes overly eager.

One of the key members of the management staff, an American executive, was liked by the shop floor for his friendliness, but he was considered a perfectionist obsessed with his work. Drawing on his devotion some would say that he, or part of his office team, would invigilate even during what would seemingly be time off work. "On the night shift the lights in the office were off, and they had windows overlooking the shop floor. People would say that somebody is there to look regardless". Even though there was a separate security service team, the office employees often functioned in worker imagination as ones who designed and supervised the invigilation system in order to make staffing decisions. The workers also speculated about the relationship of management with local police. As the earlier passage outlines, there was the belief that local policemen would get free meals at the canteen, and according to the workers, they used to visit the plant to eat. The symbiosis of unpopular police officers and management, who applied invigilation, symbolically connected two unpopular groups.

Further controversies emerged in the context of staff changes in the offices. With time, an increasing number of Romanians was hired to work in the management of the factory, replacing international employees. The workers speculated that this change brought a number of problems to the factory. Some, for instance, speculated that organization under Romanians was worse, because of a lack of transparency, technical problems or any other issues that emerged. Some workers remarked that the Western managers were also more open, visiting the shop floor and approaching it in an easy, friendly way. The workers speculated on a growing clientelisation of Romanian management and they often mentioned that Romanian office workers hardly ever visited the shop floor. Moreover, the shop floor talked about spending at corporate events, which were for management only. For instance, workers remarked on the restaurants and locations of the management's trips. One of the workers commented on the extensive spending of the investor's money by management by stating: "they are more equal – like under communism". This dynamic enforced the divide between the workforce and management, especially as the shop floor became more aware of the needs and dynamics surrounding the production process.

Lampland and Nadkarni argue that Socialist jokes, besides providing a good laugh, generated a specific version of political intimacy between joke tellers, illuminating relations of power, creating specific bonding experiences between people sharing the joke, and, most importantly verbalizing political differences that were often not present in the public domain. The same function was fulfilled by usage of humour and humorous storytelling in the plant. The workforce used joking, not only for entertainment but also for enjoying a specific line of division between themselves and "the others" who administered the oppressive system and control. Lampland and Nadkarni mention how Socialist jokes would be successful to the degree that some of party officials would share them with people, temporarily joining their side of the barricade. A similar dynamic emerged in the investment, in many cases, line managers, or even shift managers, would be remembered as open to critique only "caring so that the office did not see them having a laugh (...), [while some of them would] be like a promoted party member who forgot where he comes from [and is eager to be loyal to the party / the management]" (male worker). In this section, I have shown how in addition to the lubrication of the production process, the convention of joking has also been a tool of normalization of the relations between the workforce and the investor, serving as a main platform of resistance among workers. The stories being repeated from one person to another, their conspiratorial character and the unity produced by these narratives allowed for greater cohesion and exchange of ideas.

3 Epistemic Holes, Humour and Storytelling

> There is absolutely no clear information about how everything is being done. They hire, they think for us and everything happens somewhere far away. I don't really know where it happens. And the fact is that I don't even know who decides on that stuff. I would want to just know where this stuff happens... If it works for someone, it works, but if it does not, they just get away with anything. I asked [HR person] who decides on hiring and it was clear that he could not tell me anything, because he did not know. This whole factory is weird, people don't know anything because there is no way that they can know. (...).
>
> Older male worker

The passage above exemplifies how the decision-making process was invisible for the workers. The dispersed organization of the global value chain made it impossible to understand the complexity of production of the Nokia Corporation. Workers did not understand how the decision-making occurred and how the entire organization was structured. Lack of knowledge, with a shared inability to comprehend the investor, was apparent in several work-related spheres, including the hiring policy, contract prolongation, decision-making on the corporate level, product range as well as business decisions. Workers were unable to gather that knowledge from available sources, so in their discussions they looked for alternative explanations. Humour and speculation also helped to cope with this kind of unknown.

The passage below describes how workers coped with uncertainty and outlines the relationship between suppliers and the investor:

> I was working nights around the unloading area, and you would be surprised what they brought on the trucks. There was nothing necessary for the production of mobile phones. It would be boxes, all with Chinese signs, and there would be nothing else on them. It was weird, and I bet it was some scheme. They did not have to go through border control or maybe they did not pay tax. I saw them open it, and it would be like parts for some equipment but definitely nothing used for mobile phones. (…) Maybe it was not Nokia's but some scheme involving parts suppliers, they could definitely figure out something like that. As I remember it, they only brought it, unloaded it, somebody examined it, and they either put it aside or loaded it further to the next trucks.
> Cleaning staff member

The passage above exemplifies speculation connected to the increased movement of the delivery trucks, their unknown origin and reshuffling of transports. International license plates and trucks that were coming and leaving stimulated imagination and produced a number of stories of a similar conspiratorial character.

Pettigrew in his classical text argued that mythology is an important container of organizational culture (Pettigrew, 1979) arguing that value-imparting, justifying and reconciling qualities of myths are precisely the ones that suggest that the concept of myth has a powerful analytical role to play in studies of organizational cultures (Pettigrew, 1979: 576). In addition to humour, organization-themed myths and storytelling permit a broader expression of interpreted meanings of labour that are symbolically reflected in the position of a worker in the plant. Similarly to humour, scholars argue that myths fulfil an important function by containing meanings and value, which integrates the community of workers, answers work-related existential questions, and gives sense and direction in life (Gabriel, 1991). But perhaps the most accurate description is expanding this understanding of speculation to conspiracy, similarly to the way in which Lampland and Nadkarni explained the significance of Socialist jokes. Anthropologists Comaroff and Comaroff outline the significance of conspiracy theories:

> Conspiracy, in short, has come to fill the explanatory void, the epistemic black hole, that is increasingly said to have been left behind by the unsettling of moral communities, by the so-called crisis of representation, by the erosion of received modernist connections between means

and ends, subjects and objects, ways and means. All this in the global world that is at once larger and smaller, more and less knowable, more and less inscrutable than ever before.

COMARROFF and COMAROFF, 2003: 298.

By examining transparency, and expanding on Žižek, Comaroffs consider how we try to understand mechanisms surrounding reality with beguiling concreteness, yet, given the fact that reality is often impenetrable, and new facts or observations often cast further doubts. Lampland and Nadkarni argue that post-Socialist realities, incubate a need for transparency of social mechanisms, replacing previously easy to comprehend reality of "us and them", and give the impulse to generate new interpretations that are rarely adequate and supported by factual evidence.

While shop floor humour produced important insights into the shop floor dynamics and internal processes of the plant, conspiracy-based speculations have addressed ambiguities, for instance one related to the relationship between the investor and the state. For instance, they included a theory that Nokia was either money laundering, or avoiding taxation, moving shipments through the plant. These stories would imply that there is a second bottom to the plant's activity, serving as a cover for something bigger and unknown to the public. A number of these claims, usually described in humorous ways, were based on observations:

> There would be trucks escorting some parts, and some others would come without an escort. Sometimes an empty truck would come with an escort. (...) Why would they do that? There was no logic and it was not linked to the specific transit letter. I am not saying anything but probably there was something going on, and obviously nobody from the shop floor could know about it.
> Older male worker

The speculation would include a range of criminal offences:

> Trucks coming and going involved toys and junk from China because Chinese suppliers all had a deal and made those scams.
> Young male worker

> Once they opened a box, it was full with thick cables, just regular tangled cables, and there was no need for them. It must have been some Chinese deals.
> Cleaning staff member

SHOP FLOOR CULTURE AND ROUTINE PRODUCTION PROCESS   97

> In many cases there would be a situation where inbound and outbound stuff would not be run through any security, just packed and sent. I have no idea, but for instance, they could be selling Absolut [brand of Scandinavian vodka] to the Chinese.
>
> Older male worker

The layer of claims covered by those stories circled around the hidden and unknown powers that were invisible to a regular worker. Those conspiracies provided absurd, often unreal, stories, which drove discussion and reflection about the plant and the investor. Workers have actively looked for solutions to those challenging problems.

Another aspect of factory storytelling aimed to fill in those gaps with speculation and myth creation about the imaginary aspects of the investor's global production. The highly repeated stories have reinforced negative stereotypes, for instance about different geographies where the investor was at that time offshoring the production. These stories stirred tension and internal competition between the plant in Romania and other geographies. Typically, the Western counterparts in Western Europe would stereotypically be considered as working less and being paid better, while workers in less advanced economies, such as Eastern Asia, would be considered to be in a much worse situation and forced into severe exploitation. The workforce relied on stories pointing at specific situations that took place in the plant to illustrate these claims. A usual point was that Romanian workers are much better at assembly. The following passage could serve as an example:

> Two guys came [from a factory in Western Europe] for an exchange program. They made a bet that they can do it better and faster than the Romanians. They lost so badly that they would not talk to anybody but the managers. Everybody laughed at them so hard.
>
> Female worker

Similar stories were told about the Romanian workers' visit to a Hungarian plant:

> Their pace was much slower, their plant was older, and they did not have such strict regulations like we did.
>
> Male worker

Hungarians, and their factory located in the region, were commonly perceived as slower at fulfilling the orders but earning more than workers in Romania. Similar stories helped the workers to cope with their unclear position in the global production network and familiarized the context of global competition for production, which the plant in Romania was a part.

The shop floor also speculated about the visitations of foreign managers. They would often be protagonists of stories based on the story of "the king in the beggar's clothes". For instance, one of the workers told me:

> A big manager from Finland came and pretended he is a line operator from an experience exchange (...) He wanted to see how we are doing. [But] they stopped hiring for three weeks after which was linked to the fact that they analysed us. There would always be some rotation after a procedure like that.
> Male worker

This story of a mysterious auditor coming to the plant to gather information about the workers points to concerns connected to jobs stability and the hiring process. Other versions of the same story ended with someone getting promoted or fired. As the criteria for the contract extension were usually unknown, this story fuelled speculations about the reasons for the decision. For example, some thought that informal ties with employees in the work agency or offices in the plant protected one from the opinion of a mysterious auditor, perhaps speeding up an open-ended offer or direct work contract in the investment.

The investment's decision-making process caused numerous tensions surfacing in speculations and humour. Lack of access to information, problems connected to communication, ambiguities regarding rules beyond the shop floor as well as problems connected to defining the investment's role were at the centre of the worker's attention. Even though the myths have not improved the knowledge of these issues, their function has played a crucial role in expanding the understanding and meaning of offshoring processes.

4 Conclusions

Laughing and storytelling deeply reflected the organizational culture of the plant, fulfilling important functions in the workplace and serving as a platform to learn about the dynamics of the plant. Joking and humour helped to overcome day-to-day boredom and mechanical tasks. Laughter lightened the work atmosphere, made time at work more entertaining and pleasant, and helped to create basic forms of grassroots resistance. Jokes eased production-related stress and highly demanding physical conditions, such as standing for long hours or the invariability of the temperature. Joking supported reflection on the unknown aspects of the global production. Verbalising speculations about unspoken aspects of the investor's activity helped workers to cope with the lack of information. These organizational myths defined the position of the workers in the global production system, as the value chain was not transparent or fully understood. Despite the fact that regular participation in production made the plant a familiar physical environment, many workers felt detached from the organisation. The interpretations depicted in storytelling helped the workforce to generate ideas on how to interpret and better understand the reality of production. Many unclear aspects, such as the decision-making process, complex global structure of the Nokia Corporation or production strategy were impossible to grasp and fully understand from the shop floor level. Laughing helped to cope with product alienation as well as the ambiguous scalar configuration that the plant was in.

In the specific post-Socialist context, jokes in the factory showed significant parallels to the humour present in Socialist jokes. Joking was identified as a vehicle of a critique of Socialist regimes, producing political intimacies. In the same context, workers transformed their discomfort into humorous narratives, which in a similar way opposed the practices of the investor, including total control, surveillance, and top-down decision-making. An escalation of Socialist comparisons took place when fellow Romanians took over the management of the factory and the delegated responsibilities from transnational managers, which was interpreted as a turn towards clientelism and nepotism. Humorous comparisons to the Socialist times have also been a point of reference because existing sentiment and parallels, such as the lack of communication, egoism and mismanagement.

These narratives helped the workforce to relate one another and discuss otherwise unspoken issues important for resistance, like work conditions, pace of work, invigilation and equality among the workforce. The investment did not have a strong presence of work unions. This was mainly because of the precarious situation of workers, many of whom were hired on temporary contracts and did not feel committed to the employer. In part this was the result of the introduction of new labour regulations, which expanded usage of temporary contracts (i.e. expanding the maximum term for fixed-term employment from 24 to 36 months), increased the necessary quota of unionized workers on the company level from 33 to 51 per cent and enforced obligatory conciliation before strikes, prohibiting striking if collective agreement provisions are not implemented (Trif, 2016; Hayter et al., 2013). All these regulations, along with the precarious nature of employment limited the official actions against the employer and humour was an outlet utilised to cope with the discomfort experienced in the plant on a daily basis.

By using their imagination to fill in epistemic holes connected to the functioning of the organisation, workers developed insight into the plant's operations. Often unreal and highly improbable, they included answers to questions regarding the relationship of the investor with the state, the global position of the Romanian plant in the investor's global value chain, the strategic role of the investment, or the assessment of the Romanian workforce as compared to other similar assembly plants around the world. These explanations demonstrated the ambiguity in the investor's relationship to the state, the legality of its operations, and the role of the Romanian workforce, their efficiency and assembly pace.

Humour and narratives produced by the workforce touch on a wide range of issues that it has faced. Even though the formal mechanisms of internal resistance and critique were rather limited, relying on these narratives filled with jokes and conspiracy helps to outline the specificity of the investment and improve understanding of the shop floor's attitude toward the investor. Far from idealized, the workplace generated a number of potential issues that caused confusion and required resistance. This specific type of reflection, based on a mixture of local traditions, post-Socialist coping and a sense of humour contributed to the process of social coping and the integration of workers.

CHAPTER 5

Familial Involvement in Offshored Labour

- [...] when I finished [school], [the factory] was here, so I thought what the hell – let's go for it. I could be doing something dirty. [...] Everybody at home was pushing me to apply.
- Pushing you?
- Yes, they wanted me to be a part of it, to be close to the big thing. I was worried, but they pushed me. [Begins to imitate his mother] "look at him [the neighbour], he is two years older than you, but he works [in the factory]. He has things to do; he earns money; he has opportunities (...)". So, I went for it, and it was worth it. Besides the pay, which was not too much. But everyone at home understood that it's normal. They were happy for me, almost like it was their job [in the factory]. Or probably more [happy] than I was and cared to be. (female worker, 22)

As the quote above demonstrates, the decision of a young worker to join the factory's labour force was not solely based on her own judgment. She deliberated with her extended family. As I demonstrate in this chapter,[1] in most cases the decisions to start industrial labour in the plant were taken on the family level. This process was not only about seeking approval from the family but also the indirect involvement of the household in the factory labour process. As I will show in this chapter, a key mechanism in this process has been mutual dependency between the localised offshoring process and the local worker's household and its resources.

The post-socialist region has had a long tradition of the extended family order, based on patriarchy. Until today most households rely on the domestic labour of women. Clear gender division at home is based on developments made throughout history, embedded in peasant household organisation and the socialist approach to gender roles. Under socialism, women played an important part. The "worker-mother" model, promoted by the communist state, was based on taking care of the family and pursuing salaried employment. At the same time, men acted as "workers", as heads of families, earning more and being solely responsible for waged income (Dunn, 2004; Kideckel, 1984; Gregory et al., 1998). This gender order continued to determine coping mechanisms after systemic transition (Kideckel, 2008; Einhorn and Sever,

---

1 The findings of this chapter are expanded in Miszczynski, M. (2019). Mutual dependency: Offshored labour and family organisation in post-socialist Romania. *Organization*. https://doi.org/10.1177/1350508419838690

2003); however female at-home labour was bolstered by the work of other family members who could not find salaried employment. As a result, the organisation of the household adjusted to the period of stagnation. Some members continued to pursue salaried employment; the others, who were unable to secure jobs, worked at home, for instance by producing food or taking care of other family members. This division was a counter-mechanism for social issues emerging after the post-socialist transformation, such as alcoholism and depression, especially strongly affecting men (Kideckel, 2008; Cook et al., 2010). Today, the post-socialist household organisation continues to play an important role when populations are confronted with new types of influences, such as pursuing low-paid industrial employment in offshored investments.

This chapter addresses the complex nexus of relationships between familial organization and offshoring production. I put forward a conceptualisation of "mutual dependency", a phenomenon outlining relationships between foreign capital and familial organization in a host community. In particular my analysis contributes to the discussion concentrating on the granular effects of foreign direct investments. In formulating my understanding of the relationship between production and the workers' families I show the effects often omitted from studies of offshored value chains. This view shows the on-the-ground side of the process and offers insights into the complex situation of post-socialist communities receiving foreign investments. In contrast to the predominant view of the literature focusing on the economic side of foreign investments (Bandelj, 2004, 2008; Pavlinek, 2004), I demonstrate how worker families are positioned in these investments, being both beneficiaries of the investment and providing their own resources to facilitate it.

Inspired by ethnographic studies of global production (Dunn, 2004; Ong, 1987; Salzinger, 2003), I present the position of post-socialist worker families in global offshoring networks and the symbolic, economic and professional dimension of this process. By addressing how workers and their families engage through multiple dimensions into offshoring labour, as well as how they evaluate and reflect upon it, I expand the discussion of offshoring effects, providing an additional dimension to studying Eastern Europe's obsession with foreign investors (Pavlinek, 2004). This part exemplifies simultaneous conflicting reactions and tensions encompassing foreign investments and, in doing so, makes a contribution to the micro-level analyses in the context of familial and professional lives. It also touches on issues regarding the significance of the geographical dispersion of global value chains, which is an important field that requires further examination (e.g. Sturgeon et al., 2008).

1 Prior to Investment

> How am I supposed to be able to support myself, buy a home, have kids and be able to feed and send them to school? I think families are not made for the times we are in now.
> Male worker, 26

> You know, there is really nothing in places like this [village] in Romania. Everybody just dreams about making money, living in a city, being wealthy and having a more international life. Instead, most people either try to live life that they don't have [refers to taking loans]. (...) Or they just give up and start drinking. That's easy when you have nothing. (...) When they started building the [industrial] zone everybody believed that this is the end of being stuck. That [the investment] will bring a big change. I would never believe that Nokia's coming is at all possible. (...) I am not sure how to understand [the investment]. It was change but not like I expected.
> Male worker, 32

As these two passages from the male workers illustrate, prior to the investment the village struggled with stagnation. Since 1989, its population was neither able to re-establish large-scale agricultural production, nor find stable employment in other sectors, resulting in the breadwinners' daily struggles. As the next quote illustrates, in these difficult conditions many families pursued strategies such as small-scale subsistence agriculture and low-skilled jobs outside of the village, also migration. "Take my life as an example. When I finished school, I had no options, seriously, none. Because it is not an option to go [emigrate] to Italy if you don't have money or to work shitty jobs for shitty money commuting for two hours every day" (female worker, 23). As this woman suggests, limited local opportunities for salaried employment encouraged daily commuting to urban areas, which was time-consuming and costly. Precarious jobs in cities offered a stable monetised income, seen as an important asset for the household. However, many of these positions were based on informal contracts, a common local practice in order to reduce employer costs. This meant that many workers, being officially unemployed, lacked medical insurance or any form of social protection: "Imagine, I worked [in the factory in the city] helping clean [rubble after demolition] in the summer, all in dirt and rusty machinery from old times. If something happened, like I got pulled into [the construction machinery], I would have to pay for the operation and lie where it happened. Everything was about money [moving] from one hand to another [informal transactions]" (male worker, 26). This interviewee emphasizes the risky and precarious character of his temporary job. His case was not a unique example and many young adults from the community faced the same problems, i.e. a low and informal income and lack of medical protection. In terms of salary, the pay scale had a strong gender dimension. Men, paid significantly more, tended to work in more dangerous and physically demanding industries, such as agriculture and construction, and women found jobs in service and manufacturing industries, usually working longer hours and being paid significantly less. All community members shared a vision of stagnation and many discussed migration, either to the city or West European countries.

The rural character of the village determines its pace of life. The multi-generational family model is prevalent in the hosting village, embedded in traditional village culture especially with regards to sharing duties and modes of food production (Goldschmidt and Kunkel, 1971) and strongly motivated by economic causes. The families are agricultural producers who own the land they cultivate. They produce primarily for their own subsistence needs and sometimes also for exchange or sale (Wade, 1978). In Eastern Europe, subsistence agriculture is an important element of one's livelihood. Delayed industrialization, limited business potential in the agricultural sector, and global competitiveness of food production delayed the growth of Eastern Europe's food producing sector. With time, small-scale agriculture became separated from larger-scale farming as an effect of the industrialization of food production. In Romania, subsistence farming is important, cultivated on 37 per cent of the total agricultural land, which is the highest figure in Central and Eastern Europe (Mathijs and Noev, 2004). Even though the EU's subventions have opened a new chapter for the sector in Eastern Europe, since its accession in 2008 Romania still remains one of the smallest beneficiaries of EU structural funds (Moga et al., 2012). Subsistence food production plays an important role as a social protection mechanism, which utilises the labour of unemployed family members and remains an important source of the food supply.

The hosting village's trajectory serves as an excellent illustration of the changes in rural Eastern Europe. Under communism, this village used to be the pride of the region and a leading agricultural hub. After the collapse of large-scale collective farming and the transition, hectares of land remain uncultivated. Agricultural activity is continued by large-scale farmers, consolidating hectares of the best land. The decline of this sector is hurtful for inhabitants. One of them remarked, when walking me around the fields:

It's unbelievable how much land there is left. I feel like I was looking at a crime scene. I remember how my whole family needed to work here (...) I would come back from town and help my parents. (I16)
Worker

As this passage demonstrates, the interviewee is emotional and discontent while observing the current state of agriculture in the region. The official statistics note an enormous decrease of community members employed in the sector. In 1990 nearly 75 per cent of the entire labour force of the hosting village worked in local C.A.P. (Directia Regionala de Statistica Cluj, 2012). Since that time, the active labour force has systematically decreased. Many villagers take up unregistered employment in the agriculture, usually by taking up jobs in the months of agricultural season.

The most important element of local agriculture are the family gardens, which span about 15–20 acres of land or the equivalent of the *"unitat de existentă"*, an portion of land next to the village house, delineated and provided to rural inhabitants during the collectivization process. Resulting subsistence agriculture helped rural households deal with the difficulties of transition in Eastern Europe (Caskie, 2000; Seeth et al., 1998; Kostov and Lingard, 2002). But this form of small-scale farming was also practiced during the socialist times, forming a functional symbiosis with collective farms (Juhasz, 1991). Rural families today continue subsistence food production using their technical means, small portions of land and traditional household organization. This activity, simply called "gardening" by the villagers, is an important source of food and support for home budgets. Each of the gardens provides kilograms of fresh produce each year.

The organization of village life is centred around duties connected to food production. Land usage and in-house food production reflects the folklore traditions of the region (Brunvand, 2003). From spring until early winter many households' activities focus on cultivating and processing foods. The most important stage of the food production process is the summer kitchen (*Bucateriă de Vară*). It is usually a small wooden hut, separate from the inhabited house and located between the house entrance and front gate. It usually is about 2 feet above the ground, just a few steps from the entrance. The oldest summer kitchens are often very decorative, painted in bright colours and with a sloping roof. The other ones are often improvised constructions with a flat roof. Typically, a summer kitchen is equipped with a window and is situated in close proximity to a well. The basic function of it is to provide space for food preparation. Traditionally, the summer kitchen season starts in March or early April and ends around Christmas.

Most of the houses are made from bricks and the tiling is ceramic. Quite often the houses are eclectic constructions from different materials, an effect of constant improving over the decades. It is not uncommon to see a modified old wooden village house where thatched roofs are replaced by tiling. In general, the wooden constructions were replaced by brick houses in the post-war period. There are new developments in only in two parts of the village but very few of the houses were completed. A typical house in the hosting village has 2–3 rooms and a kitchen, plastered walls and tiled roof. Most of the construction reflects the socialist aesthetic with the strongest wave of remodelling taking place in the 1970s, during the period of prosperity.

Traditionally, a household based on semi-subsistence agriculture functions as a basic economic unit and is based on an extended family. A typical household is comprised of three generations. The scheme of labour distribution and shared budget is informal, and, usually, the burden is put on the middle and older generations. The household budget is based on multiple sources, such as waged salaries, pensions, disability annuities, income from savings accounts, or occasional sales of agricultural products. Sharing income is based on specific local household economics. Those with permanent salaried income share it and use it to pay the bills or for basic groceries. Those members often work in the city, which makes better access to resources possible, like cheaper products from city supermarkets or specialty agricultural products. Those in the family, who do not work for a salary, the elderly or unemployed family members, are burdened with other duties. They deal with the food production and maintain gardens, take care of children, or sometimes take on seasonal jobs. The household duties often function as a counterbalance to alienation from the market resources (Torres, 2011).

2   Mutual Dependencies

When an offshored plant was set up by a prestigious investor, it generated hope for stable employment and improvement of the economic situation of many families from the area. Nearly a generation had lived in stagnation, so the possibility of revival of the local labour market was perceived as a social improvement, bringing not only income but also enabling social protection, medical care and state support. As one woman commented, "There is nothing I wanted at this point more than to have a life in which I can afford to live without worrying about money or struggling for a better future. I just had [a child] then, and I was very worried about our future. (…) It is a better life, having health insurance and money" (female worker, 27). This interviewee discusses her hopes for changes brought by the investment, concentrating on the importance of a stable economic position. However, as the next quote exemplifies, the investor's practice produced poor local work conditions: "Did you think that anybody saw it coming? As soon as [the investor] arrived, it turned out that they are screwing us and won't pay us a good wage. The factory was nice, people there were nice, but an operator's wage was low. Why? Because all that mattered was to produce cheaply" (male worker, 21). Hopes were cut down to size as soon as the wages were announced by the management. Despite the high financial cost of the investment, its enormous production capacity, and the factory's important role in the Romanian economy, the workers' salaries in the plant were low, corresponding with the lower end of salary levels in the Romanian service industry. The majority of the workforce was recruited by employment agencies and hired on temporary contracts. A shop floor operator's salary ranged between 600 and 800 lei per month ($180–$240) plus additional benefits: complimentary meals during the work day and food coupons for use outside of work. As another interviewee said, "Do you know what you can buy after a whole month of working in Romania's best factory? Nothing. If our fridge broke and I had to replace it from my salary, I would have literally zero money for [utility] bills or food. Can you imagine how ridiculous this is?" (female worker, 26). Significantly, only about thirty per cent of the shop floor benefitted from direct employment in the plant and this group received a salary higher by about 120–160 lei ($36–$50) and benefits guaranteed under Romanian employment law, such as paid days off for sick leave or maternity leave. In practice, both groups shared exactly the same responsibilities and duties. The following quote illustrates how workers perceived wage levels.

> I guarantee you that no worker can survive on this wage on their own. You can't live your life working in the plant [i.e. afford to live]. But this is Romania. It's normal to live with your family and get their help. This is how it worked: people lived in their homes, with families and this is how it was all okay. Obviously, you'd never rent a place with this wage – but listen, nobody even thought about renting, that's the thing. What would you do?
> Female worker, 28

As the quote above illustrates, the plant not only failed to provide a means of living for the workers, but was also extensively dependent on family resources, which were used in order to permit industrial employment of some of the workers. Without the support of the family, this employment would not have been possible otherwise, as salaries were too low to cover the costs of living. In other words, domestic work of family members, subsistence food production, housing with extended family and other sources of monetised income, such as selling agricultural products, were all fundamental for taking up jobs in this offshored plant. As the next passage shows, family members actively encouraged others to apply for jobs in the investment:

> I have 3 sons and I wanted them all to try but only Radu got through [got the job]. The other ones don't have patience. It's not for the money that I wanted them to go there, I think it is a good place [to work]. (...) They could have earned this pocket money and learned something [laughs]. (...) Pocket money because it's not a serious salary, obviously we would need to help them, but that's no problem – look at the pantry [points at the kitchen].
> Female family member, 54

As this interviewee suggests, in many cases parents of young adults treated factory jobs in a similar way to school attendance or vocational training, gladly sponsoring and understanding offshored work as a way of personal development of their children or siblings.

To some workers who were more independent, usually over the age of thirty, employment meant an additional source of income and life security. An important role was played by the factory's shift system: "It was weird, but it made sense. You spend two days chasing your cooking, gardening, disciplining children. Then you go to work for twelve hours, come back exhausted, rest and again you have a free day" (female worker, 29). As this passage shows, the shift system was interpreted as allowing the worker to take up additional duties at home and chase other sources of income. In the plant the work schedule was 11 or 12-hour shifts, ensuring a significant number of days off: two following a night shift and one after a day shift. The 12-hour workday in the plant permitted, almost encouraged, bridging work in the plant with other roles. Many interviewees expressed relief about the possibility to pursue additional employment: "It worked well, especially with night shifts: a day off, 11 hours of work which at night was not as intense, then two days. All this was really enough to chase some extra work" (male worker, 38). So in many ways the job organization in the investment responded to the existing household model: "[The investors] thought that they can come to Romania, pay people very little and then those people would earn extra money someplace else. Like my old man under Ceausescu, he worked in a factory in town and in [the agricultural] cooperative. How else could somebody afford a living?" (male worker, 24). This man referred to the tradition of bridging jobs in the region, known as the peasant-worker model, which has very long historic traditions going back to the nineteenth century throughout the inter-war period and socialism (Beck, 1975; Szelenyi and Kostello, 1996; Czegledy, 2002). Even though he expresses disappointment, he also describes an important function of household organisation: resilience based on diversification of income. Worker families organized their lives in a similar way to worker-peasants by pursuing salaried labour, working on family land plots, and occasionally selling their produce, giving and receiving household support, such as taking care of children or the elderly, and relying on other financial sources, such as state pensions of the elderly. This complicated network of dependencies within the household created a balanced and resilient organisation. Without this balance, pursuing work in the offshored plant for the salaries on offer would not had been possible. The next section demonstrates how offshoring work and family organisation contributed to the emancipation of workers.

3 Emancipatory Forces

> Do I have to live like my mother does? And do the farming, see all that dust and be unsure of how it will be next year? All I really want is normalcy: to go to the shop, buy things, live in a nice flat with central heating. I don't need a garden or animals. I am tired of it. People get impressed [by the stereotypical village life] (...), the ecological way of life, vegetables, but it is not fun. It's actually annoying, but it keeps us living. You have five stores here, one pub. It's not a real life when you are young. What's wrong if I want to spend the money that I earned myself? [The family] are doing so much [producing food] that I can be calm about finding food on my plate.
> Female worker, 26

> I am happy and we are quite well off. Maybe we can't have everything, but it is a good living. A lot has changed in the way we see the world [after transition]. When I was his age [refers to a son working in the factory], I was already married and had two kids. He does not, but I understand it, [those were] different times. At least he works, all this complicated stuff, machines, he has plenty to do there. We can help him out, that's no problem. This work is good for him, with all the computers and stuff. It has a future.
> Parent of a male worker, 54

As both passages above illustrate, families and workers shared the perception of their symbiosis as a means of social advancement, responding to structural limitations. Years of stagnation, accompanied with the development of consumer culture, have created a desire for modernization and social pressure for upward mobility in Romania (Roman, 2003). Community members still held the belief that the industrial workplace might be a vehicle of emancipation. Throughout the history of post-socialist states, waves of peasants migrated to cities, looking for better employment and better lives (Kenney, 1997). Under socialism the industrialisation of the Eastern bloc was based on the rapid transformation of rural populations into workers, who quickly adapted to urban lifestyles and became proletarians (Stenning, 2000; Lebow, 1999). Faith in the modernising power of industrial workplace was also mirrored in attitudes to jobs in the factory, such as the statement "it has a future" in the second passage above. And even though salaries were low and the investment itself failed to provide economic elevation, an important part in elevating workers economically was played by the family: "Working in Nokia might actually change his [the husband's] life. You don't know where it can lead us. Maybe the chances are low, but definitely higher than when he worked in scaffolding" (woman, 29). As this passage demonstrates, workers' families saw work in the investment as a symbolic emancipation from the local *status quo* for their children or spouses.

Some workers emphasised that they felt disconnected from their homes and at-home duties when at work: "I completely forget about the kids, about my husband, about the world that is outside the factory. There are no windows, so I don't even think about the passing time or weather outside" (female worker, 42). The shared feeling of emancipation, even if only illusory, also emerged as positioned against household duties. The members who previously had more at-home responsibilities enjoyed delegating their duties to other family members and felt relieved: "When I am at work my mother takes care of the little ones. This works since she is at home anyway. And I need to just take a break and get out of there [for a while]". (worker, 23, female). The younger shop floor members, some of whom did not contribute to any household duties, were glad that they could find an occupation: "[My father] was going nuts with me sitting at home. He would not let me do anything, because he was observing my every move. Since I am here [working in the factory], I don't have to do anything at home. They see it as a time to rest that I earned" (male worker, 19). The at-home dynamics adjusted to the work life of the operators.

The plant was described as a very important tool for the revival of the local population: "There was a lot of impressive things [in the factory]. But I was mostly happy that I was hired. Nobody else would want me [as an employee]. And this was my way of reaching pension [age]". (female worker, 51). As this quote shows, some workers appreciated the investor's inclusive policy, based on lack of age or gender discrimination. In this context, employment signified more independence. Describing the social composition of the shop floor, both workers and families often referred to its diversity and equality. Older workers, such as the woman quoted above, stressed their goal of achieving pension age and the impossibility of finding formal, salaried employment elsewhere. Female interviewees often referred to the situation in local Romanian firms, emphasizing their difficulties in finding jobs. Their comments reflected broader trends in post-socialist labour markets: strong marginalization of feminine labour market qualities, scapegoating women as problematic employees, and in effect, exclusion from the labour market (Kostera, 1994; Turbine and Riach, 2012). In contrast, interviewees from the village stressed equality amongst the plant workforce: "We were all paid the same, we dressed the same, had the same norms. You stop thinking about where you are from. Instead, you worry about the norms [the daily production plan]" (male line manager, 29)". Workers shared a similar conclusion: even though the investor offered low salaries, comparable to low salaries in female-dominated manufacturing jobs, it also provided stable employment, medical insurance and operated in a transparent way.

The inclusiveness was also important to men: "I was sick of dirt [work in construction]. I could not carry on doing it, I simply could not keep up. In the factory, it was almost like resting [compared to the other job]. (…). I had no bully above me [like a manager in a previous job]" (male worker, 30). Male members of the shop floor, such as the worker quoted here, saw employment as much lighter and easier when compared to other available manual jobs.

Both male and female workers agreed that the egalitarian shop floor policy was a highly valued attribute of the plant. As the next quote illustrates, the workplace also reduced the perceived difference between populations from rural and urban areas: "We had people coming straight from Cluj, such as students, but also us from the village and everybody was equal. Nobody cared because we had the same clothes, the same duties and the same stress (…) I probably would not have met most of those people elsewhere" (female worker, 24). Being part of the workforce was considered an important element of both private and professional life. The next section shows how families privileged the youngest workers, seeing it as a way to achieve upward economic mobility.

4 Intergenerational Exceptionalism

Worker emancipation also had a very strong financial dimension, as salaries provided new consumption possibilities. Even though the degree of the workers' financial participation in their households varied, in general the youngest workers had the biggest amount of spending freedom and the lowest level of at-home duties. This was based on a model of intergenerational exceptionalism. Some adult workers, usually aged between 18 and 30, were not only exempt from at-home duties, such as working in the field or taking care of their younger siblings, but local culture also limited the scope of their financial contribution. Young and unmarried workers rarely contributed to the family budget, usually limiting their help to sharing food coupons and paying for occasional groceries. Below, one young man described his family's budget.

> It's really true that people work in the garden and don't spend much. My grandparents get a pension but don't really buy anything, truly. Not a single piece of clothing, nothing. Their money goes into the mattress [refers to savings] and they work in the garden and take care of the animals. My mom too. My dad makes enough money to pay the bills. She buys groceries.
> – Do you ever give them money [from your salary at the plant]?
> – No, I don't. But they really don't need it, just as most people in the village. We have never had this conversation; it's not necessary. I know they know that if they needed it, then of course. If something happened it's all theirs. We have just never stumbled upon this topic. They are happy for me, I think.
> Male worker, 22

As this passage demonstrates, the favourable situation of young workers relied on the strong capabilities of each household. The man emphasises the low consumption needs of other household members, who have reduced their expenses to the minimum. His family's situation was similar to that of other young workers' families, who did not incorporate income from the plant into the home budget but left it to the earners.

Selective solidarity therefore manifested itself in home organisation. Workers who were also responsible for organising the household, emphasised that, despite intergenerational exceptionalism and privileging young workers, their home budget is balanced. This occurred to a large degree due to the low needs of the parents' and grandparents' generations. As one family member pointed out in response to a question about his son's financial contribution:

"The Romanian peasant survived centuries of captivity, wars, and communism. We can cope and know how to cope and survive on our land" (family member, 59). However, below, passages from two different interviews show a discrepancy of intergenerational visions of organisation within the same household.

> We had a conversation about [the fact that my grandson does not have responsibilities at home] (…) with his mother. If he has a free day, he would sleep in late. Then he would get up, eat whatever is on the stove and watch TV or hang out with his pals. He is 22 years old, a bachelor, but won't help. Most things he can't do, because he has everything ready. The boy is like a king. (…) When he is working, there is a bus outside, and it takes him 15 minutes to get to work. This is an easy life.
> Male family member, mid-60s

> I wish I could help [the family], but there is no such possibility. (…) Seriously, I give them money, put it on the table. They leave it sitting there for days, but they won't take it. What can I do or give them? They don't even want to eat anything that I buy in the store. How many times have I heard that they don't want it, that they have their own [home produce], that I overpaid.
> Male worker, 21

Nonetheless, in most households the intergenerational tension was not verbalized. Instead, the privileged situation was treated in a similar way to vocational education. Families rarely discouraged the young workers from spending: "I think that he is young, and he really should have some experience of youth. He can't be sitting in a village like a peasant, like we are, instead he could go to town, buy something, meet people. He should see some of the world [laughing], meet a nice girl [laughing]" (female family member, 49). This mother strongly believed that her son should autonomously "experience youth" with his salary. Most parents of the youngest workers held a similar view. While accepting the impossibility of changing their lifestyles, they still held a belief that their children could experience this change, even if modernisation occurs at their cost. This attitude, previously not present due to the constraining power of local tradition, has changed in similar communities with the initial overenthusiasm for consumption in the market society (Kideckel, 2008; Todorova and Gille, 2010). This model was contrasted with the practice of older workers, usually married and over the age of 30, who often remembered the times of the transition and maintained traditional gender roles. In this case, their low income from the plant functioned as a supplemental source of income, which was incorporated into the household's budget and shared with other members. In addition, they often continued fulfilling household-related duties, such as the production of food.

Young workers shared the view that because of their spending freedom, they can afford a similar lifestyle to their urban counterparts, also manifested in the concepts of self-investment and self-fulfilment (Marody and Giza-Poleszczuk, 2000; Roman, 2003): "It is a joke, but we work in a factory in order to earn money to get [equipment similar to what we make]" (male worker, 26). This man jokes about the role of the salary, that it provides the means to buy consumer electronics and participate in consumer culture. In other cases the entire income from the plant was autonomously spent on clothing, going out or leisure time in the city. For example, one young woman told me: "I was tired of being a village girl. This way I can have my nails done, buy a dress, feel attractive" (female worker, 21). In a similar tone, male workers emphasised that income gives them a chance to enjoy their leisure time, for instance "get a drink, for myself and for a lady" (worker, 24) or "invite pals out" (worker, 19). One of the most important rituals of workers from this age group were Friday and Saturday night trips to the city, usually hitchhiking from the village: "When the only disco in the village was shut down, there was no way to have fun. We go to the city, but I still can't find that prince [laughing]" (female worker, 24). The salary functioned as a catapult, letting workers experience a previously less accessible world, at the cost, and with full acceptance, of their household.

The work environment and salary also provided opportunities to date and meet new people from outside of the community context, especially during work-related events and meetings. Both male and female workers emphasised their sexual freedom and attempts to be independent of traditional familial structures and pressures to get married early:

> It is not the right time; I am not living like they [the parents] did. I am not going to worry about marriage. I don't feel like it's quite the moment yet.
> Male worker, 27

> Thank God I have this job. I can still feel young and attractive. I really like that. I won't lose it by sitting at home.
> Female worker, 29

To many, employment signified higher self-perception. In this context, the workforce emphasised the aesthetics of the workplace, often mentioning that these separated them from "dirty, boring everyday life at home" (male worker, 24). Another interviewee stressed that "I simply can't afford kids now. I don't want to be living with so many people. There is enough of us in my house" (female worker, 23). As this passage demonstrates, a common claim that young workers had was that the operator's wage did not pay them enough to start their own family. Even though traditionally these young adults would have received support from their families in this instance, many emphasised their need for independence and ambitions to live without any external help.

A desire to be independent and single coincided with practical reasons. An important role in this domain is played by historical traditions, the parenting experience of parents and grandparents and the fact that after the reforms this system has collapsed, making it difficult for young families to manage. Under socialism, the conditions in the Romanian state were especially favourable to young families in that they provided special working arrangements and privileges to mothers, which coincided with the unavailability of contraception and zero tolerance for abortion (Baban, 2000; Verdery, 1996). After transitioning this situation changed and it was usually the extended family who was responsible for providing childcare, since state-provided support was very limited. At the same time, the systemic shift changed attitudes connected to parenthood and marriage, which were catalysed by the presence of the investor. A few female workers emphasised to me that they are unwilling to be worker-mothers: employed outside of the home, responsible for the household, organising and fulfilling most household duties: "I do not have a candidate for a husband; I don't feel like cooking, cleaning, breeding and working at the same time. That's just what my mother did" (female worker, 22). Both female and male workers also argued that their generation does not have as many forms of institutionalised family support as their parents' generation had.

5 Mutual Dependency in a Broader Context

To date, working class families and their relationship to offshoring has been given most attention by labour scholars, who predominantly have concentrated on the globalisation of service industries (e.g. Golpelwar, 2015; Scholarios and Taylor, 2010). In this chapter, I have analysed reciprocal relationships between worker households and offshoring, considered the emancipatory power of this relation, and addressed it as a mechanism of highly specific economic mobility. The intersection of long-lasting effects of the post-socialist transition and results of labour commodification in the offshored investment provoked agency at the family level, which at the same time reflects broader issues of adjusting to today's precarious work conditions in the manufacturing sector (Brooks, 2007; Kalleberg, 2009). A key role in this adjustment was played by at-home work of family members. Historically, the fundamental theorisation regarding commodification of labour and its relation to at-home work was laid down by Karl Polanyi in analysing the historical development of English working class. Polanyi focused on workers, while considering their familial settings and observing the destitution of workers in industrialised England, identifying the diminishing role of traditional collective culture as the driving force of this process:

> There is no starvation in societies living on the subsistence margin. The principle of freedom from want was equally acknowledged in the Indian village community and, we might add, under almost every and any type of social organization up to about the beginning of sixteenth century Europe, when the modern ideas on the poor put forth by the humanist Vives were argued before the Sorbonne. It is the absence of the threat of individual starvation which makes primitive society, in a sense, more human than market economy, and at the same time less economic.
> POLANYI, 1944: 164

Polanyi's critique of capitalist practice is very relevant when applied to the post-socialist context of the present study. Even though today the relationship between the workforce and the industrial workplace has evolved, familial organisation, and in this case a village largely based on subsistence agriculture, plays a key role in sustaining workers' employment. Mutual dependency between traditional households and offshored labour rests on traditional organisation, which prevents the starvation that Polanyi mentions, but also satisfies all of the basic needs of a worker by providing home, food, care, or paying for shopping and utility bills. This chapter has given an account of mutual dependencies emerging in response to structural limitations, based on the depreciating levels of wages in the industrial sector, local stagnation and a slack labour market.

The redistribution within the village households acts as an enabling mechanism for pursuing offshored work but also leads to economic and social upgrading. Mechanisms of household organisation permitted economic elevation and emancipation from tradition, even though their scale was much lower than the local population had anticipated prior to the investment. The household provided a means for consumption of salaries, strongly privileging young workers. As I have demonstrated, due to low salary levels this agency was driven by non-financial motives of families, shaped by the desire for modernization, upward mobility and urbanisation for their younger members. The spending freedom given to younger workers provided families with a chance of intergenerational economic progression. The special status of young workers was in many ways similar to the protection of youth attending school. It was often encouraged by their parents and grandparents who believed that, in order to abandon the peasant household, the children need to have time for study and leisure. This belief is parallel to "nesting" practices of Western households, prolonging the duration of time that young adults live at home, which also emerge mainly from economic limitations (Mitchell, 2011; Rossi, 1997). However, in the case of post-socialist societies, the basis of structural limitation is deeper and to a large degree formed during the social reconfiguration that followed the transition. Post-socialist worker populations have faced a major industrial decline; however, unlike in the experiences of the changing configuration of the working class in the West, manifested by the shift from manufacturing to tertiary sector employment or the precariousness of work, the post-socialist decline was of systemic origins and enveloped the entire social system. Since 1989, post-socialist workers not only faced stagnation following the transition but also hoped for the lifestyle, privileges and work conditions of their Western counterparts, even though they were extensively diminishing in recent decades (Blyton and Jenkins, 2012; Cowie, 2010; Hochschild and Machung, 2012; Mollona, 2009). This stance was also influenced by a goal present in the local culture, i.e. avoidance and abandonment of "dirty work", such as construction or agriculture. This stance, typical of stagnated populations of post-socialist Europe, privileges any type of work which is not "dirty" manual labour, even despite potentially higher salaries and job availability. This partially explains why offshored employment, realised in a clean and technological environment, was a temporary way of reaching modernization and social upgrade. Employment in the plant therefore allowed for temporary abandonment of traditionally "dirty" lifestyles and household duties.

The familial reliance on a relationship of reciprocity with foreign investment has also brought significant benefits. Working life in an off-shored plant often means that professional and personal life become both connected and separated. As shown, commodified labour in the plant had an important value in itself, providing a means of emancipation through channels such as a work environment outside of the home or new social settings. Paradoxically, the distinction was significant to workers embedded, and sometimes trapped, in traditional rural structures. The experience of the production process was very different from what Polanyi's "early labourer" experienced: "where he felt degraded and tortured, like the native who often resigned himself to work in our fashion only when threatened with corporal punishment, if not physical mutilation" (Polanyi, 1994: 57). As I have demonstrated in Chapter 4, very few workers considered the work environment oppressive – it was rather interpreted as harmonious. This also applies to the familial context: despite repetitive and physically demanding activities involved in the manufacturing process, such as long hours of standing and manual assembly, taking up employment signified liberation from the traditional constraints and rural environment. Older workers, usually more extensively involved in work at home, often mentioned that employment provided a respite from their everyday duties, which were often delegated to other household members. Moreover, emerging reciprocity between households and the investment was not only a foundation for the manufacturing employment process but also, on the family's part, a tool of social and economic upgrading. Kideckel, who studied populations of socialist and post-socialist workers in Romania, identified *an* inability to fulfil traditional social roles, such as breadwinning, as a main source of social problems in stagnant communities (Kideckel, 1984, 2008). The present investment has partially reversed this order by giving workers more agency. Every working day, often the same in terms of work assignments, nonetheless provided a distinctively different experience to the daily life in the stagnated community, which fulfilled an important function and on its own was considered as a way of social advancement.

To summarise, the mutual dependence of familial life and offshoring labour emerges from a need embedded in local conditions and employment opportunities. Yet, mutual dependency partially emerges out of familial choice, acting as an enabling mechanism for social upgrading. Most often, however, its roots are based on both need and choice since for many families salaried income is only supplemental to household income, yet central to some workers' independence and personal lifestyle. In those cases, the offshored workplace leverages the social position of select family members, often the younger generation of adults, permitting new experiences, connecting them to new social networks, and allowing separation from traditional culture, often considered as oppressive. Finally, the mutual dependence is a source of economic upgrading, which rests on spending autonomy provided by the family to the worker. In order to fully grasp the processes underpinning industrial employment it is thus necessary to concentrate on the processes of household, by considering both economic, symbolic and professional dimensions of employment.

This argument could also be extended to a wider context. Post-socialist Europe provides a specific case of rapid internationalization and economic globalization through the introduction of the market economy. This systemic transformation was among the biggest neoliberal experiments in history. Positioning my research in a wider theoretical context, this chapter demonstrates on a micro and meso level how societies cope with the influence of the free market. Neo-Polanyian writings show that reactions to the market can be seen as "an essentially disconnected set of national movements, each with goals and strategies determined by the place of its own nation state within the larger global market" (Evans, 2008: 273–274). As the industrial labour markets have evolved towards flexibilisation, workers and families who are connected by them are left to fend for themselves and cannot be protected from the potential chaos of unregulated circulation of capital. Today this process intensifies with globalization, with industrial production at its heart. This chapter provides a new perspective on the market participant: a worker who cannot defend their social well-being in the market context, who by participating in the labour market instead extensively involves – or relies upon – their family. As part of this, familial involvement could be included in the matrix of more recognised global industrial production employment issues such as health care, family leave, living wage campaigns, consumer boycotts, working conditions or wages. In other words, this chapter has demonstrated a Polanyian-type struggle, understood as a response to the commodification of social existence (Burawoy, 2010). It supplements the work that addressed issues connected to exploitation in the workplace (Seidman, 2007; Webster et al., 2011).

This perspective, focused on identifying a broader sphere of offshoring's influence, might be treated as a voice in the ongoing discussion of industrial labour practices. The broad presence of offshored investments in the former Eastern bloc is largely based on the manufacturing cost advantage of the region, mainly based on the low cost of labour and proximity to West European markets (Neuhaus, 2006; Pavlínek, 2004). Nonetheless, my research addresses the issues related to organisational relationships guiding capitalist manufacturing by providing an instance relevant to the post-socialist context, which is its first limitation. The present study depicts participation in global competition for foreign investments through a post-socialist lens and from the perspective of the region. Even though practices such as state-run incentives aimed to attract foreign investments, like offering tax holidays and participating in investment costs, might be universal, the reception and unique familial role in sustaining labour might be limited to the post-socialist context. Within this area, further research might explore issues reflecting the experiences of other middle-income economies exposed to the free market and facing extensive presence of offshoring capital.

CHAPTER 6

Employee Reactions to the Plant Closure

How did I learn about this? They called me. They said that there will be a meeting in a couple of days. Sometimes they would organize these types of meetings (...) [At the time I thought that] maybe somebody important was coming? Each shift then had a meeting. Everyone together. Yet this time it was different. I saw that for a couple of days they were building a white tent in the parking lot. We even laughed that it looked like a circus! It was not round, more like a huge white house made of fabric. (...) Then they set the time [for the meeting] and everything, and I went to work. Everybody came in and they sat us inside. Inside they had put a lot of chairs, blue chairs. In front, there was a screen, like for all those bigger meetings, and large loudspeakers. They put a picture of a person speaking on the screen. (...) So we sat there and the meeting started. A woman dressed in pink from the office started to talk. She described exactly what was going on, that basically they are going someplace else. It made me more than angry. But I did nothing, what could I do? Everybody was immediately texting. There was a big storm of messages and calls. (...) Many people could not believe it; how would they leave us if there is still production going on?
 Male worker

It was a chilly autumn in 2011, and the highly unexpected relocation was just announced. Upon hearing the news, I drove to the industrial zone quickly. I noticed dozens of journalists immediately. About thirty minutes prior to my arrival the first shift of workers had left the plenary meeting. On the day of announcement, the air around the plant was dense. Many workers were surprised and frozen in disbelief. I noted people smoking and discussing the handouts outlining the timeline and plan of the closure, while journalists interviewed the workers and discussed the situation amongst themselves. Everyone gathered around this area agreed that this situation was impossible to predict. Prior to the decision, the production floor had run at high capacity. The opening passage of this chapter mentions a presentation which was given during the meeting. The management provided a short justification connected to a strategy of austerity and cutting labour costs. Officially, the decision was motivated by the production costs and the distance to Asian markets, where many of the mobile phones produced in the hosting village were sold. The workers were given handouts outlining the layoff process and compensation amounts. The workforce was informed that the plant will run until the end of the year. Then, everything was to be shut down and production lines de-assembled. The investor's exit strategy was based on a closure plan which was shared during the plenary meetings with the workers. Until the closure, the workers were going to be paid double. In the last months of the assembly operation, employees with direct contracts could sign up for vocational training intended to prepare them to find work in other sectors. The employer provided a list of options. The workers would also receive compensation equal to three months wages plus one month's wage for each year of work. In total, the payment could be equal to a maximum of about $3000. It took almost six months to terminate the operation and completely shut down the plant. Both groups of employees, on direct and agency contracts, were potentially eligible for state unemployment support, the time and amount depending on their period of work in the plant.

This plan and the decision was hard to believe for many. Because of the low-cost of assembly labour involved, the investor's activity in Romania had been understood mostly as dependent on the availability and the continued low cost of the workforce. It was assumed that the investor's presence would lead to improved work conditions and an idealised middle-class urban lifestyle, limiting the amount of cheap labour available. This was based on an understanding of modernity, urbanization and the hope that it would bring nothing less than Western industrial modernity to the region. Until that became a reality, because of the low wages, the workforce considered the investor's presence to be justified and economically efficient. Workers believed in the fantasy of modernization, neoliberal economic development and urbanization. The lived experience of the shop-floor and familial support strengthened that belief. At the investment's initial stage, the community had produced certain expectations that were based on a shared idea of progress. Despite the high reliance on local support, the assembly plant helped to deepen a sense of optimism about capitalism, a positive opinion about the investor, and faith in the neoliberal vision of the future.

Because production networks incorporate new geographies and locations, transformations occur as a result of adaptation, and, as I show in this chapter, they cause a very specific form of dependence on external capital and its artefacts. For different reasons, foreign investments appear and disappear. New workplaces and industries emerge in new locations, often replacing former, more costly manufacturing facilities located in more costly geographies. In the literature, an important point of reference for such transformation are the studies of the Zambian Copperbelt, which modernised rapidly through extensive involvement in the international economy. Zambian economic growth was based on natural resource exploitation, geographically tied to place and dependent on the availability of resources, while also exploited by external capital. Writings on this region show how modernization destabilises local identity through processes such as detribalization (Wilson, 1968), cultural contact with Europeans (Wilson, 1936), establishment of trans-local networks and migrations to the city (Mitchell, 1969; Mayer, 1971) or the urbanization process (Epstein, 1973). The shifts connected to the inflow of external capital and rapid modernization of the region were grounded in a belief that "an epochal leap in evolutionary time" was taking place locally (Ferguson, 1999: 4). But modernization of the Copperbelt area has come to an end, resulting from the exploitation of natural resources, causing a deep crisis and social problems that were caused by high reliance on the outside capital.

Investments relying on labour arbitrage function as a carrier of inequality, creating a class of the working poor (Fields, 2012; Hurrell and Woods, 1999), while being shifted to different sites and leaving their workers behind. Strategies that concern the optimization of global value chain operations react to external and internal challenges, connected to corporate problems, market changes or political turbulence. Global production seeks to save on labour costs, often causing economic, political, technological and cultural difficulties and leaving behind social problems connected to the abandonment of the workforce. For the transnational managerial class, it is much easier to follow the workplace as part of a corporate career, which often relies on managing different parts of value chains in different locations. The situation is much more dramatic for the immobile workforce, left behind to be dependent on another investment. The binary between the highly mobile and the immobile also resonates with Zygmunt Bauman's perspective on space compression. The immobile are attached and dependent on the place and local conditions, unlike the transnational who can afford mobility and travel for any reason (Bauman, 1998). The workforce has strongly experienced the immobility, being faced with few local alternatives and also feeling unable to migrate for work after the closure, mostly due to their limited financial resources.

In this chapter I illustrate the local consequences of the investor's decision, outlining the initial reaction of the workforce. As I show, the reaction to the relocation resulted from the specific adaptation process to the investment. Its elements included changing the self-perception of the workforce and building up specific expectations about the future. Reliance on the investor manifested on multiple levels. By studying the reactions among workforce, I first lay out their interpretations of the closure, then study Romanian public opinion and the coping and support mechanisms activated by the state and local elites.

1   The Good Investor's Bad Decisions

Immediately following the announcement, the workforce was surprised and in disbelief. One of the workers commented on the promptness of the decision: "just like a heart attack, no warning, no symptoms, no problems. See you in another world". Given the high volume of output and persistent production increases, the layoff came as a complete surprise. Another worker, an employee for over 3 years, commented: "It would have been understandable if [the investor] decreased production gradually, but the volume was growing". Until the relocation was publicized, the operations inside the plant had not shown any signs of crisis, mismanagement or poor investment. In fact, the workforce believed that the actions of the investor were very well orchestrated, and they admired the plant's organization and volume of production. The next passage describes the initial feelings shared by the workforce.

> I really don't have anything against [the investor]. It was definitely a good employer. It might sound crazy, but I can't stop feeling sad for them. This was probably the best job that I will ever have. You might ask me why? I don't really see how somebody might come to us and trust [the workforce] so much. It is about the approach that [the investor] had towards us. They were really serious. They did not cheat [refers to regular payments and transparency of employment]. There are some people, of course, who would say that it didn't work, and we were in a bad situation. It was hard work that caused people's backs and legs to hurt. (...) But these accusations, in my situation, were not too important. This job was good for me, and I am glad I worked there. I think that because of this [employment] I regained my confidence. I met so many people. I learned so much, not really about work but about how we can expect work to be. Even he [refers to the husband present in the house during the interview] was saying that I look more happy since I started working there. I will really miss those stupid, long hours spent at their production facility.
> Female worker

As this passage illustrates, the workforce has trusted the investor's good will, and even though the investor decided to leave Romania, the general positive feelings have persisted. The interviewee relies on her own judgements of the experiences at the workplace, and by accepting compensation after the closure, she experiences sadness at the discontinuation of production. Similarly, the next interviewee expresses grief connected to the loss of the company and the quality time he spent on the line.

–   It's a big scandal that [the investment] will close. It is upsetting to be part of that thing (...). I have really mixed feelings. To me it feels like we were done with school.
–   What do you mean by this reference to school?
–   It is the same thing in many ways. I like going there. Even though the time at the line would be boring, just like in school, we would hang out and have a good time. Maybe going there every day was annoying, but at the same time, what else could I be doing? What I'm going to miss is mostly the atmosphere and seeing my buddies so regularly. That was the beauty of it. We would do stuff that we had to do but also meet other people, it was a really nice thing. Now that it's all going to be over. I'm just sad, and I realize that nothing can ever be sure. (...) The compensations sound good. I mean we will get paid more, and it will be quite a sum if they keep their promises. But the hardest part is the fact that with or without money there will be no way back. (male worker)

To this worker, the investor's departure signified the end of a specific social configuration. The disappearance of the workplace is compared to school, because the layoffs were compared to the end of school term. Even though this worker says that the compensations are acceptable, in fact, he is really sorry about the fact that all that he experienced in the plant will be soon over.

Some members of the workforce expressed understanding of the investor's decision. Paradoxically, the rationality-based decision of the investor was seen as entrepreneurial and reasonable in order to protect corporate interest. Given the mounting problems of the Nokia Corporation, some workers agreed with it. A worker in her twenties told me: "if in China the work is cheaper, it is normal to go to China and save. I won't work for 25% less but somebody there will". During the same conversation, the worker also pointed out that the plant was previously relocated from Germany, a more expensive country, so it could be expected that an investor might look for an alternative, less expensive place. Another worker stressed that if he was the decision maker, "he would have done the same". This simple rationalization is hard to believe, but it was recurring in many conversations with the workers. At the same time, it was coupled with common sense and understanding of the situation. For instance, some compared it to a small business and argued that a release of the industrial zone can be based on the same workforce:

> It is heart-breaking to think that so many people will now have nothing to do. But, on the other hand, let's remember that this can all be rented. All businesses, places like shops, bars, and restaurants sometimes fail and then they get rented, or somebody else opens something there. This is

what can happen with the factory. (...) So another company will come and will be looking for employees and you don't want to start a shit storm. I think that this one is already lost. [The investor] was nice but there is nothing that can be done to change that situation, maybe except for the fact that they can give us some more money, but that's not really up to us. So pretty much, as we are a cut off from the source, the only thing that we can do is to just stay professional. Professional. There is nothing like emotions; of course, people are sad, and it's annoying, but Nokia left for only one reason, because we stopped being needed or did they didn't have money to have us anymore. I respect that decision even though it brings really hurtful feelings and emotions.

Male worker

This passage provides an important perspective. Not only is this worker criticising the investor, but he also openly shares his view that the workforce should remain professional by not damaging its reputation, for instance through protest or resistance. The worker also argues that despite the unclear grounds of the relocation, he respects and understands it fully. The passage exemplifies an often-repeated argument that the workers have no agency over this situation, and it is impossible for them to react in any other way than to wait.

Another worker commented on the future investor and the possibility of continuing production in the industrial zone:

They promised us that there will be priority hiring for people who have worked at [the investment]. And I believe that. Now as [the local officials administering the zone] are there looking for the new investor, people need to bounce back and wait it out. But definitely the factory is modern and can be used by any type of manufacturer who can do anything. We are cheap, so that's a good reason to rent it. They will need employees in there. And as so many of us [refers to workforce] were doing a really good job, it shouldn't be a problem to find us. Anyway, I don't have high expectations, as long as it is something similar to what [the previous investor] did. I liked how they picked us up [refers to transportation system]. I liked that we were there for 12 hours [refers to shift organisation], and I liked how they paid on time. That's really not much to expect from the new firm.

Male worker

Both men above reflect on the situation and emphasise the fact that the investor was leaving behind a modern industrial zone and a workforce with a good reputation. None of the interviewees believed that the relocation meant the end of the manufacturing process in the zone, like it sometimes happens in Western states experiencing relocations (Mollona, 2009; Blyton and Jenkins, 2012). Instead, it was more usual to hear that the interviewees felt that despite their effort to adapt and work well, it was the investor's fault, given their inability to innovate and maintain competitiveness. As a result, most workers believed that the relocation was caused by the irresponsible actions of the investor. Paradoxically, some of them saw it inside the production hall:

> I think that this company was just too obsessed with ensuring that everything works well in the factory. Once they put our factory together, they already had big problems and couldn't do anything. They just were making sure that everything works according to plan. It made sense, and it was OK or actually more than OK. But in fact the problem started much earlier, and it wasn't fault of anyone else but Nokia.
> Male worker

> The more people you meet, the more opinions you hear, but my opinion is that they overdid it inside the plant. Instead of thinking how they should be fighting Apple... The whole thing was just too much. They produced very good work conditions, but maybe this is what made them fail, because they were too good. People appreciate that probably the next hundred investors won't be as welcoming as Nokia was for people who worked at it.
> Female worker

The two workers quoted above openly criticise the investor's approach to production and management arguing that it tended to be too precise and meticulous but had failed to achieve the general vision of the corporation. According to them, this strategy ultimately led to collapse, forcing the investor out of Romania and causing problems for the workforce. The relocation seemed like the only way the investor could cope with fierce global competition. For this reason, a common opinion among workers was that the new investor would not be able to offer as good work conditions as Nokia provided. Workers often justified it with the costs associated with high workplace standards.

2   Social Mobilization

When the investor decided to close the plant in Bochum, Germany, there was a strong response from the local workforce, including mass protests, extensive involvement of trade unions and signs of social solidarity with workers. As described in Chapter 3, the protests against the relocation of the plant brought together thousands of supporters. Then the investor's decision was met with resistance from trade unions, local government and national politicians. Different parties, often not directly linked to the former operations in Germany, openly criticised the investor for such practices and generated a strong response. The reaction to the relocation was different in Romania. There was only one small and short incident of mobilization that involved about 30 workers who protested against the decision before entering the plant for their shift. About a week after the decision was publicized, a small protest of temporary workers took place by the factory's entrance. One of the protestors, a worker from Cluj who participated in the protest, told me that it was done out of the frustration.

> It is very typical. People are losing money, but they can't do anything. We tried to show that workers are against that decision. The management came, told us that it's not their fault and apologized. The other workers went straight to work. In the plant, where you had at least 700 people on the shop floor, only [the protestors] were willing to do something. What do I have to lose? Once my contract ends, I have nothing left. I won't even get the compensation.
> Worker

Instead of thinking that a new investor might soon be relocating into the zone, the workforce concentrated on securing workplaces with a hypothetical new investor. For instance, one of the female workers commented: "arguing would not help here. There is no hope for the investor here. I do not want to be the loudest because then I would be the black sheep; nobody wants an employee with a big mouth". Many workers interpreted any form of resistance as potentially damaging to their professional reputation. They felt that they are awaiting a new investor/employer and did not want to interfere in this process. At the same time, they did not feel responsible and understood the situation as the investor's fault.

Besides the small protest, there were no other signs of collective action. Even though labour unions were present in the plant, they were unable to either mobilize the workers or mediate with the investor. None of the local organizations attempted to appeal the relocation. Compared to the size of the workforce, the protest was very small. It also gained very little support from the workers, all of whom were about to be laid off. For many of them, collective action was highly unnecessary and "could not bring anything new to the situation" (male worker). Some of them believed that it might only hinder their already weak position in case the investor changed its mind. Many of the workers discussed why there should be a strong reaction to the decision in Romania. Some pointed out that the regular workers have no influence over this decision. "Bargaining? Why would you bargain? It was a setup, and you don't bargain with it" (female worker). The others expressed disappointment and claimed that they do not have a strong political group to support resistance. "[The union] had no power and knowledge that it will happen. They did not tell us. Then, they told us that it's already decided" (male worker, union activist). The workforce defended their status, feeling that despite the investor's failure and their difficult situation, there will be a safe exit from this challenging situation once there is another investor found. For instance, one of the workers contemplates:

> I don't think that it is the end of this factory. It was all the starting process, but a lot of money was put into these grounds [refers to investment made by the local authorities], so I am sure that there will be somebody [refers to the potential new investor] to continue that. And I see myself being part of that because what else do I have to do. Apple can manufacture something as can any other company. We [refers to the workforce] have proven that we can do it and that we don't have a bad attitude.
> Female worker

One of the local publicists wrote in the paper that the media also ignored the strike:

> There has been no strike at the plant. [To quote a comment made by the investor:]"We had a constructive dialogue with a group of employees with temporary contracts". It reminds me exactly of the times of Ceausescu. He was always the one that had constructive dialogues and excellent bilateral relationships with anyone he could name.
> *Mesagerul de Cluj*, 2011.10:12–23

In this exemplary quote, the publicist has negatively assessed not only the reaction of the workforce but also the media perception of the strike and the management's position.

Poor mobilisation was also the result of existing labour regulations. Romania's union traditions are strong, having significantly influenced discussions about privatisation or labour laws, but their role has shifted since the introduction of the new Labour Code in 2011. The law change, officially justified by increasing the attractiveness of Romania as an investment destination (Vincze,

2015: 135), has undermined nation-wide unionising and self-organisation as well as fully supported fixed-term employment. The changes included expanding maximum fixed-term employment from 24 to 36 months, eliminating mandatory pay for union officials for their time to work on unions, and allowed for their removal after their mandate expires, if they are not needed in the workplace. These changes have put a lot of pressure on the workforce and unions, which suffered severe problems with membership and support already after the legislation changes. This was partially due to their weakening influence over state policy since the 2000s when privatisation and other events influenced the strength of the union movement (Adăscăliței and Guga, 2015; Varga and Freyberg-Inan, 2015). Along with the labour code, the Social Dialogue Act, which created administrative barriers for the registration of new trade unions, removed national cross-sectoral agreements, changed the criteria for union representation on the company level from 33 to 51 per cent of unionized workers, and enforced obligatory conciliation before strikes, which prohibited striking if collective agreement provisions are not implemented (Trif, 2016; Hayter et al., 2013). All these elements that shifted at the state level made it very challenging for the unions to operate in the plant. The situation of the investment was specific because the workforce was generally happy about the work conditions, and, unlike former socialist plants privatised by the investors, the plant did not yet develop patterns of formal resistance.

2.1   *Familial Involvement*

Reactions to the investor's decision were strongly influenced by the workers' status addressed in the chapter concerning mutual dependencies. Multi-generational households provided active support during the period of employment. Once the layoffs happened, many workers returned to work in semi-subsistence agriculture and other household duties, looked for temporary jobs, and relied on the support of the household. For many members of the workforce the plant was not a sole source of income. Those eligible for unemployment support were in a more comfortable position. Many workers have gone back to traditional duties, done before the investor came and continued during the period of employment. Resilience came from the traditional village household. Household chores immediately filled the gap that unemployment left. Some workers immediately started working around their households, cultivating soil, producing vegetables, and breeding animals. Semi-subsistence agriculture once again helped to get through a transitory moment. One of the workers remarked on this role of the rural household: "Romanian peasants survived communism, wars and centuries of occupation, people know how to carry on living". Many workers took hourly-paid jobs, either in agriculture or in the construction industry in the city. A few workers whom I interviewed decided to temporarily migrate to join their families outside of Romania.

This situation was challenging for families. In extreme cases, it generated a financial problem due to existing loans or future plans. For example, a 39-year old mother comments:

> This decision is a nightmare. I don't know what to do because I have just taken out a loan. I will need to pay my debts, and I am not sure what I can do to figure that stuff out. Obviously only the salary [from the job] would not have been enough to pay any of debt. But the salary I was getting was always solid and stable, transferred to my account every month. And now I will have to again hunt for jobs. (...) I am a cook and even when I was working at Nokia, I was working part-time in catering. So I will probably just take anything and also do more permanent stuff. I will have to cope somehow, but it is very, very stressful.
> Female worker, 39

Similar to the description above, the situation has proven to affect the eldest workers, typically managing the responsibilities of the household, the most. Many of them had taken the jobs to gain retirement eligibility while working at the plant. They suddenly lost the ground underneath their feet and experienced disappointment and upset. With this group I witnessed many tears and expressions of helplessness because of the job loss. Workers in this age group often brought up an argument similar to this statement: "it is too hurtful to experience another collapse". They referred to their professional path: from the collapse of communist-run enterprises and the painful process of systemic transformation and then the investor's departure. Below is a passage from an older woman who was one of the most loyal employees of Nokia. Before the relocation she told me about how much she loves working in the plant and her co-workers.

> I'm too sad to do anything, even now. Then I was sad, really sad. If you are my age, you just want get to retirement. Look at [the neighbour, who later rejected an interview] maybe she did not want to speak to you because she thought you are a creditor from a bank. She took loans, way too many loans! Man, she's a wreck now. I met with her, and she was really angry. I am not like that. All I am fighting for is just something to do in life and the pension. To live to an age when I am not worried about the future.
> Older female worker

Many reactions were fundamentally based on new worker roles formed in the plant. The discontinuation of production in Romania signified their ending. Since the announcement of the closure, workers' expectation of continuing activity in the industrial zone was high. A number of speculations developed immediately. Workers discussed questions of who could continue production in the industrial zone, how many people could be hired, and how much the positions could pay. The best fit was another producer of consumer electronics. Paradoxically, a common opinion was that the new investor would not be able to offer as good conditions as the mobile phone producer had. A male worker told me: "The dream was over. It was too perfect". A different worker tried to convince me that if the shop floor conditions had been more crude and simple, without the numerous and often unnecessary benefits, the price of production would have been cheaper, and it perhaps could have saved the plant in the village. But, despite the decision, I still hear that the conditions of factory work were good, some workers say "perhaps like in no other factory in Romania". Below, another illustration based on a passage from a former operator:

> Technically speaking what this situation has showed me is the fact that I can take any job in any type of production, and I will be OK. Before I worked in really dirty and hard jobs like construction, farming, or lumber. I really did not know anything about computers or mobile phones before. I made the decision; I applied; I learned everything, and I think that when the next company comes I will also be able to adjust. It wouldn't be a problem for me to do anything they would want to be doing there. I think this is what will really matter for this next company. To know that there are a lot of people willing to put in really hard work in order to meet their requirements and work there. (…) It is of course annoying to learn about what's going to happen with the factory, but to be honest with you, I have plans for my future, and I will probably just use my compensation to put up an extension on our house. We were planning to do that a while ago, but since everybody worked, there was never enough time. Now that I am jobless I can do it full-time and take care of it. And with the money, it's OK. We won't be hungry or anything like that.
> Worker

2.2 *Intermediaries*

Workers hired through intermediaries accepted the flexible nature of employment, unsure about the length and future of their contracts. Some of these workers openly admitted that they often felt like "second-class" employees, underpaid and unwilling to engage in corporate and union activities. "I was not sure if I would get my contract prolonged in November, but given the plant's closure, I just immediately started looking for something else" (young female worker). At their base there is deep individualization, embedded both in local labour culture as well as in the model of employment that Nokia offered. Workers, who have often been hired on temporary contracts for extensive periods, have in part been prepared for the situation that their contract may not be extended. As a result, each time a contract was nearing its end date, it was a stressful and unsure situation for them. When the closure took place, this situation seemed in a way understandable and acceptable to many of them. For instance, one of the female workers who worked in the plant for 14 months on temporary contracts, commented on the closure:

> What am I mostly annoyed about is the fact that I had to apply twice [refers to discontinued employment]. And every time I was hired through an agency; and every time something weird happened, so last time they fired me and now the factory is getting shut down. I think that [not receiving a contract extension] was fate telling me that it's not going to work. And now as they are really leaving forever, it's never going to work. I do not really respect that kind of attitude [of the investor] when they hire you, but they don't [refers to agency work], and they assure you that you are their employee but you're not [refers to status of temporary workers]. (…) Whatever, my sister really thinks that we should try to go to Italy for the summer. She has a friend who works there so maybe that will be one of the options. If not, I will just find something like a job in the shop or in production. I'm not really afraid of any kind of job. Christmas is over it's so time to come back to reality.
> Female worker

The interviewee quoted above points at a number of problems connected to agency employment. This form of work generated relationships of low trust between the workforce and the investor. The woman emphasizes the fact that despite the investor's assurance of her equal status, she was not treated equally because her contract was temporary. This passage reflects the attitude of many members of the workforce for whom employment in the plant generated similar anxieties. Faced with the relocation, the workers who have been exposed to this situation fully accepted it and understood it as a strategy that they had already experienced.

Workers hired through intermediary contracts expressed very low interest in mobilization or protest against the investor's decision. For them, it was seen as highly unnecessary since their work contracts typically did not extend beyond several months of employment. Below an example from a female interviewee:

Since I learned about this situation, [my husband and I] are trying to just except it and find a way of coping with it, which probably in our case would mean that I will be looking for jobs around here or just stay at home with the kids, and [my husband] will need to work on his own. I told you what I think, but this money wasn't really anything special, and we were kind of aware that they might cut us off any time [refers to flexible employment]. So we are losing a lot of extra income, but it doesn't mean we're sinking [refers to going in debt] or anything like that. In the last months they paid us more, and we were better off financially and that I see as a bonus. I'm going to miss the free transfer to work, but oh well, nobody ever told us that it will last forever.

Female worker

This interviewee emphasizes the fact that she appreciates the higher salary during the last months of the plant's operation, and, at the same time, she describes how her family was prepared for this turn, mostly because of the flexible nature of the employment.

The temporary nature of the contracts also informed the employees' lack of enthusiasm for collective action, representation, and unionization. For this group the idea of joining the union was highly unpopular as these workers did not see any benefits of representation. Typically, when asked about the idea of unionizing, these workers expressed the opinion that the representatives are troublemakers. The defined period of employment and relatively transparent conditions of labour made temporary workers feel like unionising would be a waste of time and resources, not to mention bargaining with the management. Moreover, absenteeism and a disenchanted work attitude were prevalent among temporary workers. Assuming that the investor's actions are clear, fair and reasonable, just as the physical conditions in the plant, the workforce believed in the investor's genuine, albeit rational, intentions.

3   What the Plant Changed

The months after the plant closed passed quickly. Late spring 2012 brought warm weather, and as I sat with one of the workers in his mother's kitchen, she served us coffee and we talked about the plant. Her opinion is that the plant showed people "what the world could look like (…) and how much there is to appreciate". His view differed. He thought that the plant has actually not changed anything. He argued: "It [the work in the plant] did not give me skills that can be used in some other place". Moreover, the salary was too low to buy anything significant. In fact, he was still living with his parents who were still supporting him (and brewing his coffee). His father yelled from the garden that, "maybe then it was a stipend – not a job". The man took out his mobile phone and showed it to me, saying, "This is basically what's left from this job". He got it from the plant as a work award, but he soon planned to get a different one. This one quickly became too basic and outdated. He emphasised that he has not purchased anything significant with his salary. "The money evaporated, and so did my job". Since the layoffs, the man tried to find a new job in the city. When we met, he was considering getting a taxi license.

After the closure I regularly walked around the industrial zone. Once the plant was shut down, the investor's logo was removed from the production facility, leaving a frame for the potential new investor. Padlocks were put on all gates. In the doorkeeper's lodge, where the workers used to enter, there was only one security guard. When I visited the zone once, he sleepily told me that the only reason to come to the zone would be the ATM. Even though the plant stopped working, it was still in order and regularly maintained: "It is so empty that it almost feels like I am watching over an empty grass field", he says. In fact, the zone was completely deactivated, and the infrastructure was overgrown by the surrounding plants. The roads became dusty and dirty. Hardly any cars entered it; the pavements were unused; the train platform hid in the bush. Some men living close by mow the grass in the zone in order to feed their animals in the summer. I was told that some motorcycle enthusiasts from the city organise a drag race in the zone on the surrounding asphalt lanes.

The golden age of Nokia in Romania began in 2007 and ended in 2012. The events that followed the investor's decision about leaving illustrate the well-proved argument that nation states are completely unable to control the processes of globalization. Once the decision took place, the community of workers completely failed to organize, mobilize, protest or react in any other way than to grieve. They completely gave up their bargaining power and permitted others, like the media and politicians, to deal with their problem. The hosting community reacted in a similar way. Literally every party involved in the investment on the Romanian side was shaken by the decision, but the reaction was dealt with privately. Local officials denied comment on the situation for months and followed everything that happened in the media discussion. Regional authorities and the national government also ceased activity around the issue. The decision about the location also took place outside the control and influence of the local world.

The trajectory of the plant in Romania shows how the geographic mobility of production nodes challenges the local *status quo*. In recent decades, thanks to free trade agreements led and initiated by "advanced" economies, the process of mobilizing a previously excluded labour force has intensified. Labour markets, such as Eastern Europe, offer geographic proximity, political stability, and encourage foreign investments. The activity of geographically mobile elements of production re-shapes local labour markets by engaging with workforces with limited mobility. In transforming economies, such as Romania, due to legal regulations connected to the adjustment to global economy, there are very few limits to capitalist penetration. The political process of economic integration further encourages incorporation of peripheral zones, with collapsed or former industrial activity, into the global labour force. For hosting economies, new industrial activity is considered valuable. It offers economic growth and often is seen as a countermeasure to a slack labour market. The industrial zone in Romania that I studied was custom-built for the investor by the local authorities using regional funding. Local commitment to the investment was very high.

Workers felt naïve and betrayed, but they tried to understand the relocation's motive and be emphatic to the investor's decision. The rational decision was better understood thanks to the good experience that the plant provided. Even though it was considered unfair and disappointing, workers still believe that Nokia was a good employer which offered excellent work conditions. This optimism might have been possible thanks to the extensive support provided by the traditional village organization. For the workforce, it immediately filled the gap that the unemployment created. Many workers went back to housework and continued to oversee their family plots. Thanks to this semi-subsistence economy the transition to reality after the relocation was easier. As most workers did not lose their sole source of income, they were able to wait for another investor and believe that there will be a place for them in the new organization.

The production node was shut down after four years of activity. When the plant closed, the dreams of modernization were also put on hold. The workplaces disappeared, and the production processes were over, to be reorganised in China. The movement of investments across political economies and production regimes propels the informalisation of labour and results in declining workers' rights and entitlements such as wages, social benefits or job security. Labour arbitrage is a form of capital accumulation by dispossession (Harvey, 1990). In new locations, investments cause enthusiasm, transformation and social change. At the same time, each of the new locations is competing with an unknown, geographically distant labour force that might end the benefits of the investment's presence (Cowie, 1999). The switch from Germany to Romania and further to China is a symbolic journey of the manufacturing industry. The old Western working class fails to be competitive, losing to the transitioning but geographically close Eastern Europe. As the case of the plant in Romania shows, other production regimes, such as dormitory production in China

(Pun, 2005; Pun and Smith, 2007), also influence this competition, participating in it on a global scale and outbidding other geographies.

The investor's logo was imprinted on the region's identity, and it took a long time to fade out. When talking about the changes caused by the investment, one of the community members told me that for a while the factory had been a "patron" of the village, which in Romanian means an employer and a boss, but also a caretaker, a saint. Even the church struggles with proving that saints actually help those who believe in them. The production node emerged as a promise to the local community. It was a highly visible modernizing agent. It signalled that change is inevitable, despite the fact that it was not instant. Many workers found it astonishing to be part of the plant producing phones for international markets. As one of the workers put it: "the phones ended up on the shelves of shops in Germany, France, Poland and other states in Europe. Some even went to Africa or Asia – the boxes were labelled, it was clear how far they can go". Over the course of the years the region got used to the plant. The experiences that I have described in this chapter reveal how the global capitalist system can be both oppressive and empowering. As the accounts show, workers that joined the labour force were on the one hand satisfied and committed to the job. Their job benefits and work environment were considered good and rarely contested. On the other hand, flexible contracts and low level of wages prevented them from achieving the desired upward mobility. The story of the plant complements other studies of labour in transiting economies (Cowie, 2005; Dunn, 2008; Nadeem, 2009), reflecting the turbulence and growing local expectations. The period of the investment's presence and the level of local engagement provide enough evidence to suggest that the mobility of production nodes is increasingly becoming a social issue. With the material I presented I hope to contribute to the visibility of this issue. It is a timely topic that needs to be further addressed in the context of the global production systems. I believe that the ethnographic account in this chapter provides the reader with a contextual, personal and emotional view that advances understanding of the reality of manufacturing work in the global economy.

CHAPTER 7

Coping with Loss: Local Agency and Offshored Labour

Similar to the events in Germany, the plant's operation was terminated, the workers were laid off and the plant's equipment was dispatched, while one of the other plants in the investor's global value chain took over the tasks of the production facility in Romania. The plant was left empty and to be leased to another investor. In this chapter, I concentrate on a number of relocation processes by reflecting on the reactions that took place in Romania after the investor's decision. I show how difficult it was to accept the fact that the investment ended. The relocation made major headlines and became a national issue. As I argue, coping with this decision was made additionally difficult due to the new sense of opportunity and quality of life offered by the investor that connected the town to the global capitalist system.

Accepting the end of capitalist production proved to be impossible. Stakeholders and commentators attempted to consider a new investor for the industrial zone, which could continue the production process. Various stakeholders tried to cope and an excessive amount of assets were developed to meet the expectations of the investor. The dissonance of the new situation was high. The relocation became a threat to perceived social progress and highly dependent on success of state reform and interest of outside capitalists. The relocation not only limited the opportunities for local work but also Romania's vision of future. It hurt the already weakened national self-esteem that went through a lot of suffering during the transition process. An important symbol of Romania's change all of a sudden moved and prematurely stopped the expected outcomes. Local workers and public opinion believed that the impasse connected to the relocation would be over once a new investor is found. Instead of a direct response to the investor's decision, Romanians chose to wait and believed that it was inevitable that a new investor would arrive.

Speculations over why the investor left, looking for fault in the global economy or Romania's political class, and diminishing the impact to prove that Romania might exist without Nokia, were all coping strategies. Vladimir Lenin referred to the capitalist practice of locating plants where highly immobile peasants could become factory workers as "when the factory goes to the muzhik", which applies to this situation (Lenin, 1967). Capital moves fast, surprising local populations not only by their arrival but also by their unexpected departure. Receiving communities face new challenges of rapid industrialization and modernization. Those that are left, try to cope. The new attitude of the local community, waiting for another investor, reveals features of Karl Marx's description of a "reserve army of labour" in *Das Kapital*. The reserve, composed of the proletariat, is an effect of the growing productivity of labour. The willingness to work is not enough in the face of a cost-based competition for labour. Understanding this notion helps to explain why the workforce and the public believed that the arrival of the new investor is inevitable and that waiting is the best strategy to undertake, instead of negotiating compensations or protesting.

> The greater the social wealth, the functioning capital, the extent and energy of its growth, and, therefore, also the absolute mass of the proletariat and the productiveness of its labour, the greater is the industrial reserve army. The same causes which develop the expansive power of capital, develop also the labour power at its disposal. The relative mass of the industrial reserve army increases therefore with the potential energy of wealth. But the greater this reserve army in proportion to the active labour army, the greater is the mass of a consolidated surplus population, whose misery is in inverse ratio to its torment of labour.
> MARX, 2001: 707

A concept that well compliments the idea of a reserve army of labour can be found in contemporary organisation studies. Jana Costas and Christopher Grey posited the concept of "imaginary future selves" to shed new light on the interplay of the workplace and subjectivity. They put forth:

> These imaginary future selves can be understood as postalgic; they are constructed around the fantasy of a better future self, which resists the professional self of disciplinary power regimes. Thus, they display the articulation of an alternative and more "positive" articulation of selfhood necessary for resistance. Imaginary future selves place an accent on the future; that is, the present self is approached through the fantasy of the future.
> COSTAS and GREY, 2014: 18

The case of the investor's relocation supports this claim. Despite the low-income nature of the positions offered in the plant, the community believed in the transformative power of the investor. The fantasy was based on middle-class dreams of development, urbanization, and progress. Nokia's industrial activity activated a broad spectrum of processes that attributed to Romanians' changing perception of their own position in the world, resulting from socio-economic shifts occurring after 1989.

Companies in global value chains leave more expensive locations and seek cost savings in cheaper locations. Costs shrink as a result of exploited populations and encourage further mobility. One of the pioneering works that described this process and its outcomes was Jeff Cowie's *Capital Moves* (Cowie, 1999). In the book, Cowie depicts how the RCA Corporation, American manufacturer of home electronics, changed its locations in response to the price of labour. Cowie, a historian of labour, starts in the 1930s when the plant's initial location was Camden, Memphis. Then, he outlines a series of moves, including to Bloomington, Indiana and Memphis, Tennessee. His story ends in Juarez, Mexico. Cowie's observation provides a really important and valuable insight into the nature of today's work. Cowie's approach laid the foundation for work and employment studies which study the dynamics of production relocations:

> The tile "Capital moves" implies not only geographic mobility but an entire series of social changes that industrial investment sets in motion on the local level. The rhythms of change pounded out at each site hardly cause North American workers to march in unison, but they do merge into a sort of staccato beat of social transformation. The excitement and civic plant of being awarded a plant by a major corporation, the initial awe inspired by labouring side by side with thousands of other workers in a vast industrial complex. (...) In all instances, however, any sense of entitlement was vulnerable as RCA workers found themselves competing with workers in distant places. Their locational and cultural resources were restricted and at times totally undermined by what to them was an abstract and faraway alternative to their own place.
>
> COWIE, 1999: 23

The strength of Cowie's argument lies in focusing on a single value chain, which is the constitutive element of the "race to the bottom", occurring over decades. The process of moving to different locations is propelled by the process of accumulation by dispossession, bringing informalisation of labour, and the decline of workers' rights and entitlements (Harvey, 1990). In this approach, a value chain emerges like a carrier of inequality, causing economic transformation in the newly penetrated locations. This theorization reflects the movement and allows us to understand the after-effects of the process. The example that Cowie describes illustrates how capital reshapes and reconfigures different geographies and local processes.

Another aspect of this shift is the neoliberal transition of receiving economies. Countries such as Romania, undergoing transition but not yet advanced economically, are labelled as middle-income economies in the literature. Typically, they show great reliance on foreign direct investments. Offshoring production stimulated economic activity in these states, often giving jobs to formerly peripheral communities. At the same time, some of them fell into a middle-income trap, unable to compete in export markets with lower-cost producers from elsewhere. This has been the case in Mexico, which faced the increased inflow of offshoring production since the 1960s that was consolidated in the 1980s and intensified after the signing of the North American Free Trade Agreement (NAFTA). Another case has been Eastern Europe, which plays a similar role in the European Union's integration process since the systemic transformation. Using low-cost labour resources, the manufacturing sector in both regions has bloomed in the last two decades. Labour in states that gradually underwent internationalization became a part of global production chains. The story of the investment in Romania exemplifies challenges taking place in these zones.

In the literature, a symbol of this transformation is the *maquiladora*. This production model is defined in Mexico by the Decree for Promotion and Operation of the Export Maquiladora Industry as "an industrial or service process that implies transformation, elaboration or repair of merchandise of foreign origin, permanently or temporarily imported for its later export" (translation by: de la Garza Toledo, 2007: 399). In the literature concerning labour, maquiladora became the name for offshoring practices based on exploitative labour. The notion of maquiladora production goes beyond the geographic area of Mexico and is applied to industrial zones in Latin America, Southern Asia or Eastern Europe. Maquiladora syndrome does not have any cross-national comparative value, however, and in the literature it serves as a conceptual model of low-cost industrial production, based on the assembly of imported components (Ellingstad, 1997; Pavlínek, 2004). The issues stemming from the "maquiladora syndrome" or "maquiladora industry" are transplanted to different socioeconomic contexts and reflect the relationship between low-cost labour and external capital in the semi-periphery. The maquiladora production process symbolizes production for export, mostly because of low internal demand, deskilling workers, extensive outsourcing with just-in-time parts delivery, and production in a geographically concentrated location often supported by migration from zones with a slack labour market (Ellingstad, 1997). The concept of maquiladora also carries powerful social implications, such as a power imbalance between workers and capitalists enforced for instance by responsibility-free hiring through subcontractors, low-paid work, few opportunities for unionization, job insecurity and part-time and temporary work (Bonacich and Appelbaum, 2000).

1 The Secrecy of the Contract

In Romania, the discussion about the relocation took place in reference to a number of stereotypes. Commonly capitalist reality was compared to communist Romania. A journalist that I met with on numerous occasions told me: "they did not tell the people anything under Ceausescu, and poor Romania got screwed. Now it's supposed to be a democracy, but the same thing is happening. Nobody gives a shit about the people. Everything is secret!" Another commentator, a local academic, was trying to convince me that the relocation reveals the incompetence of the elites. "Romania is still a communist place. Look at it. Nobody knows what happened. They create ministries and departments and give out the title of director to anybody who is simply loyal". The more facts about the industrial zone were revealed, the more radical that the public voice became. Despite the fact that Romania had been gradually opening to the global economy, it was still hard to believe that it was changing. The investor's exit re-activated already forgotten fears of a failed transformation as well as negative self-perception. In order to deal with the dissonance between the investor's exit and hopes for change, the public interpreted events in a paradoxical way that collided with their hopes (Burke and Stets, 1999). Psychologists understand familiarity functions as a mechanism of maintaining one's own personal assessment and coping with anxiety (Zajonc, 1968; Swap, 1977). Despite a big desire for change, many Romanians still pessimistically believed that their society is unable to reach the desired level of transition. Relocation again provided supportive evidence for this scepticism and served as confirmation. This caused a strong emotional reaction and launched adamant discussion about the future of transition.

The national discussion touched on broad, yet fundamental issues. In the winter of 2011, Romania witnessed a series of general protests. Hundreds of protestors marched every day in the major cities to address a range of interests, from opposition to austerity measures to support for putting former communists on trial. One of the leaders of the protests in Cluj-Napoca yelled the following in the freezing cold:

> Ministers ought to speak Romanian; look at what happened in Jucu. They don't represent the interests of the nation. They are traitors. They behave like they were employees of Nokia, not the public. They all bring shame to this nation.
> Protestor

A similar tone echoed on the streets, in the buses and everywhere where politics was debated. Often peopled posed this rhetorical question, expressing their inability to take action: "what can we do about it?"

These emotions were at the heart of the reaction of the media and public opinion. They gave birth to many speculations about the contract signed with Nokia. The contract was signed in 2008, and the Romanian public did not know what it contained, as it was confidential, and its conditions have not been publicised. After the decision to relocate the investment, the media speculated about the contents of the agreement as they usually contain a specific minimum stay period. One of the newspaper illustrations from that time contained a picture of a file with an inscription of "Nokia" and the "Top Secret" stamp (*Faclia*, 2011.10.1–2). Other voices urged that it is "secret even though access to this information is of public interest" (*Gazeta de Cluj*, 2011.10.24–30). The media pointed out that the Cluj County built necessary infrastructure as well as invested in elements that the investor had never used, such as the train platform for workers in the industrial zone. Another local academic told me what he thinks about the contract: "Of course [the authorities] must have an interest in protecting themselves. It's obvious that they must have either taken a bribe or been really stupid to sign a contract like that".

Alin Tișe, serving as the president of Cluj County in 2012, said at a press conference: "we are analysing all of the possibilities that are compliant with the contractual agreements. Some of them would be a violation of mandatory clauses made by Nokia, but I would say that this contract was very, very, very, very well done for Nokia" (*Ziua de Cluj*, 2011.10.06). His comment outraged the public. It signified that the agreement signed in 2008 was unfair to the Romanians. Instead of representing public interests, the officials were thought to be desperate to secure the investment and did not negotiate. Tișe continued:

> In the same measure we are analysing this contract very thoroughly, because as you know, Nokia has ninety hectares in the park [refers to the whole industrial zone, including space intended for the suppliers], not only the thirty where the plant is located. There are ninety hectares which were reserved for Nokia and which were supposed to be occupied

by subcontractors. This did not happen there. So now we are analysing the contract with Tetarom, including clauses concerning subcontractors.
>   *Ziua de Cluj*, 2011.10.06

The news astonished the public and caused speculation. Some of it was very far-reaching and held accusations of corruption and sabotage. Opinions, such as the one described above, appeared in the media and resembled a discussion about publicizing the secret service files in post-communist states. The hypothetical content of the contract was an emotional subject. The more the public opinion was pressing the officials, the more details were revealed. Leaks appeared in the media. The discussion brought on another speculation-based controversy, namely that the officials did not keep the promises stated in the contract. Even though the official version of the document has never been revealed, a leaked list of legal obligations of the local authorities contained a large list of infrastructural projects. Some were never started.

One of my interviewees, a junior-level employee from the local government, described the situation in the office to me and the initial reaction of authorities.

> Once the news got to my boss, the news dragged us down. Nokia is a global firm but even they lost during the crisis. Then everybody got paranoid, there was no minimum time in the contract. Shit! That was a stupid mistake that [the officials] made. The only obligation that Nokia has towards Cluj County is that in case they leave they are supposed to leave the industrial park in the same way they received it, so without the plant. But the other thing is that there is a possibility to negotiate to buy the production halls from Nokia. In case the authorities say no, Nokia can renegotiate with other parties.
>   Junior-level government employee

The contract with the investor did not define the minimum time or penalize the investor in case the factory was closed or its activity suspended. There was no way to sanction the investor. The fact that there was no way to stop the decision caused panic among authorities, which was amplified by the media storm. Very few among the journalists and readers were sympathetic to the officials. One of the Romanian politicians told me that in his opinion it was an obvious mistake which should be used to blame only the authorities.

> Would you think that somebody who invested 90 million euros would leave after four years? Seriously, would you put a minimum-stay period

> in a contract with a really serious partner? It would have been offensive. It was all decided on the county level. The central government had nothing to do with it. The zone was built from Cluj County's budget and everything was done through the County officials. If people are angry, they should look for the reasons at home, in Cluj.
>
> Romanian politican

This interviewee emphasized that a similar mistake could have happened to anybody, as the scale of the investment was tremendous. In his view the blame of the local government and its advisors was apparent.

Similar opinions were taken by opposition members, blaming the current rulers. Around the time of the investor's departure, one of the strongest opponents of the local authority's actions was Marius Nicoară, a member of parliament and a former president of Cluj County council, who participated in the negotiation of contract. His party, the National Liberal Party (PNL) was at that time the second biggest party in Romania. He argued the following in one of the press interviews:

> We signed [the contract] and promised that we will turn this field into an industrial park. We made roads, added water, energy. It was about 15–16 million euros. In fact, there was also an obligation to make a landing strip for cargo airplanes which was supposed to be finished by 2010. Not much was done and there is no development in that domain. All of it was going to Budapest. Nokia was looking for a cargo terminal so that they can send stuff to Mexico or India. Nokia invested about 60 million euros for which the factory was built and equipped.
>
> *Faclia*, 2011.10.1–2

For the public it was difficult to believe that the investor's decision could be based solely on rationality and the cost of labour. The media transmitted a chaotic message about the underlying causes and predicted effects, implying that there could be many other reasons. The claims were often contradictory to one other. The buzz about prospective investors, reasons for relocation, and the difficult internal situation was omnipresent.

One of the articles commenting on the situation was entitled "Bye-bye Nokia: A lesson for Romania". The author argued that the state should go through the loss but finally learn a lesson and respect the investors:

> We have to change the attitude that we base our actions on the activities of Romanian investments. I am not saying that we are against foreign

investments; they bring a lot of investment potential. We should treat them correctly by not blocking them.

Mesagerul de Cluj, 2011.10.3–9

In another article entitled "Good bye Nokia, Welcome, Bosch!" another author wrote:

Referring to the title of this editorial, I don't know if Bosch will come to Cluj County for sure, but I am certain that foreign firms will find us. And now we need to be hospitable. A friendly environment is an obligatory condition for the infusion of capital.

Gazeta de Cluj, 2011.10.24–30

In 2011 Romania witnessed a wave of protests that were aimed against the introduced austerity measures connected to Romania's difficult economic situation. The lack of interest in supporting foreign investment appears in almost all of the commentaries and political discussions about Nokia. Fatalism manifested in almost zero trust in the ruling class. When the factory announced its departure in autumn, the internal situation in Romania was quite difficult. The state was facing austerity measures, which cut down public wages. The economic crisis slowed down the Romanian economy and despite accession to the European Union, Romania was very slow to use structural funds. When the factory closure was announced, it caused further disappointment. A protest leader that I met asked me rhetorically: "Who leaves something that's good?"

2   Smartphone Controversy

When Romanians faced the fact that the highly appreciated investor is leaving the country, they also tried to find blame in its actions. Even though the workplace practices in Nokia's plant were regarded as fair, transparent and worker-oriented, it was the corporate management of the global value chain that received criticism. Around that time, the investor's position in the world-scale market was shrinking. Many Romanians believed that it was because the products of the firm were outdated, often evidenced by the range of products assembled in the Romanian plant like lower-segment phones for both Western economies and the emerging markets. With the investor's problems, it was clear that it lost not only its own global position but also affected Romanians. The day the relocation was announced, I spoke to one of the workers who expressed his disappointment and repeated that wrong decisions caused the investor's failure: "they should produce phones people want to buy". This argument became one of the coping strategies. I call it the "smartphone controversy" as its main symbol is a mobile phone equipped with advanced computing capabilities and connectivity. The difficult situation of the investor was tied to the failed innovation process. Innovation made the investor a world leader long before the smartphone era.

Nokia's difficulties started in the mid-2000s, many years before the plant in Romania was established. Between 2008 and 2010, so the time of early operations of the plant, Nokia was still a strong actor on the global market, but its profits and leadership started to shrink. In its history, the manufacturer won the most important battles on the mobile phone market, such as popularising mobile phones with high definition cameras or integrating data transmission with broadly distributed mobile phones (Syrett and Devine, 2012). Even though Nokia was persistently setting trends and remained the synonym of "cool" for a decade, it failed to win with Apple, which introduced the iPhone in 2008 (Sjöblom and Terhi, 2013). From this moment, Nokia stopped being an icon and a prestigious symbol of modern technologies, and it turned into a synonym of failed ideas and strategies. The popularity of the new generation of mobile phones created an entirely new mobile phone experience (Giachetti, 2013). The iPhone had a large 3.5-inch display and instead of a traditional keyboard it was equipped with a touch screen. Instead of a basic operating system, such as Nokia's Symbian, iPhone used colourful animated icons and offered numerous applications. It was fully integrated with the internet. Users could check e-mails, browse the internet and install often updated applications. Even though the competitors, including Nokia, already offered similar technological parameters, it was Apple that integrated those elements in an easily navigable device that was also portable and innovative in its design (Fisk, 2010). The iPhone was costly, but very quickly it became one of the most desired gadgets and its popularity has not faded.

The problems of the Nokia Corporation were observed in Romania. At a conference that I attended in 2010, a consultant from a multinational audit firm said: "Nokia is shaking, but they have enormous budgets. They will figure it out and eat Apple. They had the touch screen ready in 2001. The market has enough space and Apple is for snobs; it's not good and too expensive". But even in 2010 it was already clear that Nokia's future was unsure. Since 2009, Nokia started to adapt to the smartphone market and refocus to change its strategy. One of the attempts to regain leadership was the launch of the Lumia series, a collaboration between Nokia and Microsoft. Their first phone, Nokia Lumia 800, almost like the first cousin of the iPhone, was launched on October 26,

2011 – about a month after the closure. Romania's most read economic newspaper reported:

> The problems of the Nokia Corporation are not new. The company underwent major changes in the last years, in general because of a failing corporate strategy. The market has changed substantially in the last three years after 3G was introduced, which supports fast data transfer. The Finns were first in line with intelligent terminals, like the Nokia Communicator, a telephone which cost 1000 euro, the best in its sector. But then the iPhone was launched by Apple. The Apple revolution changed mobile telephones and put the company in the first place. The niche was also taken by Google and Android, which is in most of the non-Apple devices including Microsoft [which provides the system for the Nokia devices], which has lost the battle for this segment of operating systems. Nokia was losing with time (...) Profits were sustained but the devices use Symbian operating system. It became a dinosaur operating system. With time, clients started to give up. The Finns are not the only ones who lost terrain; similarly RIM, the maker of Blackberry, is not sustaining its place and its market shrunk.
> *Capital*, 2011.10.10–17

The smartphone controversy reflected Nokia's inability to innovate and the realities of the industrial workforce manufacturing the phones. In Romania this controversy had two dimensions. Firstly, the problem lay in the fact that the manufacturer did not produce phones in Romania but only assembled them, and thus its role was much less significant than it was commonly thought. Public discussion strongly emphasized this fact. Secondly, the problem was rooted in the fact that the plant in Romania was assigned the models from the lowest segment of Nokia's offer. As the lower-end mobile phone market was shrinking in Europe, the decision to focus on the cheaper products put the jobs in Romania at risk, or, as my interviewees argued, resulted in the factory's closure.

When the investor was coming to Romania, public opinion expressed the enthusiasm for Nokia's products. With its departure, and because of the smartphone controversy, Nokia's products became a symbol of failure. A headline of Romania's biggest economic newspaper called the plant "a factory of stupid-o-phones" (*Capital*, 2011.10.3–9). Radical criticism was echoed in the mainstream media with a number of buzzwords and catchy phrases. Nokia's official slogan "Nokia – Connecting People" was turned into "Nokia – Disconnecting Romanian people" to describe the situation (*Servus Cluj*, 2011.09.30). The other comments included very inventive slogans, such as "Osana Fin Landen" (*Academia*

Catavencu, 2011.10.5–11). A comic strip from one of the most important satirical journals in Romania, *Academia Catavencu*, summarises Nokia's departure by depicting an employee, who is about to be dismissed, listening to this message: "[Nokia officials] – When we leave, we will give you a phone. [employee] – If it could have a camera…" (*Academia Catavencu*, 2011.10.5–11). The employee's request might be read as an expression of worry that he is afraid of getting one of the phones produced in Romania.

The smartphone controversy presented the investor as a bad decision maker that was not interested in Romania's most valuable asset: its intellectual potential. As one of the local government employees commented: "Nokia saw Romania as a low-income country. We are not. We have a highly qualified workforce and if they used it maybe they could have been ahead on the smartphone market". A repeated argument against the investor was the fact that it focused on cost-cutting rather than innovation. At the same time the management of Nokia emerged as unaware of the effects of the decision. One of the commentators explained: "I think that the news is incredible. I have said that it's impossible to understand how you can do an investment and close it within two years. I don't think that it has amortised" (*Ziarul Financiar*, 2011.10.5).

A side effect of the smartphone controversy was increasing hostility towards the investor. Emotional reactions were stimulated by the tabloid press. Taxi drivers, a specific mirror of society, kept convincing me that the investor should be sanctioned. "Nokia fooled Romanians and it should get the treatment that it deserves [refers to the idea of state confiscation of the plant's equipment]". On the political scene, Romanian populists reacted to the investor's decision by stressing the dark intentions of foreign investors. Ioan Rus, a former Minister of Internal Affairs stressed that Nokia is an "industrial predator" and argued that, "the representatives of the Romanian state have been fooled with the promises of the Finnish corporation". (*Ziua de Cluj*, 2011.10.8). A local official diagnosed that Nokia just "started a war with the Romanian economy". Another interviewee, an employee of the shop floor, told me his reaction: "I am pissed off. Nokia made Romanians believe in its good will and now it turned its back. I get red [from anger] any time I think about looking for a job".

3   Romania in the Global Economy

The relocation showed that political agency was limited. The political class did not have any capacity or experience in negotiating with a relocating investor or representing workers' interests. The decision makers operated on symbols and emotions. Media speculations about the future of the zone heated up the public discourse. On all levels, the decision makers strongly criticized the decision, showing sympathy towards the workers. President Traian Basescu made a strong speech, condemning the investor for leaving Romania. He also criticized other foreign manufacturers for a smaller than promised scale of production and employment. For instance, he mentioned an automotive producer that "instead of producing cars, as planned, produces small trailers". The comments of politicians reflected the feelings of Romanians – disappointment from the impossibility of realizing the ambitious plans of foreign investors mixed with anger at their rational, often cruel strategies. There was no effective way of stopping the investor from leaving or renegotiating the decision. No procedure existed for coping with similar exits. The regional agency, which collaborated with the investor and managed the industrial zone, was helpless. Its officials were rejecting contact with the public yet promised to find a new investor for the zone. Some of them confidentially emphasized that because of the experiences with the investment, the priority in the future negotiations with new investors will be the minimum presence period. A contract with Nokia did not contain such a clause. Few weeks after the decision was made public, a brochure with the plant's rental offer was issued.

During the existence of the global production node, two parties of the FDI transaction co-existed in a seemingly perfect symbiosis. Even though the investor's decision was based on rational calculation, local observers appreciated the choice of the Nokia Corporation and in a way felt honoured by its presence. Once the global production node was about to be relocated, they realized that the seemingly special position is nothing more than an illusion. The experience with the relocation generated new awareness of Romania's own position in the globalizing world. The investment was large in its scale and it affected thousands of livelihoods. The symbolic power of relocation embraced the whole nation. Romanians realized for the first time how illusory neoliberal progress could be.

> We foresaw what was happening in the world since the spring. Everything happens in the context of global crisis. Multinationals do not have a mom, or a dad, only their filthy interests. They all move to Asia which has cheaper production, and there is the chance that the other multinationals will leave Cluj too.
>
> *Mesagerul de Cluj*, 2011.10.23–30

Economic instability caused problems throughout Europe since the economic crisis had started. Eastern Europe was touched significantly. Nokia's decision was often perceived as an effect of external economic conditions. It became clear that global economic problems have potential impact on the performance of the Nokia Corporation's value chain and its plant in Romania. The decision to relocate the plant was an impulse for further considerations about national economy's protection and prevention of similar problems.

> Romania cannot develop without foreign capital in the next 20–30 years. There is no strength in internal capital, the workforce is decreasing, and those factors do not permit fast economic growth. We are an emerging economy and need FDI.
> *Ziarul Financiar*, 2011.09.30

Experts, expressing their opinions in national media, postulated changes in the way to approach investors. These included introducing new measures that could support Romanian firms, perceived as less dependent on global capital and thus less prone to external influence. Cornel Itu, a member of Parliament from PSD, argued:

> The global economic crisis and the episode with Nokia gave us a lesson. The future is gloomy. What can we do? Two things: decrease taxes that firms and the workforce pay until we can have the smallest level in the region, including VAT, and support the development of Romanian firms.
> Cornel Itu, member of Parliament

The most radical discussions mentioned an argument that multinationals ought not to be trusted because their decision about where to locate is not permanent and based solely on economic interest. Because of the lack of sentiment, the only motivation for these actors is profit. The same argument was further continued by Itu:

> Everything was constructed for [for Nokia], completely how they wanted. But in fact, nobody in Romania should expect them that they will stay. If a company does not belong to one place, economic decisions are made quite easily. Production is cheaper in China. Of course, they go to China. I think that this should be an impulse to appreciate Romanian companies. They never left Romania, despite hard conditions in Romania. Of course, they can move production, but many don't do it.
> Cornel Itu, member of Parliament

Another argument points at the other geographies, notably Southeast Asia, which was one of the key markets for phone models produced in the industrial zone in Romania. It echoed a perspective raised by the Vice-President of Nokia, Eric Anderson, who publically admitted that the plant produced lower-end phones for Asian markets from Asian components. According to him, production in Romania did not make sense logistically:

> Your position was firm in the sense that it had nothing to do with conditions in Romania and your economic conditions. An important aspect which led to this decision was the fact that our subcontractors are from Asia and transport of the materials to Romania is very expansive for Nokia. This is why we preferred to move the activity to another existing plant in order to use the components from Asia for products in Asian markets.
> *Gazeta de Cluj*, 2011.10.24–30

The discussion of markets in which the investor has operated brought about arguments connected to price of labour and compared security and employment conditions in Romania. The commentators often argued that the workers' situation in Romania is much better than in the lower-income countries. In fact, Romanian workers have received low wages despite being protected by the law; their situation was far from ideal. But the media commentators were highly sceptical about life there, most often pointing at China and its lack of freedom and poverty. At the same time, my local interviewees often mentioned all kinds of imagined low-income states such as Morocco, Bangladesh, Turkey, Vietnam, China or India and expressed their disapproval of the starvation wages. Those opinions expressed the fear about competition with Asia, backed by claims about the investors' immoral practices and arguments that presence in the low-income markets might not be morally justifiable. For instance, an editorial entitled "I got myself a Blackberry", emphasizes how unethical practices play a key role in world production.

> Nokia is moving to Bangladesh and I see that their people are not used to eating three times a day. And this is what all multinationals do. Why don't they go to Sweden or Finland where the taxes are high and you have to pay the workers 3–4 thousand euro per week? They came from Germany and Bochum here, and they made us bankrupt. And now the Germans can't be mad anymore… Nokia is going? Go! Africa is not colonized, so the Aborigines are waiting… This is my small protest, an essential need, my tribute to Maslov; I eat three times a day.
> *Servus Cluj*, 2011.09.03

The passage illustrates how global labour relations were understood by those who were affected by the relocation. The author of this editorial points out that a similar situation happened in Germany, before the investor left for Romania, and asks about the new direction. Similar stereotypical judgments emerged on the Romanian streets. Once, in an informal conversation, I spoke to a man who emphasized that wherever the investor moved, people will be working "for a bowl of rice" (I3). Many of my interviewees did not hold it against the investor, arguing that the exploitative potential of Nokia was limited by different measures, including the European Union.

The comparison to Germany had an important function in understanding the situation. It helped to see the inevitable force of relocation. The understanding relied on the following perception: Germans were unable to cope with the decision made by the investor, so it is near impossible to argue with the investor for Romanians. However, observing the way in which Germans dealt with the relocation by accepting it but strongly negotiating compensations for the layoffs, inspired many ideas. The questions about the amount of received compensations seemed like a test for the role of Romania in the international market. Because German workers' wages were very high, as some newspapers reported, "ten times higher than Romanian" (*Adevărul*, 2011.10.02), German compensations were also high. Some Romanian newspapers literally wrote about fortunes. The media was building up the expectation of increasing the compensations by inviting numerous experts, also from Germany. For instance, a column entitled "Bye, bye Nokia! Compensations of 200 million" described the experience of Bochum (*Mesegerul de Cluj*, 2011,10.10–16). The main part of it was an interview with the leader of a German union. Ulrike Kleinebrahm represented IG Metal Bochum and was in charge of German negotiations with Nokia. In the interview she stressed, "Categorically, the workers of Nokia ought to benefit from these compensations". The most important question that was asked in the paper was "how many salaries will Romanians receive?"

The relational value of compensations was fed by the statistics and costs that Romanian authorities have covered in order to prepare the investment. For instance *Adevărul* counted:

> Germans received 60 salaries in compensations, Romanians – only six. When the factory in Bochum was closed, Finns paid the value of 200 euros in the form of compensations and requalification courses. Each of the 2.300 employees got more or less 80,000 euros [$110,000], which is the equivalent of 60 salaries. Nokia paid 30 million to the local government as a form of reimbursement".
>
> *Adevărul*, 2011.10.02

Similar calculations were also discussed by one of the employees of the local government. The employee has showed me the notes with his own calculations:

> After the German precedent, Romanian authorities should get part of the money spent in order to prepare the investment in order to attract Nokia to Cluj: value about 20 million euros. Nokia received 90 of 157 hectares in the Industrial Park Tetarom III and local government allocated 12 million euros [$16 mln] in infrastructure. Only connecting the utilities to the estate cost about 3 million euros [$4.5mln]. Ten million [$14mln] came from the local authorities and the rest from the state.
> Local government employee

The general conclusion of these comparisons and summaries was that Romania ought to approach the investor and strongly negotiate. The emphasis was often put on Romania's membership in the European Union. As one of the reporters told me during one of the interviews, "we are in Europe and we should be treated like the other countries".

4 The New Investor

The most important question asked in Romanian media was about the future investor. The region, as well as national commentators, hoped that the zone could start living again. People waited in the belief that Nokia's presence in the area had integrated it with the global economy and made it a competitive location. The industrial zone was understood as a gateway to the global economy. The necessary infrastructure already existed. The workers experienced the modern work environment and adapted to the organization of work. The hosting community gained experience in dealing with an investment of such scale. Observing the discussion surrounding the investor's departure, it is apparent that it caused a strong reaction requiring adaptation to the situation. The main coping mechanisms aimed to re-establish faith in continuous activity in the industrial zone and sustain the established scalar order.

Despite the investor's plan to move the production, the media transmitted the message that many other work opportunities exist in Romania and it is still an attractive destination for other investors. For instance, an optimistic prognosis was present in the article entitled "Romania will be the new Poland with or without Nokia" (*Ziua de Cluj*, 2011.10.08). Even though these statements were often not backed by facts, they stimulated local faith. The more statements were circulated, the easier it was to accept them and believe in the colourful future. Phenomenologists would point out that this process is connected it to self-direction and group processes (Brehm and Brehm, 1981). An interviewee, a consultant from Bucharest, shared this view: "The discussion makes sense because the investment will be made because it is an excellent location and an up-to-date plant. Hungary is just four hours from Cluj!" (I11)

Diminishing the role of Nokia helped to forget about it and supported the belief that it was not the only large-scale investor that could be investing in Romania. Many arguments focused on showing the stability of Romania's economic situation and broad availability of other opportunities and investments. In an interview with the Minister of Transportation Anca Boagi titled "The whole world wants to invest in Romania", the Minister assures readers that there is a strong interest in continuing investments, and despite the economic crisis, Romania remains a very attractive destination for foreign investors (*Adevărul*, 2011.10.14). Similarly, opinions of representatives of multinational corporations in Romania claimed that the country provides an excellent environment for business. For example, the CEO of one of the multinationals assured: "There is no motive for Evaluserve to consider leaving Cluj. The labour market in Cluj is rising to the level that we want. Outside of talent, high qualifications and education, Cluj offers cultural proximity which our European clients need". (*Servus Cluj*, 2011.09.30). All opinions of experts confirmed the region continues to be an attractive location for international business.

The recovery from the initial shock was based reconnecting the industrial zone, as well as Romania, and reengaging with the world. As initially there were no decisions made regarding the zone's future, the commentators in the media argued that there is a market competition for investments in Romania. The head of the institution administering industrial parks in the region, commented on investor's departure:

> Nokia's departure from Cluj will affect the decisions of other investors. There is a big interest in the zone. But in a very positive sense. It's evident that there is an unused niche of about five thousand people ready to work. There is actually a lack of a workforce because the unemployment rate is about 3% and it's difficult to accommodate all of the needs of investors.
>
> *Mesagerul de Cluj*, 2011.10.3–9

Local newspapers kept a similar tone by painting a vision that the perceived failure might actually bring positive outcomes because the established, trusted investors might expand their activity to the abandoned industrial zone, hiring the workforce.

> Life after Nokia exists and major multinationals have "major plans" in Romania. (...) The closing of the plant by Nokia does not mean that the other multinational corporations will leave. Emmerson, Evaluserve, Bombardier and other multinationals are continuing the process of expansion in the region. The risk that Nokia generated a domino effect does not exist.
> *Servus Cluj*, 2011.10.03

Headlines brought information depicting visions of new developments. Removal of dependence on Nokia stimulated alternative visions of the future. One of the largest newspapers wrote about "Our foreign investments of 160 million euros" and showed "the other side of the medal" so future investments, which potentially could bring "a massive amount of hires and millions of euro" (*Adevărul*, 2011.10.06). The claims blurred the sense of a loss. Instead, a specific resistance to the relocation was born and restored transactional power of decision-making taken away by the investor.

Romania's Prime Minister Emil Boc assured that the region "is like *El Dorado* for investors" (*Bursa*, 2011.10.10). The possibility of realizing investments was reinstated. The most important question was to identify who the next investor would be. Romania was excited about the speculations. They started immediately when the investor's decision was made public. The discussion included questions about what type of industry there could be instead of mobile phone production, how many people hired, and what outcomes and profits it could bring. The informal "leaks" started to appear in the press: "two new investors are interested in buildings of Nokia in Jucu" (*Monitorul de Cluj*, 2011.10.07) or "Chinese want the Nokia plant" (*Monitorul de Cluj*, 2011.10.19). My study revealed fourteen company names that were mentioned as interested in moving into the industrial zone. The nominated major successors of Nokia were:

- IBM – interested in creating 3000 workplaces in Romania
- Tata Motors – interested in realizing investment in the Nokia's zone in proximity to the initial plant's location
- Bosh – a hardware producer
- Huawei – intentions were declared to create a centre of global support with plans of creating over 1500 jobs
- Ericsson – no details
- ZTE Group – no details

The investor's departure was a strong impulse for Romanian entrepreneurs. Some of them expressed interest in taking over the plant and expanding their activity in the building that was soon to be abandoned by Nokia. The most spectacular proposal was by Irina Schrotter, a Romanian fashion designer. Schrotter expressed interest in investing in the zone by sending a letter of intent and claiming that she would be potentially interested in opening a production unit in the former factory (*Ziua de Cluj*, 2011.10.05). The news was broadly commented in the press. Some voices were rather sceptical.

The radical voices used the rhetoric of economic nationalism and postulated closing for foreign investors (D'Costa, 2012; Helleiner and Pickel, 2005). Those opinions included visions of supporting Romanian firms, which could have the potential to expand their activity into the global market. The state could support them by giving exclusive tax benefits and real estate allowances. One of the experts, working for the Ministry of Finance, had the idea to start the activity of a Romanian plant producing mobile phones.

> I present our intention to invest in Jucu where the Nokia factory was in order to realize a Romanian mobile telephone based on Romanian patents. (…) I think that this is the best moment for the Romanian industry so that it could be reaffirmed in our country. We could profit fast, with technological structure and personnel from Nokia that could be engaged in a Romanian firm.
> *Ziua de Cluj*, 2011.10.04

The view that the Romanian economy has great potential and ought to be supported by the state was also repeated during the meetings of political leaders with workers. The temporary nature of the investment did not prevent Romanians from feeling connected to global production. The unexpected departure of production lines proved that the feeling of connectedness to global production is less stable than it is commonly assumed. There clearly was a shared view that no matter what happens, the role of the investor had expired. What was left was an existing connection, which permitted participation in global production and experience of "global labour", knowledge of the work culture or modern equipment. All workers were hoping for a new investor and new positions at the plant. And so did all Romanians.

5 Discussion: National Reaction to the Issue of Relocation

Nokia's investment in Romania began in 2008 and ended in 2012. The events that follow the investor's decision to depart illustrate the argument that nation states are unable to control the processes of globalization. Middle-income economies, due to their lack of experience, prove to be more exposed to the effects of the global race to the bottom. Once the decision to relocate happened, the community of workers completely failed to organize, mobilize, protest or react in any other way than grief. They completely gave up their bargaining power and permitted others, media and politicians, to deal with their problem. National media immediately picked up the topic, reflected on the problem of relocation and analysed it. The industrial zone's relocation became a front-page issue. The decision of the Nokia Corporation caused a national discussion about the state, its ruling class, and the level of systemic transition. Because of the investor's decision, the general assessment was low, pairing with self-held stereotypes and existing problems. Difficulties in coping with the reality of the outcomes resonated nationally. In a short moment the industrial zone went from national success to failure. Fatalism gave birth to speculations and theories about the contents of the secret contract with the investor. The public realized that participation in the global value chain might also do harm. Wrong actions and decisions made on the corporate level have led to problems. The end of the investment in Romania showed how unattainable the mechanisms of the global economy are. Learning the strength of the impact of the investor's decision also permitted an understanding of the German experience, who previously lost the plant to Romania. Like what has already occurred in the Western world, capital movement caused layoffs and problems also in only recently transiting Romania.

For Romanians the relocation became a symbol of the negative effects of involvement in the global economy. At the national level, the possibility of intervention was rather limited. It was impossible to change the decision. Global events caused confusion. Romanian authorities admitted their mistake of not defining the minimum time of the investor's presence in the contract. The commentators and media also showed how there was no good way out of it and the only possibility was to accept the fact that the investor left. A similar strategy was already undertaken by the workers and the hosting community. The experience of the investment reflects the difficult position of the emerging markets in the global economy. The drive to adapt to market realities of those economies and a desire for global competitiveness often causes oversight of the potential side effects of neoliberalism. The pressure for social normalization and economic prosperity, the desires of middle class idyll, made it difficult to think about the possible problems caused by the global economy.

With the investor's departure, its former workforce joined the global reserve army of labour, waiting for new opportunities from another investor. It was a painful experience for all stakeholders to learn that they were only a stage in the race to the bottom. Romania's seemingly competitive position in Europe, geographically close to West European markets, politically stable, with a relatively inexpensive labour force, industrial zones and offering numerous benefits, turned out to be not enough for the investor. The only reason given to the hosting side was that the relocation happened because of a cost-cutting strategy. It remained unclear and unexplained why the investor left and despite the official justification, it was only considered one of the interpretations. Factors, such as lack of transparency, gave birth to speculations. For instance, investor's competitiveness has been identified as key factor influencing the relocation. Accepting the rational explanation of the global cost-competition was difficult as so many resources were mobilized in response to the investor's activity. All of the investment-specific infrastructural and cultural elements described in the previous chapters were generated in order to meet the investor's needs in Romania. As a result of the investor's exit, all parties involved in the investment were determined to continue it. With this situation, it became clear that the way out of this situation is to find a new investor. Romanians believed that this was not the end of industrial production. They believed that in the nearest future the industrial zone would continue its activity with another large investor. A lottery of names of possible investors circulated in the press and in local discussions. Many expected the new investor to be as large and as successful as Nokia was when it arrived to Romania. Those actions strongly proved international dependence. The labour force turned into the reserve army of workers, ready to be mobilized whenever needed and believing in its own role and the importance in the global production chain.

CONCLUSIONS

Labour Arbitrage, Modernity and the Realities of Offshored Labour

The globalisation of production has caused the workforce to be very dependent on the condition of international markets. Regardless of the sector, competition on the global labour market has become fiercer. The central concept that drives offshoring is labour arbitrage, which is based on the savings that an organisation may make by hiring labour in a location abroad where it is cheaper to do so (Hollinshead et al., 2011). Labour arbitrage effectively reduces the bargaining power of employees in favour of their employers. Offshoring practices, the relocations of businesses from one place to another, transform not only organisations but also the way employees engage in work. In the new locations, the introduction of new regimes of production offers lower labour costs, new organisation of work and improved efficiency (Brass, 2011). Factory workers in more advanced economies lose.

Labour arbitrage is a social issue. Offshoring leads to wealth creation for organisations but not necessarily for countries, regions, or foremost employees (Levy, 2005). Nation states, progressively integrating both economically and politically, struggle to control production processes. With offshoring, their sovereignty remains challenged in a vast number of spheres (Sassen, 1996; Krasner, 1999; Cohen, 2012). Complete lack of protection and control over the labour process leads to the intensive cost-competition race between hosting populations (Rudra, 2008; Brass, 2011). No geography is left aside. Advanced Western economies with long industrial pasts face factory closures (Rousseau, 2011; Mollona, 2009; Blyton and Jenkins, 2012), adapt to offshoring (Nadeem, 2009) and try to cope with industry re-structuring. Participating in this competition, the contenders, usually less powerful economies, actively expand their global engagements by offering privileges and lower costs of labour. As this competition has no end, it is known as the "race to the bottom" in labour costs (Rudra, 2008; Collins and Mayer, 2010). The further down the costs go, the bigger the potential net profits. The decrease in costs is proportional to the decrease not only in salary levels and work conditions but also in the scope of labour movements and workers' rights (Clawson, 2003; Silver, 2003).

Grand theories of economic globalisation interpret distant, forgotten geographies as a source of energy for the process of economic development. My research has provided an ethnographic account of the East European periphery to convey the meanings, lived experiences and emotions experienced locally by a global production node of a foreign investor. Michael Burawoy argues that the ethnographer has privileged insight into the lived experience of globalisation (Burawoy, 2000). For Burawoy, global ethnography means "releasing fieldwork from solitary confinement, from being bound to a single place and time" (Burawoy, 2000: 4). Similar to classically understood ethnography, the underlying assumption of this research approach is that it is possible to gain an analytical and critical understanding of the described experiences by examining how specific actors reflect on them or call them into question.

In this book I have shown how ethnography can be an important tool for studying the on-the-ground effects of global capitalism, specifically those of a manufacturing plant on a post-socialist population. In the study, I understand the plant as a place of global assemblage (Ong and Collier, 2005), which represents the transformation caused by the interaction of diverse scales of social processes. This notion exposes the specific context and outcomes of the production node's presence, such as the new arrangements of culture and power. Bridging the perspective of global political economy with context-specific ethnographic data, I have outlined the double meaning of offshoring. On the one hand, it encourages middle-class dreams and fantasies, and on the other, it functions as a source of social problems and tensions resulting from the global arbitrage.

"Rational choice is the heart of the microeconomic model of economic man, who is portrayed as a logical thinker who evaluates options and inputs consistently and coherently, and selects those that maximize his utility" (Oritz, 2005: 63). In this study I have explored the dynamics of the encounter between the global economy and local realities. Neoliberal rationality penetrated the workforce in the region and the local participation in the global production of the investor generated a challenge to the status quo. After more than 20 years of economic turbulence, the Romanian population expected change. In the first decades of the transitions, the country struggled with transitory realities, problems with the legal framework, a disappearing industry and shrinking job market. In the next decade, despite celebrating small steps towards the normalization of life, the system started to open, but at the same time, in trying to ensure competitiveness, it conformed to free market realities by adapting neoliberal policies and reducing the amount of worker protections and welfare benefits. These attempts were strengthened by the global economic crisis, which in Romania resulted in radical austerity measures in the public sector and further legal changes that removed worker protections. One of the most radical changes has been the new labour law, which impacted the labour market with a set of new regulations increasing the flexibility of contracts and reducing the amount of employer responsibilities.

In this work, I have depicted the dynamics of two different forces: the rationality of the investor and the local culture. Similar to other transforming geographies of Eastern Europe, local adaptation to neoliberal policy was bound with rationality and coped with the transformative social environment of the evolving state. The local population, just as in other states in the region, adopted the free market and the development models of old Western economies and the view that it is a way towards economic growth and lifestyle change. From the beginning it was clear that calculation and economic rationality were the driving force behind the investment. Aside from rational calculation there could be very few factors influencing the decisions of the investor regarding the location of production. It is highly probable that coming to Romania was probably influenced by the fitness of Romania's political-economic system and the characteristics of the local labour market, such as good human resources, its strategic location and relatively good infrastructure. For Nokia, the investment in Romania seemed the most efficient solution, which brought the high promise of profit.

This rationality was however partially shared by the host population, the workers and local authorities. The plant offered a distinct and different space and sensory experience that was highly valued by the workforce. The jobs provided excitement and empowerment. The investment influenced identities and sociocultural contexts but also put the community in a new transitory situation. The community and workforce started to live a fantasy based on imaginary participation in the globalized, capitalist world. The workforce and their families activated the desire of living a middle-class life that stands in opposition to traditional village experience. The plant in the village was a promise, a mirage of an entirely different life. Nokia did not cause a revolution but promised change. Local workers participated in the life of the plant. It was a valuable and appreciated experience. The workforce underwent adaptation. Getting used to the organizational culture, work attire and internal procedures cost effort and stress. Entering and leaving the plant on a daily basis was compared to a journey. Its internal reality was different from the everyday lives of the local populations. Once a worker left the plant, the same familiar local world, where priorities included land cultivation and other duties embroiled in traditional livelihood, was all around.

Despite being embedded in a fantasy of modernisation, new ways of thinking about local life have played an important role in the functioning of the investment. In only five years, the region changed its understanding of its own position in the world through re-scaling. The new connections helped the community feel attached to global production and formed new desires based on their visions for progress. A number of new cultural elements, activated by the investment, contrasted with the workers' post-socialist realities and the challenging transitory reality of Romania. The materialization of the investment in the rural zone outside of the main city was seen as a project of unique quality and organization. The new hosting community admired the orchestration of the construction works and complexity of the industrial zone intended not only for the main investor but also for its future suppliers and the facilities needed by them. When the investor officially opened the facility, some of the members of the local population participated in its opening, hoping for gifts and benefits from the investor's presence.

Once the investment's preparations were complete, workers from the surrounding areas were recruited to work in the plant. They were offered relatively low pay, a meal, food vouchers and free transportation to work. From the recruitment stage the workforce experienced an entirely new quality of work organization. Cultural specificity of the workplace was an important factor influencing the overall assessment of the investor and the work in the plant. Highly regulated work procedures, along with the pristine work environment, strongly contrasted with other workplaces in the manufacturing sector in the region. The work required complex workplace adaptation to elements such as: language, consisting of phrases specific for production procedures in global facilities of the multinational; work attire, intended to protect the equipment from any traces of dirt; temperature and light; as well as diet and breaks during the working hours. As a result of these adaptations to new procedures, the workforce often related to their work using terms that used the metaphor of a journey – emphasizing the complexity of the differences of the workplace. At the same time, adaptation to these realities, as well as their experience, was understood as valuable and an escape from everyday realities.

Despite the perceived attractiveness of cultural distinctiveness, the production process in the plant was physically demanding and took place under highly regulated and supervised conditions. In response to this oppressiveness, the workforce developed coping mechanisms. A central mechanism of workplace culture was workplace humour. It provided a distraction during repetitive workplace duties, helping to deal with the assembly process, and improving workplace morale. Humour also helped to cope with oppressive control, creating a sense of resistance among those who joked about security measures, managers, and those who failed to cope with extensive monitoring of the workforce. This showed parallels to jokes told under socialism, which exposed the absurdities of the day-to-day class struggles faced by the layman and those who gained privileges through party membership. Lastly, shop floor culture developed humorous and absurd storytelling mechanisms, which helped to deal with global production and the organisation of the investment. These stories produced important insights into the functioning of the organisation and the role of the facility in the global value chain of the investor, and it speculated on important aspects, such as the relationship to the Romanian state officials.

One of the main disadvantages of the shop-floor work was salary levels, which were on the low end of the scale in the manufacturing sector in Romania. I have shown how the offshoring work was possible due to the mutual dependency between the family organisation and offshoring labour. Prior to the investment many of the worker families lived lives similar to those of thousands in peripheral villages in Eastern Europe, highly reliant on semi-subsistence and safety-first strategy (Lipton, 1968). For those families, waged income of family members was only one of the sources of balancing the household's equilibrium. The variety of household inputs and family labour is crucial and proves to be the best buffer in transitory moments. Once the investment happened, the wages from the plant in the village did not significantly change the situation of local families, who still supported workers, providing housing, sharing food and taking over some of their duties. In reality, despite their members working in the plant, traditional roles continued to be dominant. For those families, the work of their members was understood as a way of intergenerational economic mobility, mainly through participation in consumption and exposure to new social circles in the plant. Probably very few workers of the plant were able to achieve full financial independence only through the salary from the plant. Even though the mutual dependence had a significant gender and age dimension, highly privileging young men, to a different degree most of the workers in the investment experienced the outcomes of this familial orientation.

For the local population, the investment was understood as a change of reality. All of the sudden the region became the stage for national events, a symbol of Romania's integration to the local economy. The workforce strongly believed in the transforming power of the plant. Once the decision that the investment will be relocated was publicized, it was taken with strong disbelief. Prior to this decision, the workforce understood the investment as a long-term commitment by the investor, based on the low-price of labour and high availability of the workforce. Because these perceived criteria have not changed, the decision to re-locate was a complete surprise. Despite leaving, the workers still perceived the investor in largely positive terms, trusting its good will and paradoxically understanding the officially given argument connected to the reduction process of labour costs. Despite the decision, the majority of the workforce strongly dismissed the idea of mobilizing against it. One of the leading beliefs was that the industrial facility will soon be a home to a new investor and creating tensions might worsen the situation of the workforce and individual workers. A key part of reacting to the relocation was also played by the precarious status of the workforce hired on temporary contracts by workforce agencies. These workers, used to the temporary nature of their labour, took the decision in a similar way they would have taken a non-prolonged contract by the agency. The dominating strategy of workers after the investor's departure has been a return to at-home duties or temporary jobs, or duties that they fulfilled prior to the investment. The well-received investment proved to the immobile workforce their main limitation: that the work may be replaced at any time and with few barriers. Moved from Germany, it already proved to be very mobile. The inability to cope with the investor was apparent in multiple actions of the decision makers. Both the local authorities and Romanian government explicitly expressed that they are awaiting a new investor. The media heated up the discussion by exposing some contents of a secret contract with the investor, including the mistake of not defining the minimum stay period of the investor. Further media discussions contained the analyses of the investor's failed innovation strategy and its impact on the Romanian economy. The departure of the investor forced a reflection about the position of Romania in the context of global labour relations and the problematic cost competitiveness with less advanced economies. Media discourse circulated around daily speculations about a new investor taking up the former Nokia production facility, including highly recognized producers and Romanian entrepreneurs. All parties shared the belief that the industrial zone needs to continue activity and the labour force is competent, price competitive and fit for any type of production.

Nokia's production in Romania ended in 2012. In four years Romania witnessed the whole lifecycle of a global industrial node. It began with a joyful welcome and it ended in an atmosphere of scandal and grief. The moment of localisation occurred when the prestigious investor built an extremely modern factory. It was unexpected and later highly appreciated. The investment brought back faith in Romania's ability to keep up with the other European counterparts. When the plant left, it was leaving a different setting. The zone offered itself as a new home for a new investment. The asset specificity connected to the plant's presence held back the protests and instead made public opinion look for an investor in the same sector. The community was upset but strongly believed in the return of a global production firm. The four-year presence of the plant generated the belief about the involvement of the community in global production. Even though Nokia left, this faith was sustained, and most local workers and members of the hosting community believed that by being already incorporated in the global reserve army of labour, the industrial zone would continue production with a new investor.

Production practices of multinational enterprises are the object of strong critique. It is a fact that multinationals shift their production to countries with reduced labour market standards in order to decrease operating costs. In response, host economies have an incentive to sustain or increase the inflow of FDI by keeping labour standards low (Olney, 2013), as well as by offering tax holidays and participating in location costs. The global competition for FDI is fierce. Industrialised economies have been experiencing factory closures connected to cost-based competition for decades. Because of their industrial experience, they are equipped with social protection mechanisms and prepared to re-train the workforce. Their counterparts, industrializing states, participate in the race by offering alternative labour regimes and liberalising their labour markets. Their experience and ability to cope with relocations proves to be limited.

This book's goal has been to give an account of one of the communities that found itself between a rock and a hard place. The case of the investment reflects a situation of similar communities in middle-income economies, showing the paradoxes of their in-between situation. The investment's establishment followed a typical course of FDI location in the industrializing economy. The Romanian state supported it fully by providing the necessary infrastructure under the investor's guidelines and financing the construction of the industrial zone. In return, the state hoped for labour market improvements and economic growth. However, the investor's departure largely reflected the experiences of escaping capital associated with the developed economies. Largely unexpected, justified by costs, it again proved to be an inability of the nation state to cope with globalization. However, unlike the industrialised world, the state was inexperienced and unable to win any additional concessions and compensations from the investor, partially because of ineffective labour protection standards and political inability of decision-makers. The Romanian reaction to the investor's plant location initially displayed enthusiasm and hope for change. With the later relocation it was replaced with helplessness and discontent. The lack of agency when faced with layoffs displayed the vulnerability of middle-income economies as well.

This vicious circle of global competition for labour creates difficulties also for the local labour force in the middle-income states, such as Romania. With production node's mobility a specific local adaptation emerged. Despite the strong desire for a radical change of the economic situation, it did not occur. Instead, waged income from the plant became part of a diversified household income. This is not a singular case, and it is not limited to the Eastern European countryside. Foreign investments usually resonate extremely well locally, responding to limited perspectives for industrial employment in the locality.

Desperate for work nearby, in order to stay close to their households and family, workers are very often willing to compromise by fully accepting low wages and decreased work standards. Even though the latter was not the case with the investor, the workforce was given no other option but complimenting industrial employment with alternative sources of income. In the situation when the investor left, the workers shared a common opinion that a potential decrease in work conditions would be acceptable and hypothetically might stop another investor from leaving.

The present case also expresses the multiple impacts that investments bring to host economies. Whether foreign direct investments provide a desirable outcome depends on one's view of employment protection rules, labour employment standards and economic development. The investor's arrival was locally considered largely positive. The investment generated the belief about involvement of the region in global production. The commonly appreciated outcomes include the improved situation of the host community, economic growth of the national economy and changing reputation of the region. Even though the investor left, most local workers and members of the host community believed that having already been incorporated in the global reserve army of labour the industrial zone will continue production with investors and grow in size. As I have shown, this belief has also inspired a lack of industrial action during the closure. The investor's plant replaced former post-communist stagnation with local dependence on foreign investments. Facing a slack labour market and sceptical of migration, the region awaited continued production in the zone and hopes for the fulfilment of the visions that the investor activated.

In the end, deLonghi, the Italian producer of consumer electronics, took over the plant. In the proximity of the plant, another producer, Bosch, located its industrial operations. Some of the hires included staff that formerly worked in the mobile phone plant. The industrial zone continues to operate, however, at present, none of the investors achieved a scale similar to the initial investment.

Bibliography

Ackroyd, S., & Thompson, P. (1999). *Organizational misbehaviour*. London: Sage.

Adascalitei, D., & Guga, Ş. (2015). Decentralization, union power and contention episodes: the case of Dacia workers. Marie Curie Changing Employment ITN Research Paper Series, 15, Accessed at: https://ub-madoc.bib.uni-mannheim.de/37854/ [2018-11-19].

Adăscăliţei, D., & Guga, Ş. (2016). Coming apart or joining hands? The crisis and current dilemmas of the Romanian trade union movement. In V. Pulignano, H.D. Köhler and P. Steward (Eds.) *Employment relations in an era of change* (pp. 37–55). Brussels: European Trade Union Institute (ETUI).

Andreev, S.A. (2009). The unbearable lightness of membership: Bulgaria and Romania after the 2007 EU accession. *Communist and Post-Communist Studies*, 42: 375–393.

Asmussen, C.G., Larsen, M.M. & Pedersen, T. (2016). Organizational adaptation in offshoring: The relative performance of home-and host-based learning strategies. *Organization Science,* 27(4): 911–928.

Avolio, B.J., Howell, J.M. & J.J. Sosik. (1999). A funny thing happened on the way to the bottom line: Humor as a moderator of leadership style effects. *Academy of Management Journal,* 42(2): 219–227.

Baban, A. (2000). Women's sexuality and reproductive behaviour in post-Ceausescu Romania. In S. Gal and G. Kligman (Eds.), *Reproducing gender: Politics, publics, and everyday life after Socialism* (pp. 225–256). Princeton, N.J.: Princeton University Press.

Bacon, W. (2004). Economic Reform. In H.F. Carey (Ed.) *Romania since 1989. Politics, Economics, and Society*. Lanham, MA: Lexington.

Balcerowicz L. (1995). *Socialism, capitalism, transformation*. Budapest: Central European University Press.

Bandelj, N. (2003). Particularizing the global: Reception of foreign investment in Slovenia. *Current Sociology*, 51: 375–292.

Bandelj, N. (2004). Negotiating global, regional, and national forces: Foreign investment in Slovenia. *East European Politics & Societies*, 18: 455–480.

Bandelj, N. (2008). *From Communists to Foreign Capitalists: The Social Foundations of Foreign Direct Investment in Postsocialist Europe*. Princeton: Princeton University Press.

Bandelj, N. (2009). The Global Economy as Instituted Process: The Case of Central and Eastern Europe. *American Sociological Review*, 74: 128–149.

Barrientos, S. and Kritzinger, A. (2004). Squaring the circle: global production and the informalisation of work in South African fruit exports. *Journal of International Development,* 16: 81–92.

Barrientos, S. and Rossi, A. (2011). Economic and social upgrading in global production networks: a new paradigm for a changing world. *International Labour Review,* 150 (3–4): 319–340.

Bartram, D. (2013). Migration, return and happiness in Romania. *European Societies,* 15: 408–422.

Bauman, Z. (1998). *Globalization: the human consequences.* New York: Columbia University Press.

Beck, S. (1975). The emergence of the peasant-worker in a Transylvanian mountain community. *Dialectical Anthropology,* 1(1): 365–375.

Blyton, P. and Jenkins, J. (2012). Life after Burberry: shifting experiences of work and non-work life following redundancy. *Work, Employment & Society,* 26(1): 26–41.

Bohle, D. and Greskovits, B. (2007). Neoliberalism, embedded neoliberalism and neo-corporatism: Towards transnational capitalism in Central-Eastern Europe. *West European Politics,* 30(3): 443–466.

Bonacich, E., and Appelbaum, R.P. (2000). *Behind the label: Inequality in the Los Angeles apparel industry.* Berkeley: University of California Press.

Borman, K.M. (1988). Playing on the job in adolescent work settings. *AEQ Anthropology & Education Quarterly,* 19: 163–181.

Brainerd, E. (2000). Women in transition: changes in gender wage differentials in Eastern Europe and the former Soviet Union. *Industrial & Labour Relations Review,* 54(1): 138–162.

Brass, T. (2011). *Labour regime change in the twenty-first century: Unfreedom, capitalism, and primitive accumulation.* Leiden; Boston: Brill.

Brecher, J., Costello, T., & Smith, B. (2006). International labour solidarity: The new frontier. *New Labour Forum,* 15(1): 8–18.

Brenner, N. (1998). Between fixity and motion: Accumulation, territorial organization and historical geography. *Environment & Planning, Society and Space,* 16(4): 459–481.

Brenner, N. (2001). The limits to scale? Methodological reflections on scalar structuration. *Progress in Human Geography,* 25: 591–614.

Bridger, S., Kay, R., & Pinnick, K. (1996). *No more heroines? : Russia, women, and the market.* London; New York: Routledge.

Brochner, J and Haugen, T.I. (2004). *Power and supply chain relationships.* Bradford, England: Emerald Group Pub.

Brooks, E.C. (2007). *Unraveling the garment industry transnational organizing and women's work.* Minneapolis: University of Minnesota Press.

Brooks, E.C. (2007). *Unraveling the garment industry: Transnational organizing and women's work.* Minneapolis: University of Minnesota Press.

Brubaker, R., Feischmidt, M., Fox, J., & Grancea, L. (2006). *Nationalist politics and everyday ethnicity in a Transylvanian town.* Princeton: Princeton University Press.

Brunvand, J.H. (2003). *Casa frumoasa: The house beautiful in rural Romania.* Boulder; New York: Columbia University Press.

Budhwar, P.S., Luthar, H.K., & Bhatnagar, J. (2006). The dynamics of HRM systems in Indian BPO firms. *Journal of Labour Research,* 27(3): 339–360.

Burawoy M. (1979). *Manufacturing consent: Changes in the labour process under monopoly capitalism.* Chicago: University of Chicago Press.

Burawoy M. (2000) *Global ethnography: Forces, connections, and imaginations in a postmodern world,* Berkeley: University of California Press.

Burawoy, M. (2010). From Polanyi to Pollyanna: The false optimism of global labour studies. *Global Labour Journal,* 1(2): 301–313.

Burawoy, M., Lukács, J (1992). *The radiant past: Ideology and reality in Hungary's road to capitalism.* Chicago: University of Chicago Press.

Burke, P.J. and Stets, J.E. (1999). Trust and Commitment through Self-Verification. *Social Psychology Quarterly.* 62: 347–366.

Capital (2011, December, 14). Băsescu reproșează Nokia și Ford că nu s-au ținut de promisiuni. Capital, p. 3.

Capital (2011, September 29). Guvernul nu deține informații privind intenția altei companii internaționale de a părăsi România, p. 1.

Carroll, J.M. (2012). *The Neighborhood in the Internet: Design research projects in community informatics.* London; New York: Routledge.

Caskie, P. (2000). Back to basics: Household food production in Russia. *Journal of Agricultural Economics,* 51: 196–209.

Clark, E. and Soulsby, A. (2012). Constructing post-Socialism: organisational identity and the experience of international joint ventures. *Europe-Asia Studies,* 64(2): 257–280.

Clauwaert S., Schömann I. (2013) *The crisis and national labour law reforms: A mapping exercise. Country report: Romania.* Brussels: European Trade Union Institute (ETUI). Accessed at: http://www.etui.org/content/download/7466/71681/file/Romania+January+2013_final.pdf. [2018-12-1].

Clawson D. (2003). *The next upsurge: Labour and the new social movements.* Ithaca: ILR Press.

Clyne, M.G. (1994). *Inter-cultural communication at work: Cultural values in discourse.* Cambridge; New York: Cambridge University Press.

Cohen, J.L. (2012). *Globalization and sovereignty: Rethinking legality, legitimacy, and constitutionalism.* London: Cambridge University Press.

Collins, J.L., and Mayer, V. (2010). *Both Hands Tied: Welfare Reform and the Race to the Bottom in the Low-Wage Labour Market.* Chicago: University of Chicago Press.

Collinson, D.L. (1988). "Engineering humour": Masculinity, joking and conflict in shop-floor relations. *Organization Studies,* 9: 181–199.

Comaroff, J. & Comaroff, J (2003). Transparent fictions; or the conspiracies of a liberal imagination: An afterword. In H.G. West & T. Sanders (Eds.), *Transparency and*

Conspiracy: Ethnographies of Suspicion in the New World Order, Durham: Duke University Press: pp. 287–299.

Constantin, D.L. (2012). Middle of the road: Romania's regional policy in the current EU programme period. Working Paper of the 52nd Congress of the European Regional Science Association. Accessed at: https://www-sre.wu.ac.at/ersa/ersaconfs/ersa12/ersa12acfinal00922.pdf [2018-12-14].

Cook, J.A., Cylke, O., Larson, D.F., Nash, D., & Stedman-Edwards, P. (2010). *Vulnerable places, vulnerable people: Trade liberalization, rural poverty and the environment*. Cheltenham, UK and Northampton, MA: Edward Elgar.

Cornelius, W.A. (2009). *Migration from the Mexican Mixteca: A transnational community in Oaxaca and California*, San Diego, Calif.: Center for Comparative Immigration Studies, University of California, San Diego.

Costas, J., & Grey, C. (2014). The temporality of power and the power of temporality: Imaginary future selves in professional service firms. *Organization Studies*, 35(6): 909–937.

Cowie J. (1999). *Capital moves: RCA's seventy-year quest for cheap labour*, Ithaca, N.Y.: Cornell University Press.

Cowie, J. (2010). *Stayin'alive: The 1970s and the last days of the working class*. New York: The New Press.

Cowie, J. (2001). *Capital moves: RCA's seventy-year quest for cheap labour*. The New Press: New York.

Cravey, A.J. (1998). *Women and work in Mexico's maquiladoras*. Lanham, Md: Rowman & Littlefield.

Crowley, S., & Ost, D. (Eds.). (2001). *Workers after workers' states: Labour and politics in postcommunist Eastern Europe*. Rowman & Littlefield.

Culpan, R., & Akcaoglu, E. (2003). An examination of Turkish direct investments in Central and Eastern Europe and the commonwealth of independent states. In S.T. Marinova & M.A. Marinov (Eds.), *Foreign direct investment in Central and Eastern Europe* (pp. 181–199). London: Ashgate.

Czegledy A. (2002). Urban peasants in a Post-Socialist World: Small-scale agriculturalists in Hungary. In P. Leonard P and D Kaneff (Eds.) *Post-socialist peasant? Rural and urban constructions of identity in Eastern Europe, East Asia and the former Soviet Union* (pp. 200–220). London: Palgrave Macmillan.

Daianu, D. (2004). Fiscal and Monetary Policy. In H.F. Carey (Ed). *Romania since 1989: Politics, Economics, and Society*. Lanham, MA: Lexington.

Danford, A. (1998). Work organisation inside Japanese firms in South Wales: A break from Taylorism? In: Thompson P., Warhurst C. (Eds.) *Workplaces of the Future* (pp. 40–64). Palgrave, London.

Daveri F. and Silva O. (2004). Not only Nokia: what Finland tells us about new economy growth. *Economic Policy*, 19: 117–163.

D'Costa, A.P. (Ed.). (2012). *Globalization and economic nationalism in Asia*. London: Oxford University Press.

de la Garza Toledo, E. (2007) The Crisis of the Maquiladora Model in Mexico. *Work and Occupations*, 34: 399–429.

Deacon, B. (1992). *The new Eastern Europe: Social policy past, present and future*, London: Sage Publications.

Delbridge, R. (1998). *Life on the line in contemporary manufacturing: The workplace experience of lean production and the 'Japanese' Model*. Oxford University Press: Oxford.

dePauw, W. (2008). Expert Report on the Fight against Corruption / Cooperation and Verification Mechanism. Acessed at: https://www.economist.com/media/pdf/romaniacorruption.pdf [2018-12-14].

Directia Regionala de Statistica Cluj. (2012). Fisa Localitatii Jucu – manuscript.

Duneier, M. (2004). Scrutinizing the Heat. *Contemporary Sociology*, 33: 139–150.

Dunn, E.C. (2004). *Privatizing Poland: Baby food, big business, and the remaking of labour*, Ithaca: Cornell University Press.

Earle, J.S. and Telegdy, Á. (1998). The results of "mass privatisation" in Romania: A first empirical study. *Economics of Transition*, 6: 313–332.

Economist. (1998). Old Habits. The Economist Europe. Acessed at: https://www.economist.com/europe/1998/06/25/old-habits [2018-12-14].

Economist. (2008). The logic of Logan: Success on Four Wheels. The Economist Europe. Acessed at: https://www.economist.com/special-report/2008/05/29/the-logic-of-the-logan [2018-12-14].

Economist. (2011). Internet Speed: World Wide Wait. Acessed at: https://www.economist.com/babbage/2011/10/28/world-wide-wait [2018-12-14].

Einhorn, B. (1993). *Cinderella goes to market: Citizenship, gender, and women's movements in East Central Europe*, London; New York: Verso.

Einhorn, B. and Sever, C. (2003). Gender and civil society in Central and Eastern Europe. *International Feminist Journal of Politics*, 5(2): 163–190.

Ellingstad, M. (1997). The maquiladora syndrome: Central European prospects. *Europe-Asia Studies*, 49(1): 7–21.

Eriksen T.H. (2003). *Globalisation studies in anthropology*. London; Sterling, VA.: Pluto Press.

European Comission (2011). Report from the Commission to the European Parliament and the Council: On progress in Romania under the Co-operation and Verification Mechanism. COM (2011) 460 final (EN). Acessed at: https://ec.europa.eu/info/sites/info/files/comm-2017-751_en.pdf [2018-12-14].

European Comission. (2012). Statement by the European Commission on Romania, MEMO/12/529.

Eurostat. (2010). EU *Economic Data Pocketbook Quarterly*, 4.

Evans, P. (2008). Is an alternative globalization possible? *Politics & Society*, 36(2): 271–305.

Fabry, N. and Zeghni, S. (2006). How former Communist countries of Europe may attract inward foreign direct investment? A matter of institutions. *Communist and Post-Communist Studies*, 39(2): 201–219.

Farole T. and Winkler D. (2014). Making foreign direct investment work for Sub-Saharan Africa: Local spillovers and competitiveness in global value chains. Accessed on-linet: https://openknowledge.worldbank.org/bitstream/handle/10986/16390/9781464801266.pdf?sequence=1. [2018-11-26].

Ferguson, J. (1999). *Expectations of modernity myths and meanings of urban life on the Zambian Copperbelt*. Berkeley: University of California Press.

Fernández-Kelly, M.P. (1983). *For we are sold, I and my people: Women and industry in Mexico's frontier*. Albany: State University of New York Press.

Fields, G.S. (2012). *Working hard, working poor: A global journey*. New York: Oxford University Press.

Figueiredo, P. (2011). The role of dual embeddedness in the innovative performance of MNE subsidiaries: evidence from Brazil. *Journal of Management Studies*, 48: 417–440.

Fish, M.S. (1997). The determinants of economic reform in the post-communist world. *East European Politics & Societies*, 12: 31–78.

Fisk, P. (2010). *People, planet, profit: how to embrace sustainability for innovation and business growth*. London; Philadelphia: Kogan Page.

Florida, R.L., Kenney, M. (2004). *Locating global advantage industry dynamics in a globalizing economy*. Stanford, Calif.: Stanford University Press.

Fold, N. (2002). Lead firms and competition in bi-polar commodity chains: Grinders and branders in the global cocoa-chocolate industry. *Journal of Agrarian Change*, 2: 228–247.

Forester, J. (2004). Responding to critical moments with humor, recognition, and hope. *Negotiation Journal*, 20: 221–237.

Fortuny, M., Nesporová, A., Popova, N., et al. (2003). *Employment promotion policies for older workers in the EU accession countries, the Russian Federation and Ukraine*. Available at: http://www.ilo.org/public/english/employment/strat/download/ep50.pdf. [2018-12-1].

Foster, J.B., McChesney, R.W., & Jonna, R.J. (2011). The global reserve army of labour and the new imperialism. *Monthly Review*, 63: 1–31.

Frankfurter Algemeine Zeitung. (2012). Wir werden die Entwicklung in Rumänien nicht ignorieren. Acessed at: https://www.faz.net/aktuell/politik/ausland/amtsenthebung-basescus-wir-werden-die-entwicklung-in-rumaenien-nicht-ignorieren-11813233.html [2018-12-14].

Fraser, N. (2017). Crisis of care? On the social-reproductive contradictions of contemporary Capitalism. In: Bhattacharya, T. (Ed.) *Social Reproduction Theory*. London: Pluto, 21–36.

Fudge, J., & Strauss, K. (2013). Temporary work, agencies and unfree labour: Insecurity in the new world of work. In J. Fudge & K. Strauss (Eds.) *Temporary work, agencies and unfree labour* (pp. 17–41). London: Routledge.

Funk, N. and Mueller, M. (1993). *Gender Politics and Post-Communism: Reflections from Eastern Europe and The Former Soviet Union*, New York: Routledge.

Gabanyi, A.U. (2004). New Business Elite: from Nomenklatura to Oligarchy In: H.F. Carey (Ed.) *Romania since 1989: Politics, Economics, and Society*. Lanham, MD: Lexington.

Gabriel Y. (1991) Turning facts into stories and stories into facts: A hermeneutic exploration of organizational folklore. *Human Relations* 44: 857–875.

Gallagher, T. (1998). Romania's desire to be normal. *Contemporary Politics*, 4: 111–125.

Galster, G.C. (2012). *Driving Detroit: the Quest for respect in the Motor City*. Philadelphia: University of Pennsylvania Press.

Ger, G., Belk, R.W. & Lascu, D.-N. (1993). The development of consumer desire in marketizing and developing economies: The cases of Romania and Turkey. *Advances in Consumer Research*, 20: 102–107.

Gereffi, G. and Korzeniewicz, M. (1994). *Commodity chains and global capitalism*. Westport, Conn.: Greenwood Press.

Gereffi, G., Humphrey, J., and Timothy, S. (2005). *The governance of global value chains*. London: Taylor & Francis.

Getto, G., & Amant, K.S. (2015). Designing globally, working locally: Using personas to develop online communication products for international users. *Communication Design Quarterly Review*, 3(1): 24–46.

Ghemawat, P. (2003). The forgotten strategy. *Harvard Business Review*, 81(11): 76–87.

Giachetti, C. (2013). *Competitive dynamics in the mobile phone industry*. Basingstoke: Palgrave Macmillan.

Glassner, V. (2013). Central and Eastern European industrial relations in the crisis: National divergence and path – dependent change. *Transfer: European Review of Labour and Research,* 19(2): 155–169.

Gligorov, V. (1994). Gradual shock therapy. *East European Politics & Societies*, 9: 195–206.

Goldschmidt, W., and Kunkel, E.J. (1971). The Structure of the Peasant Family. *American Anthropologist,* 73: 1058–1076.

Golpelwar, M.K. (2015). *Global call center employees in India: Work and life between globalization and tradition*. Berlin and Heidelberg: Springer.

Gooris, J. and Peeters, C. (2014). Home–host country distance in offshore governance choices. *Journal of International Management,* 20(1): 73–86.

Goschin, Z., Dachin, A., Constantin, D.L., et al. (2012). The absorption capacity of European funds for rural development in Romania: Estimates of the factor influence. *International Journal of Foresight and Innovation Policy*, 8: 272–291.

Gregory, A., Ingham, M., and Ingham, H. (1998). Women's employment in transition, 1992–4: The case of Poland. *Gender, Work & Organization*, 5(3): 133–147.

Grosescu, R. (2004). The political regrouping of the Romanian nomenklatura during the 1989 revolution. *Romanian Journal of Society and Politics*, 4: 97–123.

Gross, P. and Tismaneanu, V. (2005). The end of postcommunism in Romania. *Journal of Democracy*, 16: 146–162.

Grubb, E.A. (1975). Assembly line boredom and individual differences in recreation participation. *Journal of Leisure Research*, 7: 256–269.

Gruner, C.R. (1997). *The game of humor: A comprehensive theory of why we laugh*. New Brunswick, N.J.: Transaction Publishers.

Grzymala-Busse A. and Luong, P.J. (2002). Reconceptualizing the state: Lessons from Post-Communism. *Politics & Society*, 30: 529–554.

Guillen, M.F. and Garcia-Canal, E. (2009). The American model of the multinational firm and the "new" multinationals from emerging economies. *Academy of Management Perspectives*, 23 (2): 23–35.

Gusfield JR. (1975). *Community: A critical response*. New York: Harper & Row.

Häikiö M. (2002). *Nokia: The inside story*. London; Boston: FT Prentice Hall.

Haney, L.A. (2002). *Inventing the needy gender and the politics of welfare in Hungary*. Berkeley: University of California Press.

Harvey, D. (1989). *The urban experience*. Baltimore: Johns Hopkins University Press.

Harvey, D. (1990). *The condition of postmodernity: An enquiry into the origins of cultural change*. Oxford [England]; Cambridge, Mass., USA: Blackwell.

Haukanes, H. and Pine, F. (2005). *Generations, Kinship and Care: Gendered Provisions of Social Security in Central Eastern Europe*. Bergen: University of Bergen.

Hayter S., Vargha C. and Mihes C. (2013) The impact of legislative reforms on industrial relations in Romania, Budapest, International Labour Office.

Hayter, S., Vargha, C., & Mihes, C. (2013). The impact of legislative reforms on industrial relations in Romania. *ILO*, 13, 1.25, accessed on-line: https://www.epsu.org/sites/default/files/article/files/ILO_Romania_-_Impact_legislative_reform_on_IR.pdf [2018-11-19].

Helleiner, E., and Pickel, A. (2005). *Economic nationalism in a globalizing world*. Ithaca, N.Y.: Cornell University Press.

Henderson, J., Dicken, P., Hess, M., et al. (2002). Global production networks and the analysis of economic development. *Review of International Political Economy*, 9: 436–464.

Herod, A. (2011). *Scale*. London; New York: Routledge.

Hochschild, A. and Machung, A. (2012). *The second shift: Working families and the revolution at home*. New York: Penguin.

Hollinshead, G., Capik, P., and Micek, G. (2011). Beyond Offshore Outsourcing of Business Services. *Competition & Change,* 15(3): 171–176.

Holmes, J. (2000). Politeness, power and provocation: How humour functions in the workplace. *Discourse Studies,* 2: 159–185.

Hunya G. (1998). Romania 1990–2002: Stop-go transformation. *Communist Economies and Economic Transformation,* 10: 241–258.

Hurrell, A. and Woods, N. (1999). *Inequality, globalization, and world politics.* Oxford; New York: Oxford University Press.

Ianos, I., Peptenatu, D., Pintilii, R.D., et al. (2010). The insertion of highly disadvantaged areas in regional environments. *Analele Universitatii din Oradea,* xx: 159–166.

International Monetary Fund. (2003). *Romania: Financial Stability Assessment,* Washington D.C: IMF.

International Monetary Fund. (2012). *World Economic Outlook Database*: October 2012.

International Organization for Migration. (2008). *Migration in Romania: A country profile 2008,* Geneva: IOM.

Isen, A.M., Daubman, K.A., & Nowicki, G.P. (1987). Positive affect facilitates creative problem solving. *Journal of Personality and Social Psychology,* 52(6): 1122–1131.

Jefferson, T. and King, J.E. (2001). "'Never intended to be a theory of everything': Domestic labour in neoclassical and Marxian economics". *Feminist Economics,* 7(3): 71–101.

Jensen, P.D.Ø. (2009). A learning perspective on the offshoring of advanced services. *Journal of international Management,* 15(2): 181–193.

Jessop, B. (2000). The crisis of the national spatio-temporal fix and the tendential ecological dominance of globalizing capitalism. *International Journal of Urban and Regional Research,* 24: 323–360.

Juhasz, J. (1991). Large-scale and small-scale farming in Hungarian agriculture: Present situation and future prospects. *European Review of Agricultural Economics,* 18: 399–415.

Kalleberg, A.L. (2012). Job quality and precarious work: Clarifications, controversies, and challenges. *Work and Occupations,* 39(4): 427–448.

Kalleberg, A.L. (2009). Precarious work, insecure workers: Employment relations in transition. *American Sociological Review,* 74(1): 1–22.

Kass, S.J., Vodanovich, S.J., & Stanny, C.J. (2001). Watching the clock: boredom and vigilance performance. *Perceptual and motor skills,* 92: 969–976.

Katz, R. (1978). *Time and work: Towards an integrative perspective.* Cambridge; Mass.: Alfred P. Sloan School of Management, M.I.T.

Kenney, M., Goe, W.R., Contreras, O., Romero, J., & Bustos, M. (1998). Learning factories or reproduction factories? Labour-management relations in the Japanese consumer electronics maquiladoras in Mexico. *Work and Occupations,* 25(3): 269–304.

Kenney, P. (1997). *Rebuilding Poland: Workers and Communists: 1945–1950,* Ithaca: Cornell University Press.

Kideckel, D.A. (2001). Winning the battles, losing the war: Contradictions of Romanian labour in postcommunist transformation. In: S. Crowley and D. Ost (Eds.) *Workers After Workers' States: Labour and Politics in Postcommunist Eastern Europe*. Lanham, MD: Rowman and Littlefield, 97–120.

Kideckel, D.A. (1984). Drinking up: Alcohol, class, and social change in rural Romania. *East European Quarterly*, 18(4): 431–446.

Kideckel, D.A. (2008). *Getting by in post-socialist Romania: Labour, the body and working-class culture*. Bloomington, Ind.: Indiana University Press.

King, R.F. and Sum, P.E. (2011). *Romania under Basescu: Aspirations, achievements, and frustrations during his first presidential term*. Lanham, Md.: Lexington Books.

Kinnie, N., Purcell, J., & Adams, M. (2008). Explaining employees' experience of work in outsourced call centres: the influence of clients, owners and temporary work agencies. *Journal of Industrial Relations*, 50(2): 209–227.

Knorringa, P. and Pegler, L. (2006). Globalisation, firm upgrading and impacts on labour. *Journal of Economic and Social Geography*, 97(5): 470–479.

Kojima, S. and Kojima, M. (2007). Making IT offshoring work for the Japanese industries. In: Meyer, B. and Joseph, M. (Eds.) *Software engineering approaches for offshore and outsourced development*. Berlin and Heidelberg: Springer, pp. 67–82.

Kopinak, K. (1996). *Desert Capitalism: Maquiladoras in North America's Western Industrial Corridor*. Tucson: University of Arizona Press.

Korczynski, M. (2011). The dialectical sense of humour: Routine joking in a Taylorized factory. *Organization Studies* 32: 1421–1439.

Kostera, M. (1994). Beyond the social role: The case of Polish female professionals. *Scandinavian Journal of Management*, 10(2): 99–116.

Kostov, P., and Lingard, J. (2002). Subsistence farming in transitional economies: Lessons from Bulgaria. *Journal of Rural Studies*, 18: 83–94.

Kovács Kiss G. (2011). *Studies in the history of early modern Transylvania*. Boulder, Colo.; Highland Lakes, N.J.; New York: Social Science Monographs; Atlantic Research and Publications; Distributed by Columbia University Press.

Kovács, J., and Zentai, V. (2012). *Capitalism from outside? Economic cultures in Eastern Europe after 1989*, Buapest: Central European University Press.

Kramer, M.W. (2010). *Organizational socialization: Joining and leaving organizations*. Cambridge, UK and Malden, MA: Polity.

Krasner, S.D. (1999). *Sovereignty: organized hypocrisy*. Princeton, N.J.: Princeton University Press.

Kshetri, N. and Dholakia, N. (2009). Professional and trade associations in a nascent and formative sector of a developing economy. *Journal of International Management*, 15(2): 225–239.

Kwon, Y.-H. (1994a) The Influence of appropriateness of dress and gender on the self-perception of occupational attributes. *Clothing and Textiles Research Journal*, 12: 33–39.

Kwon, Y.-H. (1994b). Feeling toward one's clothing and self-perception of emotion, sociability, and work competency. *Journal of Social Behaviour and Personality*, 9: 129.

Lakhani, T., Kuruvilla, S. and Avgar, A. (2013). From the firm to the network: Global value chains and employment relations theory. *British Journal of Industrial Relations*, 51(3): 440–472.

Lampland, M., & Nadkarni, M. (2016). "What happened to jokes?" The shifting landscape of humor in Hungary. *East European Politics and Societies*, 30(2): 449–471.

Lang J., Chinying L., & Chay H. (2010) Workplace humor and organizational creativity. *The International Journal of Human Resource Management* 21: 46–60.

Lattanzi M, Korhonen A and Gopalakrishnan V. (2006). *Work goes mobile: Nokia's lessons from the leading edge*, Hoboken, NJ: Wiley.

Lazar, M. (2003). Metastasis of ostentation: Blackand white illustrations from the tricolor city. *IDEA Arts and Society*, 15/16: 125–134.

Lebow, K.A. (1999). Revising the politicized landscape in Nowa Huta, 1949–1957. *City & Society* 11(1–2): 165–187.

LeDuff, C. (2013). *Detroit: an American Autopsy*. New York: Penguin Press.

Lee, A.S. and Trappmann, V. (2014). Overcoming post-communist labour weakness: Attritional and enabling effects of multinationals in Central and Eastern Europe. *European Journal of Industrial Relations*, 20(2): 113–129.

Lee, C.K. (2007). *Working in China: Ethnographies of labour and workplace transformation*. London; New York: Routledge.

Lefebvre, H. (1991). *The production of space*. Oxford, UK; Cambridge, Mass., USA: Blackwell.

Lenin, V. (1967). *The development of capitalism in Russia*. Moscow: Progress Publishers.

Levy, D.L. (2005). Offshoring in the New Global Political Economy. *Journal of Management Studies*, 42 (3): 685–693.

Lewin, A.Y. and Peeters, C. (2006). Offshoring work: business hype or the onset of fundamental transformation? *Long Range Planning*, 39(3): 221–239.

Lillie, N. (2010). Bringing the offshore ashore: transnational production, industrial relations and the reconfiguration of sovereignty. *International Studies Quarterly*, 54(3): 683–704.

Linden, R.H. (2004). Romania and Bulgaria between the EU and the United States. *Problems of Post-communism*, 51(5): 45–55.

Linder, C. (2011). Outsourcing as a cause for absent employee's commitment to the organization. *International Journal of Globalisation and Small Business*, 4: 114–126.

Lindholm C, Keinonen T and Kiljander H. (2003). *Mobile usability how Nokia changed the face of the mobile phone*. New York: McGraw-Hill.

Lloyd-Evans, S. (2008). Geographies of the contemporary informal sector in the global South: Gender, employment relationships and social protection. *Geography Compass*, 2: 1885–1906.

Lobodzinska, B. (1995). *Family, Women, and Employment in Central-Eastern Europe.* Westport, Conn.: Greenwood Press.

Luxton, M. and Bezanson, K. (Eds.) (2006). *Social Reproduction: Feminist Political Economy Challenges Neo-Liberalism.* Montreal: MQUP.

Lyttle, J. 2007. The Judicious Use and Management of Humor in the Workplace. *Business Horizons*, 50(3): 239–245.

MacKinnon, D. (2011). Reconstructing scale: Towards a new scalar politics. *Progress in Human Geography*, 35: 21–36.

MacLeod, G. (1999). Place, politics and "scale dependence": Exploring the structuration of euro-regionalism. *European Urban and Regional Studies,* 6: 231–253.

Mahutga, M.C. (2012). When do value chains go global? A theory of the spatialization of global value chains. *Global Networks*, 12: 1–21.

Marginson, P., Edwards, P., Edwards, T. et al. (2010). Employee representation and consultative voice in multinational companies operating in Britain. *British Journal of Industrial Relations,* 48(1): 151–180.

Marin, D. (2006). A new international division of labour in Europe: Outsourcing and offshoring to Eastern Europe. *Journal of the European Economic Association*, 4(2–3): 612–622.

Marody, M. and Giza-Poleszczuk, A. (2000). Chaning images of identity in Poland: From the self-sacrificing to the self-investing woman? In S. Gal and G Kligman (Eds.) *Reproducing Gender: Politics, publics, and everyday life after Socialism.* Princeton, N.J.: Princeton University Press.

Marshall, D. (2005). Food as ritual, routine or convention. *Consumption, Markets and Culture,* 8: 69–85.

Martin, R., & Cristescu-Martin, A.M. (2000). Industrial relations in Central and Eastern Europe in 1999: patterns of protest. *Industrial Relations Journal,* 31(4): 346–362.

Marx, K. (2001). *Capital: a critique of political economy.* London: Electric Book Co.

Mathijs, E., and Noev, N. (2004). Subsistence farming in Central and Eastern Europe: Empirical evidence from Albania, Bulgaria, Hungary and Romania. *Eastern European Economics,* 42: 72–89.

Mayer, P. (1971). *Townsmen or tribesmen.* Cape Town: Oxford University Press.

McGovern, P. (2007). Immigration, labour markets and employment relations: problems and prospects. *British Journal of Industrial Relations* 45(2): 217–235.

Meaghar, G. and Nelson, J.A. (2004). Survey article: Feminism and the dismal science. *Journal of Political Philosophy,* 12(1): 102–126.

Mendelski, M. (2011a). Romanian Rule of Law Reform: A Two-Dimensional Approach. In: P.E. Sum and R.F. King (eds.) *Romania under Basescu: Aspirations, achievements and frustrations during his first presidential term.* Lanham, MD Lexington Books.

Mendelski, M. (2011b). Rule of law reforms in the shadow of clientelism: The limits of the EU's transformative power in Romania. *Polish Sociological Review*, 2: 235–253.

Meyer, K.E., Mudambi, R. and Narula, R. (2011). Multinational enterprises and local contexts: the opportunities and challenges of multiple embeddedness. *Journal of Management Studies*, 48: 235–252.

Milberg, W.S. and Winkler, D. (2013). *Outsourcing economics: global value chains in capitalist development.* Cambridge; New York: Cambridge University Press.

Mills, M.B. (1999). *Thai women in the global labour force: Consuming desires, contested selves.* New Brunswick, N.J.: Rutgers University Press.

Mitchell, B. (2011). *The boomerang age: Transitions to adulthood in families.* New York: Transaction Publishers.

Mitchell, J.C. (1969). *Social networks in urban situations: analyses of personal relationships in Central African towns.* Manchester: Published for the Institute for Social Research, University of Zambia, by Manchester U.P.

Mitu S. (2001). *National identity of Romanians in Transylvania.* Budapest; New York: Central European University Press.

Moga, L.M., Antohi, V.M., and Neculiță, M. (2012). Usage of the European funds for agricultural and countryside development in Romanian rural areas. *European Journal of Interdisciplinary Studies*, 4: 56–65.

Mollona, M. (2009). *Made in Sheffield: An ethnography of industrial work and politics.* New York: Berghahn Books.

Mungiu-Pippidi, A. (2007). Is East-Central Europe backsliding? EU accession is no "End of history". *Journal of Democracy*, 18: 8–16.

Mureşan, M. (2008). Romania's integration in COMECON. The analysis of a failure. *Romanian Economic Journal*, 30: 27–58.

Nadeem, S. (2009). The uses and abuses of time: Globalization and time arbitrage in India's outsourcing industries. *Global Networks*, 9: 20–40.

Neef, R., & Stanculescu, M. (Eds.). (2002). *The social impact of informal economies in Eastern Europe.* Aldershot: Ashgate.

Negrescu, D. (1999). *A decade of privatisation in Romania: delegation of European Commission.* Working Paper no. 13/October 1999.

Neuhaus, M. (2006). *The impact of FDI on economic growth an analysis for the transition countries of Central and Eastern Europe.* Mannheim: Physica-Verlag.

Nicholson, B. and Sahay, S. (2004). Embedded knowledge and offshore software development. *Information and Organization* 14(4): 329–365.

Noutcheva, G. and Bechev, D. (2008). The successful laggards: Bulgaria and Romania's accession to the EU. *East European Politics & Societies*, 22: 114–144.

Office for Labour Force Migration. (2006). *Liberalization of labour market in Romania. Opportunities and Risks.* Working Paper.

Ong, A. (1987). *Spirits of resistance and capitalist discipline factory women in Malaysia.* Albany: State University of New York Press.

Ong, A. (1991). The gender and labour politics of postmodernity. *Annual Review of Anthropology,* 20: 279–309.

Ong, A. and Collier, S.J. (2004). *Global assemblages: Technology, politics, and ethics as anthropological problems.* Malden, MA: Blackwell Pub.

Ornston D. (2006). Reorganising adjustment: Finland's emergence as a high technology leader. *West European Politics,* 29: 784–801.

Palpacuer, F. (2000). Competence-Based Strategies and Global Production Networks a Discussion of Current Changes and Their Implications for Employment. *Competition & Change,* 4(4): 353–400.

Pando. (2012). *Pando networks releases global internet speed study.* Available at: http://chartsbin.com/view/2484 [2012-11-10].

Pascall, G. and Kwak, A. (2005). *Gender Regimes in Transition in Central and Eastern Europe,* Bristol, UK: Policy Press.

Pavlínek, P. (2004). Regional development implications of FDI in Central Europe. *European Urban & Regional Studies,* 11(1): 47–70.

Peluchette, J.V. and Karl, K. (2007). The impact of workplace attire on employee self-perceptions. *Human Resource Development Quarterly,* 18: 345–360.

Peterson, S.V. (2005). How (the meaning of) gender matters in political economy. *New Political Economy,* 10(4): 499–521.

Petrovici, N. (2011). Articulating the right to the City: Working-class neo-nationalism in postsocialist Cluj, Romania. In: *Headlines of Nation, Subtexts of Class*: 57–77.

Petrovici, N. (2012). Workers and the city: Rethinking the geographies of power in postsocialist urbanisation. *Urban Studies,* 49(11): 2377–2397.

Petrovici, N. (2013). Neoliberal proletarization along the urban-rural divide in postsocialist Romania. *Studia Universitatis Babes-Bolyai, Sociologia,* 58(2): 23–54.

Pettigrew, A.M. (1979). On studying organizational cultures. *Administrative Science Quarterly,* 24: 570–581.

Philbin, T. (1996). *Cop speak: The lingo of law enforcement and crime.* New York: J. Wiley.

Phinnemore, D. (2001). Romania and Euro-Atlantic integration since 1989: a decade of frustration? In: D. Phinnemore and D. Light (eds.) *Post-Communist Romania: coming to terms with transition.* New York: Palgrave-Macmillan.

Pine, F. (2002). Retreat to the household: Gendered domains in postsocialist Poland. In: Hann CM (ed.) *Postsocialism: Ideals, ideologies, and practices in Eurasia.* London; New York: Routledge.

Pîrvu, G., Gruescu, R. and Nanu, R. (2008). Romania's strategy of attraction of foreign investments. *Annals of the University of Petroșani: Economics,* 8: 87–94.

Polanyi, K. (1944). *The Great Transformation.* New York: Farrar & Rinehart.

Popescu, R. and Ungureanu, E. (2008). *Analysis of the situation of Romanian industrial parks.* Working paper.

Pun, N. (2005). *Made in China: Women Factory Workers in a Global Workplace.* Durham: Duke University Press.

Pun, N. and Smith, C. (2007). Putting transnational labour process in its place: The dormitory labour regime in post-Socialist China. *Work, Employment & Society,* 21(1): 27–45.

Quayle, Q. (2005). I am optimistic about Romania's future Romanian. *Journal of Political Sciences,* 5: 9–12.

Quinn, B.A. (2000). The paradox of complaining: Law, humor, and harassment in the everyday work world. *Social Inquiry,* 25: 1151–1185.

Radulescu, D.M. (2003). An Assessment of Fiscal Sustainability in Romania. *Post-Communist Economies,* 15: 259–275.

Rafaeli, A., Dutton J., Harquail, C.V., et al. (1997). Navigating by attire: The use of dress by female administrative employees. *Academy of Management Journal,* 40: 9–45.

Rainnie, A., Herod, A. and McGrath-Champ, S. (2011). Review and positions: global production networks and labour. *Competition and Change,* 15(2): 155–169.

Rajkai, Z. (2015). *Family and social change in Socialist and Post-Socialist Societies: Change and continuity in Eastern Europe and East Asia.* Boston, MA: Brill.

Realitatea.net. (2011) Politicienii, despre fabrica Nokia de la Jucu, în 2008: Este viitorul României. Available at: http://www.realitatea.net/politicienii-despre-fabrica-de-la-jucu-in-2008-acesta-este-viitorul-romaniei_874855.html. [2018-11-26].

Reuters. (2007). Ford offers $78 mln for Romanian Carmaker. Available at: http://www.reuters.com/article/2007/09/07/ford-romania-idUSL0789400020070907 [2012-11-19].

Riisgaard, L. and Hammer, N. (2011). Prospects for labour in global value chains: labour standards in the cut flower and banana industries. *British Journal of Industrial Relations,* 49(1): 168–190.

Roman, D. (2003). *Fragmented identities: Popular culture, sex, and everyday life in post-communist Romania.* Lanham: Lexington Books.

Romanian National Institute of Statistics (2011). *The trading balance sheet of Romania: Two decades with an annual adverse sold.* Bucharest: Romanian National Institute of Statistics.

Rossi, G. (1997). The nestlings why young adults stay at home longer: The Italian case. *Journal of Family Issues,* 18(6): 627–644.

Rousseau, M. (2011). "Post-Fordist Urbanism in France's Poorest City: Gentrification as Local Capitalist Strategy". *Critical Sociology,* 38(1): 49–69.

Roy, D.F. (1959). "Banana Time": Job satisfaction and informal interaction. *Human Organization,* 18(4): 158–168.

Rudd, E. (2006). Gendering unemployment in postsocialist Germany: "What I do is work, even if it's not paid". *Ethnos*, 71(2): 191–212.

Rudra, N. (2008). *Globalization and the race to the bottom in developing countries: who really gets hurt?*, Cambridge, UK; New York: Cambridge University Press.

Salzinger, L. (2003). *Genders in production: Making workers in Mexico's global factories.* Berkeley: University of California Press.

Sandu, D. (2005). Emerging Transnational Migration from Romanian Villages. *Current Sociology*, 53: 555–582.

Sassen, S. (1996). *Losing control? : sovereignty in an age of globalization,* New York: Columbia University Press.

Sassen, S. (2007). *Sociology of globalization.* New York: W.W. Norton.

Schmitz, H. (2004). *Local enterprises in the global economy: Issues of governance and upgrading.* Cheltenham, UK; Northhampton, MA: Edward Elgar.

Scholarios, D., & Taylor, P. (2010). Gender, choice and constraint in call centre employment. *New Technology, Work and Employment*, 25(2): 101–116.

Seidman, G.W. (2007). *Beyond the boycott: Labour rights, human rights, and transnational activism.* London and New York: Russell Sage Foundation.

Sengupta, S. and Gupta, A. (2012). Exploring the dimensions of attrition in Indian BPOs. *The International Journal of Human Resource Management*, 23: 1259–1288.

Silver, B.J. (2003). *Forces of labour: Workers' movements and globalization since 1870.* Cambridge; New York: Cambridge University Press.

Sinn H-W., and Weichenrieder A.J. (1997). Foreign direct investment, political resentment and the privatisation process in Eastern Europe. *Economic Policy* 12: 177–210.

Sjöblom, P.A. and Terhi, H.U. (2013). *Names in the economy: cultural prospects.* Newcastle upon Tyne: Cambridge Scholars Publishing.

Smith, A., Pickles, J., Bucek, M. et al. (2008). Reconfiguring "post-socialist" regions: cross-border networks and regional competition in the Slovak and Ukrainian clothing industry. *Global Networks*, 8(3): 281–307.

Smith, J. (2015). Imperialism in the twenty-first century. *Monthly Review*, 67(3): 82–94.

Smith, N. and Dennis, W. (1987). The restructuring of geographical scale: Coalescence and fragmentation of the northern core region. *Economic Geography*, 63: 160–182.

Snell-Hornby, M. (1999). Communicating in the global village: On language, translation and cultural identity. *Current Issues in Language and Society* 6: 103–120.

Solomon, M.R. and Schopler, J. (1982). Self-consciousness and clothing. *Personality and Social Psychology Bulletin*, 8: 508–514.

Spendzharova, A.B. (2003). Bringing Europe in? The impact of EU Conditionality on Bulgarian and Romanian politics. *Southeast European Politics*, 4: 141–153.

Stănescu, C. and Nedelescu, D. (2008). Evolution of the foreign direct investment in Romanian Economy. *Stiinte Economice*, XVII: 170–176.

Staritz, C. (2011). *Making the cut? Low-income countries and the global clothing value chain in a post-quota and post-crisis world.* Washington, DC: World Bank.

Stefan, L. and Sorin, I. (2011). *Nations in Transit: Romania.* Bucharest: Freedom House.

Steinbock, D. (2001). *The Nokia revolution the story of an extraordinary company that transformed an industry*, New York: AMACOM.

Steinbock, D. (2005). *The mobile revolution: the making of mobile services worldwide*, London: Kogan Page.

Stenning, A. (2000). Placing (post-)socialism: The making and remaking of Nowa Huta, Poland. *European Urban and Regional Studies,* 7(2): 99–118.

Stillo, J. (2012). The Romanian tuberculosis epidemic as a symbol of public health. In P.E. Sum and R.F. King (eds.) *Romania under Basescu: Aspirations, Achievements and Frustrations During his First Presidential Term.* Lanham, MD: Lexington Books.

Stoica, C.A. (2004). From Good Communists to Even Better Capitalists? Entrepreneurial Pathways in Post-Socialist Romania. *East European Politics & Societies,* 18: 236–277.

Stoiciu, V. (2012). Austerity and structural reforms in Romania. International Policy Analysis. Accessed on-line: https://sar.org.ro/wp-content/uploads/2012/12/Austerity-and-Structural-Reforms-in-Romania.pdf [2018-11-19].

Sturgeon, T., V Biesebroeck, J., and Gereffi, G. (2008). Value chains, networks and clusters: reframing the global automotive industry. *Journal of Economic Geography,* 8(3): 297–321.

Sturgeon, T.J. (2002). Modular production networks: A new American model of industrial organization. *Industrial and Corporate Change,* 11(3): 451–496.

Sturgeon, T.J. (2007). How globalization drives institutional diversity: The Japanese electronics industry's response to value chain modularity. *Journal of East Asian Studies,* 7: 1–34.

Sturgeon, T.J. (2008). *From commodity chains to value chains: Interdisciplinary theory building in an age of globalization.* Industry Studies Association Working Paper Series.

Swap, W.C. (1977). Interpersonal Attraction and Repeated Exposure to Rewarders and Punishers. *Personality and Social Psychology Bulletin,* 3: 248–251.

Swyngedouw, E. (2000). Authoritarian governance, power, and the politics of rescaling. *Environment and planning D: Society and space,* 18(1): 63–76.

Syrett, M. and Devine, M. (2012). *Managing uncertainty: strategies for surviving and thriving in turbulent times.* London: Economist.

Szalai, J. (2000). From informal labour to paid occupations: Marketization from below in Hungarian women's work. In: Gal S and Kligman G (Eds) *Reproducing Gender: Politics, Publics, and Everyday Life after Socialism.* Princeton, N.J.: Princeton University Press, pp. 200–224.

Szelenyi, I. and Kostello, E. (1996). The market transition debate: Toward a synthesis? *American Journal of Sociology*, 101(4): 1082–1096.

Szelewa, D. and Polakowski, M.P. (2008). Who cares? Changing patterns of childcare in Central and Eastern Europe. *Journal of European Social Policy*, 18(2): 115–131.

Tache, I. (2008). The Mass Privatisation Process in Romania: a Case of Failed Ango-Saxon Capitalism. Accessed on-line: https://www.hse.ru/data/283/636/1233/1Tache_Moscow.pdf [2018-11-19].

Taylor, P. and Bain, P. (2008). United by a Common Language? Trade Union Responses in the UK and India to Call Centre Offshoring. *Antipode*, 40: 131–154.

Taylor, P., and Bain, P. (2003). Subterranean worksick blues: Humour as subversion in two call centres. *Organization Studies*, 24(9): 1487–1509.

Terrion, J.L & Ashforth, B.E. (2002). From "I" to "we": The role of putdown humor and identity in the development of a temporary group. *Human Relations*, 55: 55–88.

Todorova, M.N., and Gille, Z. (2010). *Post-Communist Nostalgia*. New York: Berghahn Books.

Tönnies F. (1934). *Community and Society*, New York: Harper.

Torres, M. (2011), Capital, Family or Community in Postsocialist Rural Romania: Inequalities and Equalities. In: Kaneff D and Pine F (Eds) *Global Connections and Emerging Inequalities in Europe: Perspectives on Poverty and Transnational Migration*. London, U.K.; New York, N.Y.: Anthem Press.

Torres, M. (2011). Capital, Family or Community in Postsocialist Rural Romania: Inequalities and Equalities. In: Kaneff D and Pine F (Eds) *Global Connections and Emerging Inequalities in Europe: Perspectives on Poverty and Transnational Migration*. London, U.K. ; New York, N.Y.: Anthem Press.

Trif, A. (2016) Social dialogue during the economic crisis: The survival of collective bargaining in the manufacturing sector in Romania. In: A. Koukiadaki, I. Távora, & M.M. Lucio (Eds.). *Joint regulation and labour market policy in Europe during the crisis*. Brussels: European Trade Union Institute (ETUI), 395–439.

Trofor, A., Mihaltan, F., Mihaicuta, S., et al. (2009). Smoking cessation and prevention for young people – Romanian expertise. *Pneumologia*, 58(1): 72–78.

Turbine, V. and Riach, K. (2012). The right to choose or choosing what's right? Women's conceptualizations of work and life choices in contemporary Russia. *Gender, Work & Organization*, 19(2): 165–187.

Uhlenbruck, K. (2004). Developing acquired foreign subsidiaries: the experience of MNES in transition economies. *Journal of International Business Studies*, 35(2): 109–123.

United Nations Conference on Trade and Development. (2012a). *Goods and Services Trade Balance Indicators*. [2018-11-19].

United Nations Conference on Trade and Development. (2012b). Inward and Outward Foreign Direct Investment Flows, annual, 1970–2011. [2018-11-19].

United Nations Conference on Trade and Development. (2013). Global value chains: Investment and trade for development. Accessed at: https://unctad.org/en/PublicationsLibrary/diae2013d1_en.pdf [2018-12-14].

Van Maanen, J.E., & Schein, E.H. (1978). Toward a theory of organizational socialization. In: Barry Staw (Ed.) Annual Review of research in organizational behaviour. JIP Pres: New York: pp. 84–89.

Varga, M. (2013). Refocusing studies of post-communist trade unions. *European Journal of Industrial Relations*, 19(2): 109–1.

Varga, M. (2014). *Worker Protests In Post-Communist Romania And Ukraine: Striking With Tied Hands*. Manchester: Manchester University Press.

Varga, M., & Freyberg-Inan, A. (2015). Post-communist state measures to thwart organized labour: The case of Romania. *Economic and Industrial Democracy*, 36(4): 677–699.

Verdery K. (1983). *Transylvanian villagers: Three centuries of political, economic, and ethnic change*. Berkeley: University of California Press.

Verdery, K. (1996). *What was Socialism, and what comes next*. Chichester: Princeton University Press.

Vincze, E. (2015). Glocalization of neoliberalism in Romania through the reform of the state and entrepreneurial development. Studia Universitatis Babes-Bolyai-Studia Europaea, 60(1), 125–152.

Vincze, E. (2017). The ideology of economic liberalism and the politics of housing in Romania. Studia Universitatis Babes-Bolyai-Studia Europaea, 62(3), 29–54.

Vlase I. (2012). Gender and migration-driven changes in rural Eastern Romania: Migrants' perspectives. *International Review of Social Research*, 2: 21–38.

Vosko, L.F. (2002). The pasts (and futures) of feminist political economy in Canada: Reviving the debate. *Studies in Political Economy*, 68(1): 55–83.

Wade, R. (1978). A "returns to labour" theory of peasant household organisation. *Sociologia Ruralis*, 18: 23–39.

Wallendorf, M. and Arnould, E.J. (1991). "We Gather Together": Consumption Rituals of Thanksgiving Day. *Journal of Consumer Research*, 18: 13–31.

Wallerstein, I.M. (1974). *The modern world-system*. New York: Academic Press.

Wallerstein, I.M. and Hopkins, T.K. (2000). Commodity chains in the world-economy prior to 1800. In: Wallerstein, I.M. (Ed.) *The essential Wallerstein*. New York: New Press; Distributed by W.W. Norton.

Webster, E., Lambert, R., & Beziudenhout, A. (2011). *Grounding globalization: Labour in the age of insecurity*. New York and London: John Wiley & Sons.

Weresa, M.A. (2004). Can foreign direct investment help Poland catch up with the EU? *Communist and Post-Communist Studies*, 37(3): 413–427.

Wilson, G. (1968). *An essay on the economics of detribalization in Northern Rhodesia*. Manchester, Eng.; New York: Manchester University Press.

Wilson, M. (1936). *Reaction to conquest; effects of contact with Europeans on the Pondo of South Africa*. London: Oxford University Press.

Winkler, D. (2013). *Potential and actual FDI spillovers in global value chains the role of foreign investor characteristics, absorptive capacity and transmission channels.* Available at: http://elibrary.worldbank.org/content/workingpaper/10.1596/1813-9450-6424. [2018-12-1].

Woodard, M.S. and Sherman, K.E. (2015). Toward a more complete understanding of offshoring: bringing employees into the conversation. *The International Journal of Human Resource Management.* 26(16): 2019–2038.

World Economic Forum. (2010). The Global Competitiveness Report 2010–2011. Accessed on-line: http://www3.weforum.org/docs/WEF_GlobalCompetitivenessReport_2010-11.pdf [2018-11-19].

Yeung, H.W.C., Liu, W., & Dicken, P. (2006). Transnational corporations and network effects of a local manufacturing cluster in mobile telecommunications equipment in China. *World development,* 34(3): 520–540.

Zajonc, R.B. (1968). Attitudinal effects of mere exposure. *Journal of Personality and Social Psychology,* 9: 1–27.

Cited Press Articles

Academia Catavencu, 2011.10.5-11, pictorial.
Adevărul, 2011.10.02, no title.
Adevărul, 2011.10.14, Toata lumea vrea sa investeasca in Romania.
Adevărul, 2011.10.06, no title.
Bursa, 2011.10.10, Jucu, noul El Dorado al investitorilor straini.
Capital, 2011.10.3-9, Plecarea Nokia ne costa peste un punct procentual in PIB.
Capital, 2011.10.10-17, Nokia vine la China.
Faclia, 2011.10.1-2, Consiliul Judetean trebuia sa faca pista la aeroport, terminal cargo si pasaje rutiere.
Gazeta de Cluj, 2011.10.17-23, Good bye Nokia, Welcome, Bosch!.
Gazeta de Cluj, 2011.10.24-30, no title.
Mesagerul de Cluj, 2011.10.3-9, Editorial.
Mesagerul de Cluj, 2011.10.3-9, Bye-bye Nokia: O lectie pentru Romania.
Mesegerul de Cluj, 2011,10.10-16, Bye-bye Nokia, Compensatii de 200 de milioane.
Mesagerul de Cluj, 2011.10.12-23, Editorial.
Monitorul de Cluj, 2011.10.07, no title.
Monitorul de Cluj, 2011.10.19, Terapia si chinezii de la ZTE vor halele Nokia.
Servus Cluj, 2011.09.30, Mi-am luat Blackberry.
Servus Cluj, 2011.09.30, Nokia, disconnecting Romanian people.

Servus Cluj, 2011.10.03, Miltinationalele din Cluj spun ca exista viata si dupa Nokia.
Ziua de Cluj, 2011.10.04, no title.
Ziua de Cluj, 2011.10.05, Greva la Nokia.
Ziua de Cluj, 2011.10.06, Obligatiile Nokia fata de salariatii concediati sunt inexistente.
Ziua de Cluj, 2011.10.08, Evaluatorii: Nokia va fi noa Polonie chiar si fara Nokia.
Ziua de Cluj, 2011.10.8, Ioan Rus: Nokia una dintre cele main mari tepe luate vreodata de statul Roman.
Ziarul Financiar, 2011.09.30, Cea mai proasta veste pentru economie.
Ziarul Financiar, 2011.10.5, Cum se spune.
Ziarul Financiar, 2011.10.23, RTI: Updating please check again Soon.
Ziua de Cluj (2011d) ŞOC LA CLUJ. Cât estimase Băsescu că va rămâne Nokia la Jucu. Şi cât s-a înşelat, September 29.

Index

Ackroyd   17, 83, 84
age   18, 80, 108, 109, 111, 113, 130
agency work   34, 132
agriculture   14, 24, 85, 104, 105–106, 117, 130
  semi-subsistence   14, 18, 129
Apple   128, 146, 147
Asia   136, 149, 151
assembly process   61, 66, 162
atmosphere   77, 82, 87, 92, 124, 164
attire   72, 73
austerity measures   36, 40, 46, 141, 145

badge   74, 88
Bandelj   4, 21, 26, 102
Bangladesh   151
banks   25, 27, 28, 29, 34, 64, 130
Barrientos   8, 44
Blyton   1–2, 5, 14, 117, 126, 159
Bochum   55, 126, 151, 152
Bohle   4, 10
boredom   17, 83, 84, 85, 98
Bosch   145, 166
Brass   2, 44, 159
breaks   73, 77, 89, 110, 162
Brenner   45, 46
Bucharest   29, 50, 51, 154
Bulgaria   32, 33
Burawoy   6, 9, 12, 83, 90, 119, 160

cameras   13, 67, 73, 78, 88, 91, 148
canteen   76, 77, 80, 92, 93
capital   2, 6, 38, 45, 119, 122, 137, 138, 145, 147
  external   19, 121, 122, 140
capitalism   136, 137
care of children   10, 106, 109
chaos   20, 24, 25, 33
children   10, 67, 106, 108, 109, 110, 113, 117
China   12, 16, 96–97, 124, 135, 150, 151
cigarettes   77, 89
Clark   4
Cleaning staff   95, 96
clowning   84, 87, 89
Cluj   50, 127, 128, 142, 143, 144, 145, 148, 149, 151, 152, 153, 154, 155, 156
coffee   77, 80, 87, 89, 133

Collier   16, 46, 47, 160
Collinson   17, 83, 84
commodification   5, 6, 9, 11, 116, 119
communities   1–3, 6, 11, 15, 55, 58, 59, 104, 113, 121, 138, 161, 164, 165
  host   15, 102, 166
  local   3, 12, 15, 44, 62, 136, 138
competition   1–2, 32, 34, 136, 151, 159
  global   98, 119, 126, 165
computers   48, 63, 66, 70, 74, 109, 131
concept   46, 95, 114, 138, 140, 159
configurations   45
conflict   23, 33, 38, 41
conspiracy   95, 97, 100
conspiratorial character   94, 95
context
  familial   81, 118
  post-Socialist   99, 116, 119
control   8, 10, 17, 25, 40, 47, 78, 84, 88, 89, 92, 94, 134, 157, 159
corruption   25, 27, 33, 37, 39, 40, 143
Cowie   5, 9, 60, 117, 135, 136, 139
Cravey   5, 10
CV   62, 63, 65, 79

decision makers   124, 148–49, 164
Dunn   7, 101, 102, 136

Eastern Europe   3–7, 23, 24, 26, 27, 32, 34, 40, 41, 89, 90, 104, 105, 110, 119, 140
economic cooperation   28
economic crisis   16, 22, 35, 150, 160
economic growth   4, 24, 26, 30, 32, 46, 54, 122, 135, 161, 165, 166
economies
  advanced   1–2, 15, 20, 97, 134, 159, 164
  middle-income   19, 84, 119, 140, 157, 165
elections   24, 27, 30
Ellingstad   4, 140
emancipation   110, 116, 117
employees   2, 8, 34, 35, 50, 52, 61, 63–67, 111, 125, 132, 133, 148, 152–53, 159
  direct   54, 63, 64
  new   67
equipment   48, 70, 73, 74, 78, 95, 114, 162

INDEX

ethnography 11–12, 47, 160
European Commission 20, 32, 33, 37, 39, 40
European Investment Bank 35
European Union 16, 21, 22, 26, 38, 41, 43, 47, 53, 145, 152, 153
  accession 31, 32, 33, 34, 41, 104, 145
exploitation 6, 10, 90, 97, 119, 122

families 9, 10, 11, 101, 102, 103, 106, 107, 110, 111, 113, 115, 116–19, 130, 163
  extended 60, 81, 101, 106, 108, 115
  family members 102, 107–8, 110, 112–13, 116, 118, 163
fieldwork 12
food 76, 77, 78, 80, 105, 107, 114, 116
food production 104, 105, 106, 114
  subsistence 104, 105, 107
foreign investments 3, 11, 15, 16, 18, 21–26, 28, 102, 117, 119, 121, 165, 166
Freyberg-Inan 31, 36, 129
fun 77, 82, 85, 86, 89, 109, 114

gardens 53, 105, 106, 109, 112, 133
Gereffi 42, 43
German
  journalists 54, 55
  media 54, 55
  workers 55, 152
global economy 7, 15, 19, 21, 40, 41, 135, 136, 137, 141, 148, 153, 157, 160
global value chains 15, 17, 41, 43, 44, 45, 46, 94, 100, 102, 137, 139, 145, 157, 163
governance 31, 42, 43
government 16, 25, 26, 28, 29, 30, 31, 32, 33, 34, 35, 37, 54, 144
grandparents 112, 115, 117
Greskovits 4, 10
Guga 34, 36, 41, 129

Harvey 14–15, 135, 139
Hayter 36, 99, 129
Holmes 83
home 8, 10, 60, 74, 76, 77, 80, 101, 102, 103, 107, 108, 110, 113, 114–18
Hopkins 42
hosting community 11, 13, 16, 53, 134, 153, 157, 164

household duties 81, 106, 110, 115, 117, 129
humour 17, 82, 83, 84, 86, 87, 88, 91, 93, 94, 95, 98, 99, 100, 162

India 76, 91–92, 144, 151
industrial labour 3, 5, 31, 70, 101
inflation 24, 26, 27, 37
infrastructure 3, 12, 39, 46, 50, 69, 134, 142, 153, 165
intergenerational exceptionalism 112
International Monetary Fund 20, 23, 24, 26, 27, 29, 30, 34, 35, 37
internet 48, 71, 87, 146
investor 16, 50–51, 54, 56, 57–58, 123, 125, 126, 127, 137, 148, 152, 157–58, 164, 166
invigilation 91, 92, 99
iPhone 146, 147

Jenkins 1–2, 5, 14, 117, 126, 159
jokes 42, 62, 76, 84, 86, 87, 88–94, 98, 99, 100, 114
  socialist 17, 90, 91
journalists 49, 55, 57, 120, 141, 143
journey 14, 17, 161, 162
Jucu 58, 142, 155, 156

Kideckel 14, 30, 101, 102, 113, 118
King 11, 20, 30, 32
Korczynski 17, 86

labour arbitrage 1–2, 12, 135, 159, 161, 163, 165
labour code 36, 129
labour conditions 8, 10, 34, 80
labour costs 2, 120, 122, 159, 163
  lower 2, 159
labour market 3, 9, 11, 14, 28, 39, 40, 111, 119, 134, 154, 160, 165
Lampland and Nadkarni 17, 90, 93, 94, 95, 96
language 17, 61, 69, 70, 71, 72, 162
  working 70
layoffs 10, 30, 31, 54, 64, 123, 124, 129, 134, 152, 157, 165
learning 61, 67, 68, 157
Lefebvre, Henri 45
line managers 66, 70, 82, 94
line operators 63, 64, 66, 98

machines 74, 87, 109
male worker 55–56, 73, 75, 77, 78, 88–89, 94, 96, 97, 98, 103, 108, 114, 115, 125
management 38, 69, 78, 80, 83, 84, 86, 93, 94, 99, 107, 120, 126, 127, 133
Manele 86, 87
manufacturing industry 2, 4, 10, 61, 67, 75, 79, 84, 116, 140, 162, 163
maquiladora syndrome 140
Marx 15, 19
meals 76, 77, 92, 162
Mendelski 38
metal detectors 69, 88, 89
Mexico 12, 139, 140, 144
Microsoft 146, 147
migration 13, 27, 29, 34, 39, 40, 56, 103, 122, 140, 166
mutual dependencies 9, 11, 18, 101, 102, 106, 115, 116, 118, 129, 163
myths 88, 89, 95, 98

Nadeem 2, 76, 136, 159
Nadkarni 17, 90, 93, 94, 95, 96
Nokia 13–14, 34, 38, 94, 99, 124, 126, 130, 142, 143, 144, 146, 147, 148, 150, 151, 152, 153, 155, 156
Nokia Village 16, 49, 50, 58

offices 29, 39, 62, 70, 75, 92, 93, 94, 98, 120, 143
Offshored Labour 101, 103, 105, 107, 109, 111, 113, 115, 116, 117, 119, 137, 139, 141, 143
offshoring 1–4, 7, 8, 9, 10, 11, 32, 39, 92, 115, 159, 160
Ong 5, 16, 46, 47, 102, 160
opening ceremony 57, 58
organizational culture 49, 61, 67, 68, 82, 83, 87, 89, 95, 98, 161

parents 60, 105, 109, 112, 113, 114, 115, 117, 133
parks, industrial 31, 51, 143, 144, 154
Pavlinek 102
Peeters 8
pensions 56, 106, 111, 112, 130
post-Socialism 5, 7, 53, 117, 118
precariousness 40, 41, 117
press 58, 155, 156, 158
privatisations 4, 11, 20, 21, 27, 29, 30, 31, 34, 36, 38, 128, 129

protests 29, 30, 36, 54, 55, 125, 127, 132, 134, 141, 157, 164
Pun 5, 7, 10, 12, 136

recruitment 16, 62, 63, 64
reforms 16, 20, 21, 25, 26, 27, 29, 30, 32, 33, 38, 40, 58, 115
relocation 14, 15, 54, 55, 122, 123, 126, 127, 137, 141, 149, 152, 157, 158, 165
resistance 30, 34, 38, 63, 83, 85, 90, 94, 99, 125, 127, 138, 155, 162
Roman 27, 110, 114
Romania 16, 20, 22, 23, 24–26, 28–41, 46, 54, 58, 137, 141, 145, 147, 148, 150–58
    communist 141
Romanian economy 25, 27, 28, 37, 38, 40, 44, 45, 107, 145, 148, 156, 164
Romanian employment law 63, 107
Romania's Systemic Transformation 20, 21, 23, 25, 27, 29, 31, 33, 35, 37, 39, 41
Rudra 2, 44, 159

salaries 104, 106, 107, 108, 109, 110, 112, 113, 114, 116, 117, 130, 133, 134, 152
    low 17, 79, 111
Sassen 2, 44, 45, 159
scalar fixes 45, 46, 58
secrets 68, 141, 142
security 61, 87–89, 91–92, 97, 151
security guards 51, 52, 55, 89, 91, 134
shifts 51, 58, 60, 67, 68, 70, 75, 76, 85, 86, 87, 91, 92, 93, 108
shoes 72, 73
shop floor 60, 61, 63, 64, 67, 69, 70, 75, 79, 84, 87, 91, 92–93, 98, 111
shop floor culture 17, 77, 88, 162
Silver 2, 5, 9, 44, 159
Smith 1–2, 4, 10, 20, 45, 136
socialism 13, 14, 90, 101, 109, 110, 115, 162
socialist jokes 90–99
social problems 1, 10, 14, 22, 54, 118, 122, 160
social reproduction 2, 11, 14
Soulsby 4
structural funds 38, 40, 104, 145
Sturgeon 4, 42, 43, 44, 102
subsidization 25
subsistence agriculture 55, 104, 105, 116
summer kitchens 105
systemic transformation 7, 15, 20, 45, 47, 53, 118, 130, 140

INDEX

taxes   95, 150, 151
temperature   74, 80, 98, 162
temporary contracts   36, 64, 99, 107, 128, 132, 164
temporary jobs   57, 104, 129, 164
temporary work   141
tensions   3, 19, 27, 29, 37, 40, 84, 85, 91, 92, 102, 160
Thompson   17, 83
trade unions   5, 127
training   54, 65, 66, 68, 69, 71, 73
transition   4, 14, 16, 20, 21, 25, 32, 33, 37, 40, 104, 105, 117, 140, 141
Trif   35, 36–37, 99, 129

unions   23, 30, 31, 34, 35, 36, 54, 128, 129, 133
United Nations Conference on Trade and Development   4, 10, 25, 26, 27, 29, 31, 32, 33, 37, 43
urbanization   121, 138

Varga   5, 30, 31, 36, 41, 129
Vincze   21, 35, 36, 37, 128
visions   26, 39, 45, 49, 104, 126, 154, 155, 161, 166

wages   5, 6, 9, 15, 32, 34, 36, 39, 40, 107, 116, 119, 121, 135, 136
Wallerstein   42
Weresa   4
Western working class   84, 135
Wilson   122
Winkler   10, 43
work attire   17, 61, 72, 73, 80, 161, 162
workers   63, 65–82, 85, 88, 91, 92, 93, 94–95, 97–103, 107, 110, 111–14, 118, 124, 126–37
working class   5, 10, 14, 117
World Bank   16, 20, 23, 25, 26, 29, 30, 34, 35, 43, 47

Young workers   86, 88, 91, 96

CPSIA information can be obtained
at www.ICGtesting.com
Printed in the USA
JSHW021602160820
7292JS00004B/13